BUREAUCRATIC CULTURE

BUREAUCRATIC CULTURE

CITIZENS AND ADMINISTRATORS IN ISRAEL

DAVID NACHMIAS and
DAVID H. ROSENBLOOM

ST. MARTIN'S PRESS   NEW YORK

Library of Congress Cataloging in Publication Data

Nachmias, David.
    Bureaucratic culture.

    Bibliography: p.
    Includes index.
    1. Civil service—Israel. 2. Israel—Politics and government. 3. Political
participation—Israel. I. Rosenbloom, David H., joint author. II. Title.
JQ1825.P34N3 1978   301.18'32'095694   78-17638
ISBN 0-312-10808-7

CONTENTS

Contents

To our daughters,
Leah, Anat, and Sarah

PREFACE

The rise of public bureaucracy has long been of concern to social scientists, government officials, and community-minded citizens. This book builds upon that interest by advancing a theory of bureaucratic culture, which involves several elements of central importance to the relationships among public bureaucracy, democracy, and national development. One of its major themes concerns the consequences of bureaucratisation for the nature of citizenship in democratic political communities. Thus, the study investigates the attitudes of citizens and public bureaucrats towards the increasing political power of a national bureaucracy. It ascertains their reactions to bureaucratic penetration of the political, economic, and social life of the polity; assesses citizens' and bureaucrats' feelings of efficacy regarding bureaucratic policy-making; and investigates their perceived ability to influence the bureaucracy's course. Incongruence between|bureaucrats' and citizens' perceptions, attitudes, and evaluations is also analysed. Relatedly, the study examines the impact of social cleavages on bureaucratic representation and recruitment. One of our major findings is that distinct patterns of dispositions towards the bureaucratisation of public life exist among citizens and bureaucrats. Based upon the understanding it develops about bureaucratic culture, the study suggests ways of alleviating the tension between public bureaucracy and democracy.

The research was undertaken in Israel and produced with the aid of grants from the Ford Foundation received through the Israel Foundation Trustees, from Tel Aviv University, and from the University of Vermont. In addition to acknowledging our gratitude to these institutions, we would like to thank several colleagues and friends who were helpful in the evolution of the book. Alan Arian, Joel Migdal, Saadia Touval, and Moshe Czudnowski provided helpful suggestions and criticisms at various stages along the way. Joel Azaria and Barry Mart assisted us with data collection and analysis. Patricia M. Molloy rendered valuable assistance in the preparation of the manuscript for publication. A special word of thanks is due to Chava Nachmias for her aid in data analysis and support and encouragement throughout the project. Finally, we would like to thank our daughters, to whom the book is dedicated, for what they didn't do.

1 A THEORY OF BUREAUCRATIC CULTURE

Bureaucracy has emerged as a dominant feature of the contemporary world. Virtually everywhere one looks in developed and developing nations, economic, social, and political life are extensively influenced by bureaucratic organisations. Indeed, even the transmission of knowledge and culture has often become bureaucratised and to the extent that the world itself is organised, its organisation is largely bureaucratic. Nowhere has the tendency towards bureaucratisation been greater than in the realm of governance. It is increasingly evident that as governments engage in greater activity and as nations become more interdependent, no political system is likely to flourish, or even survive, if it fails to develop an effective administrative component. Regardless of ideology and political institutions, all developed nations are thoroughly dependent upon a body of highly specialised and hierarchically organised administrators. In fact, in Western Europe it is not uncommon for civil servants to claim that they are the state itself,[1] and elsewhere bureaucrats have sometimes been considered a (new) ruling class.[2] If the twentieth century is epitomised by the 'bureaucratization of the world',[3] what then are the consequences of this phenomenon?

This question could be answered, or at least addressed, on several levels. There is abundant literature on some of the political, economic, and social consequences of the rise of bureaucracy.[4] The psychological effects of working in bureaucratic organisations and interacting with them as clients has also been considered at some length.[5] Some have dealt with the development and contemporary performance of individual national bureaucracies.[6] Such studies have been concerned with both the institutional and behavioural aspects of public bureaucracies. Still other scholars have been engaged in cross-national analysis of bureaucratic structure and behaviour.[7] Nor has there been a dearth of theorising about the nature of organisation, the possibilities of ensuring efficiency and political responsiveness in public bureaucracies, or the relationship between bureaucracy and democracy.[8] All of these approaches have their utility, and we will draw on them from time to time in this study. However, they also fail to deal with at least one very crucial aspect of bureaucracy and bureaucratisation: they tell us virtually nothing about how the general population and the bureaucratic component of a political community relate to the agglomeration of personnel, functions, and power in public bureaucratic agencies. Yet this information and knowledge concerning differences in bureaucrats' and citizens' patterns of thinking and feeling with regard to public bureaucracies is of considerable importance to an understanding of bureaucratic performance, political culture, and political systems.

There is no coherent concept in the literature of public administration and political science which deals with these aspects of bureaucracy. However, the term 'bureaucratic culture', which has been used in related contexts,[9] suggests itself as a label for one. Despite ambiguity and conflicting usage in the social sciences, there is little doubt that to an overwhelming extent the administrative components of developed, and most developing nations are in fact organised along lines which almost everyone would consider bureaucratic and to manifest patterns of bureaucratic behaviour. Similarly, 'culture' has many meanings. Yet, certainly it should be used to include several major aspects of national bureaucracies, including their composition, performance, and political roles. These elements, of course, vary from nation to nation. In some countries bureaucrats are an elite, in others they clearly are not; in some, bureaucrats possess a service ethic, in others a client is an object of disdain; some bureaucracies are highly politicised and thoroughly involved in politics, whereas others are largely insulated from the political process.

'Bureaucratic culture', then, is an important, but under-researched aspect of political culture. It follows, therefore, that in conceptualising it, much is to be gained by adhering, in so far as practicable, to a standard concept of political culture. In their classic study, *The Civic Culture*, Almond and Verba define the latter as follows: 'The political culture of a nation is the particular distribution of patterns of orientation toward political objects among the members of the nation.'[10] 'Orientation' refers to:

> (1) 'cognitive orientation,' that is, knowledge of and belief about the political system, its roles and the incumbents of these roles, its inputs, and its outputs; (2) 'affective orientation,' or feelings about the political system, its roles, personnel, and performance, and (3) 'evaluational orientation,' the judgments and opinions about political objects that typically involve the combination of value standards and criteria with information and feelings.[11]

Knowledge about such elements is extremely important to our understanding of politics and political systems. It represents a major dimension of the interface between government and people and is central to the idea of political community. Moreover, it has been found that political cultures can be usefully classified in accordance with the objects of political orientation. These may be the political system in general, inputs, outputs, and/or the individuals themselves as active participants.

It is evident that a similar model can be developed to study usefully orientations towards a specific unit of political systems, such as a public bureaucracy. Yet an additional dimension must be included. The concept of political culture, as presented here, has a major shortcoming in that it fails to include the orientations of politicians and political authorities in the analysis. As such it is somewhat akin to studying a religious culture without examining the attitudes of the clergy, or to analysing economic culture without dealing with the thought-patterns of a managerial class. It is necessary, therefore, to include the orientations of bureaucrats towards bureaucracy and themselves in an analysis of bureaucratic culture. Indeed, not to do so fails to place information obtained about mass orientations into a useful framework and perspective. In administrative matters, differences in orientations between bureaucrats and the public may be of critical importance. Some of the benefits of such an approach were amply demonstrated in a study of the images held by the general population and by bureaucrats with regard to the United States Federal Service as an employer. In *The Image of the Federal Service*, Kilpatrick and associates found, for instance, that 'in many respects, the public's image of federal employment does not fit the perceptions of those who are actually in federal employment'.[12] The authors were able to explore the roots and implications of these differences and to suggest ways of making the federal service more attractive to outsiders. Other studies have shown that a significant source of general dislike of bureaucracy is an incongruence between the bureaucratic norm of impersonality and clients' demands for personalised treatment.[13]

A concept of bureaucratic culture should include, therefore, not only the orientations of publics and bureaucrats towards national bureaucracies, but also an assessment of the congruence of these sets of orientations. Specifically, the objects of cognitive, affective, and evaluative orientations can be divided into two general categories: (1) the personnel who staff bureaucratic agencies, and (2) the organisational dynamics of bureaucratic agencies. Although the precise line of demarcation may be elusive in some instances, the latter, in turn, can be divided into the sub-categories of administrative performance and political performance. With regard to the personnel, some of the major dimensions for investigation are whether bureaucrats form an elite; whether they adequately represent significant social segments of the population; and the nature of the general stereotypes concerning their personality, efficiency, and character that are held by different population groups. In terms of organisational dynamics, attributes of bureaucratic structures are of concern. With regard to administrative performance, these elements would include orientations towards the treatment of clients, efficiency, the nature of bureaucratic processes such as recruitment and promotion, 'bureaupathologies',[14] and the like. In studying political performance, questions pertaining to political responsiveness, national development, social integration, the provision of justice, and the general content of policy-outputs would be of greatest interest. Running throughout all of these elements is a concern with citizens' and bureaucrats' feelings of efficacy and ability to influence the nature of bureaucratic activities. This approach may be elucidated by organising it in tabular form, as is done in Table 1.1.

Using this format, it should prove possible to discover the existence of different patterns of orientation towards bureaucratic objects among citizens, bureaucrats, and even entire political communities. Before elaborating on this, however, it is necessary to address the nature of bureaucratic organisation in order to explain why its behaviour engenders significant levels of cognition, affect, and evaluation and why we would expect these to be distributed differentially among separate groups.

Table 1.1. Orientations Towards Bureaucratic Objects

| | Personnel | Organisational dynamics | |
		Administrative performance	Political performance
Cognition			
Affect			
Evaluation			

Bureaucracy

It is common to begin a discussion of bureaucracy by declaring that it is a perplexing term that has been subjected to many different definitions, uses, and abuses. Indeed, the term has caused so much controversy and confusion that a leading investigation into its meanings concludes that the only reasonable approach is to 'avoid the use of the term "bureaucracy" while pursuing research in the areas in which it has been employed'.[15] Unfortunately, however, ignoring the word will not bring us any closer to defining the organisational reality to which it alludes. Moreover, much of the ambiguity concerning bureaucracy is now primarily of historical interest and it is possible to identify a considerable consensus concerning the central characteristics of bureaucratic organisation. Furthermore, this consensus does not simply classify organisations, it also relates bureaucratic organisation to specific behavioural patterns.

It is sometimes easier to begin a definition of a social phenomenon with a statement of what it is not. 'Bureaucracy' should no longer be used in technical work as an invective against inefficient operation. Efficiency and inefficiency can occur in virtually all forms of organisation and there is little to be gained by referring to the inefficient operations of an organisation as 'bureaucratic' and the efficient ones as 'non-bureaucratic'. Similarly, although there has been a considerable tendency to identify *all* public administrative systems as bureaucratic, given the diversity of public organisational forms and the dissimilarity of some of these to private organisations generally referred to as bureaucratic, there is little to be gained from such an approach. Clearly, there is no justification for using the word 'bureaucracy' as a synonym for less bewildering and ambiguous terms. Once these two definitional approaches are set aside, the question becomes whether bureaucracy should be used to refer to a specific set of structural arrangements or to specific patterns of behaviour, or both.

Current consensus in the social sciences has opted for a largely structural definition of bureaucracy which is coupled with an attribution of behavioural characteristics to that structure. The most important and influential statement on bureaucracy has been that of Max Weber,[16] who provided a structural identification of the bureaucratic form of organisation and discussed some facets of its behaviour. Drawing on studies of ancient bureaucracies in Egypt, Rome, China, and the Byzantine Empire, as well as on the more modern ones emerging in Europe during the nineteenth and early part of the twentieth centuries, he used an 'ideal type' approach to abstract from the empirical world the central core of features that would characterise the most fully developed bureaucratic form of organisation. The 'ideal type' is neither a description of reality nor a statement of normative preference. It is more of the order of an identification of the major variables which characterise bureaucracy. That these might not be fully present in an organisation is not necessarily to say that the organisation is 'non-bureaucratic', but rather to say that it is not a fully developed bureaucracy. The assumption here would be that there are some militating forces which have limited the degree of bureaucratisation of the organisation. At some point, however, it would be necessary to conclude that the characteristics of bureaucracy are so lacking in an organisation that it reasonably could neither be termed bureaucratic nor be expected to produce patterns of bureaucratic behaviour.

Weber's characteristics of the 'ideal type' bureaucracy were the following:

1. The staff members are personally free, observing only the impersonal duties of their offices.
2. There is a clear hierarchy of offices.
3. The functions of the offices are clearly specified.
4. Officials are appointed on the basis of a contract.
5. They are selected on the basis of a professional qualification, ideally substantiated by a diploma gained through examination.
6. They have a money salary, and usually pension rights. The salary is graded according to position in the hierarchy. The official can always leave the post, and under certain circumstances it may also be terminated.
7. The official's post is his sole or major occupation.
8. There is a career structure, and promotion is possible either by seniority or merit, and according to the judgement of superiors.
9. The official may appropriate neither the post nor the resources which go with it.
10. He is subject to a unified control and disciplinary system.[17]

Weber's structural identification of bureaucratic organisation has been one of the most comprehensive statements on the subject in the literature of the social sciences. It nevertheless has not always been considered satisfactory. Some have argued that it includes too little, whereas others have suggested that Weber included too much in his model of bureaucracy. Anthony Downs, for example, has argued for the inclusion of two additional features in a definition of bureaucracy:

1. The organisation must be large. 'Generally, any organization in which the highest-ranking members know less than half of the other members can be considered large.'[18]
2. 'The major proportion of its output is not directly or indirectly evaluated in any markets external to the organization by means of voluntary *quid pro quo* transactions.'[19]

Victor Thompson, on the other hand, has reduced the characteristics of bureaucracy to two major ones: (1) a highly elaborated hierarchy of authority which is superimposed upon (2) a highly elaborated division of work.[20] Others have added the variable of 'administrative density',[21] that is, the ratio of line supervisors, managers and staff personnel to the total number of employees, to a conception of bureaucracy. Bureaucracy has also been defined in terms of centralisation, specialisation, and formalisation only.[22] At the same time, the literature of organisation theory and management suggests that numerous additional variables including functional dispersion, functional specificity, staff density, vertical span, vertical differentiation, professionalisation, spatial dispersion, and others can be of utility in gaining an understanding of bureaucracy and other organisational structures.[23]

Any or all of these elements could be employed in an analysis of bureaucracy. While there is dissensus, therefore, concerning precisely which of them should be incorporated into such studies, there is nevertheless widespread consensus pertaining to the definitional characteristics of *public* bureaucracy. Thus, few would disagree with Ferrel Heady that public organisations can reasonably be referred to as bureaucratic when they manifest the following 'pivotal characteristics': '(1) hierarchy, (2) differentiation or specialization, and (3) qualification or competence.'[24] Such a reduction is possible primarily because public organisations tend to be large and not engaged in the sale of their 'product', and to bear a more direct relationship to government and politics, thereby accentuating the political importance of these characteristics. There is also a general consensus that, by and large, these and the other elements mentioned should be treated as continuous variables and thereby used not only to identify bureaucratic forms of organisation, but also the process of bureaucratisation itself.

Yet, useful as these variables may be in contributing to a definition of the bureaucratic form of organisation, it would be improbable that they would do much to facilitate our understanding of how public bureaucracies operate and the nature of bureaucratic culture unless they were associated with organisational and individual patterns of behaviour. It behoves us, therefore, to turn our attention to the nature of bureaucratic behaviour and to explain why it could be expected to be an object of citizens' and bureaucrats' cognitive, affective, and evaluative orientations.

Bureaucratic Behaviour

At the most general level, there is a considerable disagreement concerning the overall nature of bureaucratic behaviour. Some, along with Weber, have reasoned that bureaucracy is the most rational and efficient form of organisation. In Weber's oft-quoted words, 'The decisive reason for the advance of bureaucratic organization has always been its purely technical superiority over any other form of organization. The fully developed bureaucratic mechanism compares with other organizations exactly as does the machine with the non-mechanical modes of production.'[25] Others, however, have argued that 'bureaupathologies' and dysfunctions characterise bureaucracy to such an extent that it cannot be efficient in its operations. Among these limitations, it has been argued, are:

Bosses without (and underlings with) technical competence.
Arbitrary and zany rules.
An underworld (or informal) organization which subverts or even replaces the formal apparatus.
Confusion and conflict among roles.
Cruel treatment of subordinates based not on rational or legal grounds but upon inhumanity.[26]

Despite this highly general dispute which pervades much of the literature on bureaucracy, there is actually a considerable area of agreement concerning more specific aspects of bureaucratic behaviour. This is because the attempt to develop a general assessment of bureaucratic performance really involves disagreement as to the consequences of less global features of bureaucratic operation. From the perspectives of bureaucratic culture, the most important of these are impersonality and political unresponsiveness.

Weber referred to bureaucracy's 'special virtue' as 'dehumanization'. While many would reject the normative element in this observation, few would argue that bureaucracy does not have dehumanising consequences for its employees and, to a lesser extent, generally, its clients. By dehumanisation, Weber meant the elimination 'from official business [of] love, hatred, and all purely personal, irrational, and emotional elements which escape calculation'.[27] Today, the term 'impersonality' is generally employed in referring to this aspect of bureaucratic behaviour. Viewed against an historical background of administrative organisations characterised by such 'irrational' elements as nepotism, personal subjugation, and capricious and uninformed judgement, impersonality can be seen as a step in the direction of greater rationality. Thus, it is generally agreed that impersonality has three major advantages. First, it increases organisational effectiveness by enabling administrators to accomplish tasks which might otherwise be too expensive in terms of human costs. In the course of their normal functioning, governments create considerable hardships for individuals. These may be in the form of punishment, taxation, conscription, the withholding of benefits, or generally coercive measures. The often elaborate system of rules and hierarchical structure of bureaucracy make it easier for bureaucrats to accomplish these functions and provide a ready rationalisation for the necessity of disrupting and even destroying individuals' lives. Moreover, to the extent that administrators work on the basis of 'orders from above', it is clear that those making decisions are often isolated from the human consequences of their choices. This is not to suggest, of course, that bureaucrats do not also bring happiness to human lives, but only to mention the advantages of impersonality in achieving the opposite.

A second advantage of dehumanisation flows from the fact that 'efficiency also suffers when emotions or personal considerations influence administrative decisions'.[28] If, for example, recruitment and promotions within an organisation are based on personal preference, or ascriptive criteria rather than competence, administration will generally be less efficient. Finally, impersonality tends to produce relatively evenhanded rule application and thereby assures procedural justice. 'Go by the book' behaviour requires equal treatment of those in the same categories.

On the other hand, there are several aspects of impersonality which are generally thought to be disadvantageous. These, too, are of importance to bureaucratic culture because they form salient aspects of orientations towards bureaucratic objects. To the extent that emotional elements must be suppressed by administrators, there is a tendency towards personality disorder. It has been argued, for example, that there is an incongruence between the needs of bureaucratic organisation and those of a mature personality. Thus, bureaucracy requires that employees be 'provided minimal control over their work-a-day world', and they are 'expected to be passive, dependent, subordinate'.[29] A healthy adult personality, however, requires precisely opposite behaviour.[30] Secondly, although impersonality may ensure procedural justice, it may also fail to render substantive justice.[31] In this case impersonality is significantly related to specialisation as well as to hierarchy and formalisation. Because bureaucrats do not generally deal with wide aspects of their clients' lives, but only with very limited and specific ones, the decisions they reach may fail to fit the individual case in terms of providing a just resolution of whatever issue has caused the client to interact with the bureaucracy in the first place.

This feature of bureaucracy has often been cited as one which does much to arouse hostility on the part of clients, and even bureaucrats themselves. Many people simply fail to accept or believe that their case is no different from those of others and they consequently reject being treated on the basis of categories to which they do not feel they rightly belong. At one time or another, virtually everyone believes that his or her case is exceptional and should not be decided under a general set of rules established to meet other needs. The nature of bureaucracy, however, is such that specialisation, hierarchy, and formalisation generally lead bureaucrats to apply established rules and procedures even when they realise that these will not provide a reasonable or just resolution of a specific problem. It has often been argued that a characteristic pathology of bureaucracy is an inversion of ends and means whereby the rules become more important than the objectives underlying their creation.

The political responsiveness of public bureaucracies and the nature of their political outputs are also of great importance to the development of bureaucratic culture. The objects of responsiveness could be political authorities, the citizenry at large, interest groups, or the bureaucracy itself. It appears that by and large, few polities are unconcerned with efforts to ensure political responsiveness to external bodies. In democratic regimes the problem of ensuring responsiveness is generally considered more acute. Indeed, one could understand almost the entire development of the United States Federal Service from the perspective of attempting to guarantee that bureaucratic policy-making would be controlled by political authorities.[32] In general, bureaucracy and democratic government require different values and structural arrangements. For instance, bureaucracy requires hierarchy, unity, long duration in office, command, secretness, and the assumption that not all citizens are qualified to partake in its activities. Democracy, on the other hand, requires equality, plurality, rotation in office, liberty, openness, and the assumption that all citizens are qualified to participate in politics. Ultimately, however, the tension between democracy (and other regimes) and bureaucracy is really over who shall rule. In discussing the power position of bureaucracy, for example, Weber observes:

> Under normal conditions, the power position of a fully developed bureaucracy is always overtowering. The 'political master' finds himself in the position of the 'dilettante' who stands opposite the 'expert,' facing the trained official who stands within the management of administration. This holds whether the 'master' whom the

bureaucracy serves is a 'people,' equipped with the weapons of 'legislative initiative,' the 'referendum,' and the right to remove officials,
or a parliament, elected on a more aristocratic or more 'democratic'
basis and equipped with the right to vote a lack of confidence, or
with the actual authority to vote it.[33]

The difficulties political authorities face in trying to regulate, control, or foster bureaucratic activity are legion. For example, although
the presidency of the United States is generally considered one of the
most powerful political offices in the world, there is ample testimony
from presidents that vis-à-vis the bureaucracy their powers amount to
little more than the power to persuade.[34] Indeed, the standard tools
used to try to ensure that a bureaucracy will at once be responsive and
efficient seem not to have been fully successful anywhere. Reorgan-
isations, regulations concerning political neutrality and loyalty-security,
the use of 'in and outers', and built-in pluralism have not made bureaucracy in any developed nation simply a neutral tool without a substantial political impact of its own. In fact, to an extent, some have
given up on this goal and have reasoned that because a public bureaucracy will inevitably play an important political role, the best route to
responsiveness is not depoliticisation, but rather representation within
the bureaucratic structure. One of the tenets sometimes advanced in a
theory of bureaucratic representation, for example, is that 'the wider
the range of talents, types, and regional and family contacts found in a
bureaucracy, the more likely it is to be able to fulfill its functions, with
respect to both internal efficiency and social setting'.[35] Many now think
that by making a bureaucracy sociologically representative of all major
groups in a society, it will in fact, and despite its structural features,
become a representative, if not responsive, institution. In some nations,
including the United States and India, this belief forms a basis for
important features of public personnel policy.[36]

Although the problem of 'Ruling Servants' is more acute in democratic regimes, it is prevalent elsewhere as well. Eastern European, Soviet,
and Chinese Communist Party officials are not less vociferous than
western politicians in criticising bureaucracy and bureaucratic tendencies.
It may appear, therefore, that the problem of ensuring bureaucratic
responsiveness is so critical as to lead to overwhelmingly negative orientations towards public bureaucracies. Indeed, it has been pointed out
that in the United States election campaigns 'always ring with denun-
ciations of the "dictatorial bureaucracy", its "demand for more power",
its "incompetence" and its "corruption"'.[37] In the Soviet Union, 'bureau-

cracy' is the only major element in the regime which is frequently subjected to criticism in the official media. Yet, bureaucracy may also be viewed in positive terms. It can be a keeper of national and public interests, lend expertise to policy formulation and implementation, provide continuity, and act as a buffer between political authorities and the citizenry in general. This line of reasoning has been well expressed by Herbert Storing:

> Not only do civil servants exercise discretion in interpreting and applying the commands of their political superiors; they participate intimately in the formulation of those commands. They make proposals of their own and fight for them; they comment on the proposals of their political superiors—and may fight against them. They make a vital contribution to the process of deciding what is to be done. Government would come to a standstill if our 'closet statesmen' in the civil service suddenly started doing only what they were told.
> . . .
> The special kind of practical wisdom that characterizes the civil servant points to a more fundamental political function of the bureaucracy, namely to bring to bear on public policy its distinctive view of the common good or its way of looking at questions about the common good . . . Like judges, civil servants have a special responsibility to preserve the rule of law.[38]

Thus, as in the case of impersonality, we can expect different patterns of cognition, affect, and evaluation concerning the political responsiveness and outputs of public bureaucracies. Here, however, social representation, as well as structural features, can be of considerable importance.

Typologising Orientations towards Public Bureaucracy

It has been argued thus far that public bureaucracy is a central feature of almost all political systems and that its structural and behavioural characteristics can logically engender different orientations towards it. There has long been evidence, albeit unsystematic, that social group and personality can condition these orientations by acting as filters through which individuals relate to bureaucratic organisation. In 'Bureaucracy and Its Clientele—A Case Study', for example, Katz and Eisenstadt found important differences in the way Middle Eastern immigrants to Israel and those of European descent related to bureaucracy. Because the

Middle Easterners did not understand the nature of bureaucratic rule application and impersonality, bureaucrats found it desirable to

> teach a client something about his (the bureaucrat's) expectations concerning how the client role is to be played. In other words, the bureaucrat teaches the client how to be a client so that he (the bureaucrat) can go on being a bureaucrat.[39]

In a more elaborate statement of the same phenomenon, Eisenstadt writes that in political communities with emergent bureaucracies,

> these bureaucratic organizations are (at least initially) based on universalistic and functionally specific definitions of the role of the official and the role of the client. The majority of the population of these countries, however, have a different orientation. In social life, their traditional orientations and structures, such as the extended family, are predominant. In these societies, most of a person's role relations are set within traditional groups; and rights and duties are defined in terms of personal relationships. Previous experience with bureaucratic organizations was restricted, and was rarely of any great significance.
>
> Thus, the contacts of the public with governmental organizations provided a framework for a wider process of political socialization. The public's accommodation to the new political structure became, to a considerable extent, dependent upon its successful learning in these situations of contact. This has very often forced the bureaucracies to go beyond their proper specialized roles and to assume various roles of social and political leadership and tutelage—without which they could not have effected the necessary changes in the behavior of the population at large. This need to foster change often extended the scope of the activities of bureaucrats beyond their specific goals, and made them reach also into the realm of family, kinship, and community life of wide strata of the population.[40]

Hence, there is a sense in which reactions to bureaucracy are intertwined with developmental processes of socialisation and internalisation of bureaucratic norms. Therefore, while instances in which segments of a society have almost totally different orientations towards bureaucratic objects are probably rare, there is considerable evidence of the existence of more limited differences among population groups. For example, several studies of the prestige and image of public bureaucracy in the

United States have revealed that blacks, the foreign-born, women and those of lower socio-economic status in general, tend to rate public employment higher than do other groups.[41]

The interface between personality and bureaucracy has long been a matter of interest to social scientists and it, too, can have an important effect on individual orientations towards bureaucratic objects. For example, in his classic study of 'Red Tape as a Social Problem', Gouldner found that individual perceptions of red tape included instances in which

> the individual's ego is challenged on two counts: (1) A claim which he believes legitimate is not taken 'at face value.' He must either supply proof or allow it to be investigated. He is, as one remarked, 'treated as a criminal'—he may feel his worth is questioned, his status impugned. (2) Not only are his claims and assertions challenged, but other details of his 'private life' are investigated. The individual enters the situation on 'official,' 'technical,' or 'public' business, and feels that he ends up by being investigated as a person.[42]

In addition, 'sensitivity to disparities of power seems to be another element in the red tape frame of reference'.[43] Thus, it appears that 'the individual who decries red tape feels that he is unable to "get to" the people who have the power, or get to them readily enough. Power centers are felt to be out of reach and the individual experiences himself and those with whom he can have some face to face contact as powerless'.[44] Finally, 'Two further character traits of clients apparently encourage them to perceive red tape where others do not. These are suspiciousness and an apparent inability to defer gratifications.'[45] These two elements are interlocked in that 'to the extent that the world is felt to be peopled with those who would do us harm and who cannot be trusted, safety lies only in the *immediate* satisfaction'.[46]

Victor Thompson is another who has given consideration to the relationship between social and personality characteristics and individual reactions to bureaucratic organisation. Although his observations are not empirically grounded in a systematic way, they are nevertheless highly suggestive. In his view,

> The bureaucratic culture makes certain demands upon clients as well as upon organization employees. There are many people in our society who have not been able to adjust to these demands. To them bureaucracy is a curse. They see no good in it whatsoever, but view the

demands of modern organization as 'red tape.' This kind of behavior is external to the organization, and is not simply a reaction to bureau-pathology. Its source will be found within the critic himself, not within the organization. It is, in fact, a kind of social disease which we propose to call 'bureausis.'[47]

According to Thompson, 'the basic ingredient of bureausis is immaturity, the dysfunctional persistence of childish behavior patterns'.[48] Those who suffer from this 'disease' are 'bureautics'. They are characterised by 'low powers of abstraction' and a 'need to personalize the world'.[49] Consequently, 'the bureautic can rarely enter successfully into an impersonal, functional, or *bureaucratic* relationship. The world is peopled only with friends and enemies; it does not have impartial, impersonal functionaries'.[50] Moreover, 'bureautics fear the world beyond, the nonpersonalized world, and they fear bureaucracy because they cannot personalize it. They feel powerless in relation to it'.[51] Finally, the bureautic has 'no confidence in securing justice through an impersonal, abstract system of norms and routines, and he interprets justice as getting what is his by right. For him, "what is by right" and what he wants are easily confused'.[52]

There are several themes running throughout these interpretations of the ways in which social group and personality characteristics filter individual orientations towards bureaucracy. They suggest, for instance, that bureaucracy is a structure of high salience to individuals and that they react differently to its procedures and output-oriented behaviour. Some are able to cope with bureaucratic organisations, whereas others find them an anathema. The features associated with bureaucracy which appear to be most central in this context are impersonality and perceived unfairness. Together, these tend to generate a feeling of powerlessness in some individuals, which, in turn, may reinforce their negative images of bureaucracy. Consequently, if these observations are correct, it should be possible to discover distinct patterns of cognitive, affective, and evaluative orientations towards a public bureaucracy among the members of a political community.

It could be reasoned that such patterns would be most readily uncovered by ascertaining individuals' perceptions of the most general structural and output-oriented characteristics of public bureaucracy. Such an approach would be inclusive of the features people associate with 'red tape', which are largely structural and procedural, as well as those associated with the actual distribution of bureaucratic services. In this study we were able to typologise individuals along two dimensions of this nature. One is the extent to which people believe public bureaucracy is 'so complicated that a person like me can't really understand what's going on'. This dimension broadly taps those structural and procedural aspects of public bureaucracy which the individual finds most salient. It includes impersonality and red tape, but nevertheless goes beyond these elements and concerns structural complexity and other bureaucratic norms and processes as well. The second dimension concerns output and determines whether people expect equal treatment from public bureaucracy. As such, this dimension characterises the individual's overall perception of bureaucratic outputs by indicating whether these are believed to be egalitarian or to benefit some individuals and groups more than others.

When the dimensions of complexity and equality are combined they yield the four types of orientations towards public bureaucracy contained in Table 1.2. Individuals in category IV perceive bureaucracy to be complex and they do not expect equal treatment from it. As will be seen later on (chapters 3, 4 and 5), they are also less aware of its impact on their daily lives, feel less efficacious with regard to it and view public bureaucracy in more negative terms than do any of the other groups. These are the individuals who see themselves as being oppressed by red tape and bureaucrats who are unresponsive to their demands. They are repelled by impersonality and consider bureaucratic outputs to be unfair. By and large, then, they are the 'bureautics' of whom Thompson speaks, and we will follow him in the use of that term.

Type I, on the other hand, consists of people who believe that public bureaucracy is uncomplicated and a dispenser of equal treatment. They are the most efficacious group and are repelled neither by the structural, procedural, nor output characteristics of public bureaucracy. For them, bureaucracy is comprehensible, rational, and fair. They are the well-adjusted administrative clients of a bureaucratised society. Unfortunately, there is no term in the literature which readily suggests itself as a label for such a group. Indeed, the overriding popular view of bureaucracy is that it is irrational, if not evil, and favourable views are rarely voiced, except perhaps by bureaucrats and sociologists. In any event, the existence of such a group has been largely overlooked. Consequently, we will take the liberty of calling them 'bureauphiles'. This term immediately distinguishes them as the polar opposite of bureautics, who are the ultimate 'bureauphobes'.

The remaining two categories consist of either (1) those who believe that public bureaucracy is complicated but nevertheless, or perhaps because of this perception, expect equal treatment from it, or (2) those

Table 1.2: Patterns of Orientation Towards Public Bureaucracy

	Expectation of Treatment	
	Equal	Unequal
Uncomplicated	I: Bureauphile	II: Bureautolerant
Complicated	III: Bureautolerant	IV: Bureautic

who view the bureaucracy as uncomplicated and do *not* expect equal treatment from it. Despite their different outlooks, these two groups can be collapsed into one analytical category because there is little difference between them in so far as patterns of orientations towards bureaucracy are concerned. For example, those in categories II and III feel equally efficacious with regard to public bureaucracy and have similar images of it. Again, there is no term in the literature which has been generally used to refer to such a group. We propose to call them 'bureautolerants', in view of their positive orientation towards either the structural and procedural features of bureaucracy or the overall nature of its outputs. Unlike bureautics, this group is not totally repelled by bureaucracy, and in contrast to bureauphiles, they are unable to accept it as wholly intelligible and fair. In short, they tend to accept bureaucracy, but only partially.

Throughout much of this study it will be shown that bureauphiles, bureautolerants, and bureautics have distinct patterns of cognitive, affective, and evaluative orientations towards public bureaucracy. It is useful to note here, however, that these categories of individuals consist of members of different ethnic and educational groups, although there is some tendency for social group and educational level to influence one's perceptions of bureaucracy. Consequently, there is no reason to believe that they are tied to a specific political culture or social sub-culture. This will become more evident as our analysis progresses.

Now that we have typologised the general membership of a political community, it is desirable to turn our attention to its bureaucratic component. Here, there is no dearth of guidance available in the literature on organisation and administration. One of the earliest empirically based typologies of bureaucrats was developed by Leonard Reissman in 'A Study of Role Conceptions in Bureaucracy'.[53] He discovered four types of public bureaucrat. The first was the 'functional bureaucrat', 'who is oriented towards and seeks his recognition from a given professional group outside of rather than within the bureaucracy'. Such bureaucrats measure success against professional standards rather than in terms of satisfying the needs of the bureaucracy or its policy objectives. 'Psychologically' this type of bureaucrat 'is facing outward and away from the bureaucratic structure.' For them, the bureaucracy is just another place to practise one's profession. Second, there are 'specialist bureaucrats'. Although these resemble the first type in their professional orientations, they exhibit 'a greater awareness of an identification with the bureaucracy'. They seek both professional and bureaucratic recognition and consequently occupy a sometimes precarious position. Specialist bureaucrats tend, therefore, to be 'overly meticulous about the rules and regulations', and attempt 'always to remain safely within these limits'. The next type is the 'service bureaucrat':

> Here too . . . a position of ambivalence is created. He is oriented in terms of the bureaucratic structure, but seeks recognition for the job he does from a group outside of it. He entered civil service primarily to realize certain personally-held goals which center about rendering service to a certain group. The bureaucracy offers a framework through which he can best function and his task is one of utilizing that mechanism to achieve his goals.

A final type are 'job bureaucrats'. They are 'immersed entirely within the structure' and oriented towards it. For them, 'professional skills only provide the necessary entrance qualifications and determine the nature of the work to be done'. They seek 'recognition along departmental rather than professional lines', and the 'improvement of the operating efficiency of the bureau'. In addition, 'His aspirations consist of achieving material rewards and increased status through promotions. He strongly adheres to the rules and the job constitutes his full center of attention and the end to be served'.

Another typology of bureaucrats was introduced by Anthony Downs.[54] These types, however, are purely theoretical and not based on systematic empirical investigation. He divides bureaucrats into the following categories:

1. *Climbers*—a 'climber seeks to maximize his own power, income, and prestige, he always desires more of these goods.' 'Climbers seek to aggrandize in ways that will create the least effective resistance.'

2. *Conservers*—'Conservers seek to maximize their security and convenience.' They 'are essentially change avoiders. In this respect, they are the opposite of climbers'.

3. *Zealots*—officials who 'act as though pursuit of the public

interest means promotion of very specific policy goals . . . regardless of the antagonism they encounter or the particular positions they occupy. Hence their conceptions are narrow in focus and stable in both in time and under varying circumstances.'

4. *Advocates*—'are basically optimistic, and normally quite energetic. However, they are considerably more "other directed" in character than zealots; hence they are strongly subject to influence by their superiors, equals, and subordinates. Nevertheless, they are often quite aggressive in pressing for what they believe best suits their organizations.'

5. *Statesmen*—are 'loyal to the nation or the society as a whole,' they 'are mainly "inner directed" in character, and therefore can persist in maintaining a generalized outlook even when their responsibilities are quite particular. However, they do not like conflict situations and seek to reconcile clashes of particular viewpoints through compromises based upon their broad general loyalties'.

A third typology has been introduced by Robert Presthus in *The Organizational Society*. Although Presthus did not address bureaucratic types in a strict sense, but rather sought to identify patterns of accommodation to the demands of working in large organisations, his observations are nevertheless relevant to the study of bureaucracy. He developed his typology at great length and based it broadly on diverse areas of social theory. However, it can be readily summarised. The first pattern of accommodation is that of 'upward-mobiles':

His values and behavior include the capacity to identify strongly with the organization, permitting a nice synthesis of personal rewards and organizational goals. A typical form of accommodation is adjustment through power and special efforts to control situations and people. His 'security operations' stress efficiency, strength, self-control, and dominance. His most functional value is a deep respect for authority.[55]

The polar opposite of the 'upward-mobile' is the 'indifferent':

The indifferent's rejection of status and prestige values often insures a felicitous accommodation. Since job satisfaction is a product of the relation between aspirations and achievement, he is often the most satisfied of organization men. His aspirations are based on a realistic appraisal of existing opportunities. He rejects the status anxiety, the success striving, the self-discipline, and the conformity demanded of self and family that confront the upward-mobile ... Escaping the commitments of the 'true believer' and the anxiety of the neurotic striver, he receives big dividends in privacy, tranquility, and self-realization through his *extravocational* orientation.[56]

Finally, there are the 'ambivalents', who can be outlined in the following terms:

The most critical item is his fear of authority which often distorts his interpersonal relations. His inability to accept the organization's collective goals, which violate his need for personal autonomy, is also at work. His 'tender-minded' view of human relations disqualifies him for the 'universalistic' decision making required for success on organizational terms. Since his preferences include a desire for creativity and for a work environment that permits spontaneity and experiment, the structured personal relations, stereotyped procedures, and group decision making of big organization prove stifling ... If his values did not include prestige and influence, a happier accommodation might be possible ... In sum, with the exception of his critical function as the agent of change, the ambivalent type is uniquely unsuited to the bureaucratic institution.[57]

It is evident that there are several common strands running throughout these typologies, and undoubtedly each clarifies something about important aspects of bureaucrats' reactions to the organisations in which they are employed. Reissman, Downs, and Presthus find both structural factors and personal motives to be of great consequence. Orientations towards one's job, chances for advancement, prestige, or status, and one's feelings towards colleagues, self, community, and other reference groups are thought to be of great significance. So is one's reaction to hierarchical authority and specialisation. At the same time that one can learn much from these typologies and the study of the elements upon which they are based, it is also clear that they are so diverse that no attempt to integrate them fully is likely to succeed. Consequently, some factors influencing bureaucrats' attitudes and behaviour must be sacrificed in any typology in order to include others. Here again, as in the case of the general citizenry's orientations towards bureaucracy, we were able to tap many of the elements involved and to borrow from the theories advanced by others by typologising bureaucrats along two broad dimensions which are associated with their patterns of cognition, affect, and evaluation concerning the organisations in which they work.

The two dimensions employed concern (1) the factors bureaucrats believe are most important in obtaining a position in the public bureaucracy, and (2) their personal motives for seeking such a post. The first of these included such elements as education, qualifications for the job, talent, age, personal connections, political connections, and luck. This dimension broadly taps the individual bureaucrat's view of personnel administrative features in the bureaucracy, which is an element that Reissman, Downs, and Presthus all find highly salient in the construction of their typologies. How one gets a job implies a great deal about the nature of an organisation, including its goals and objectives, rationality, the nature of its functions, and its stress on efficient operations. Consequently, it also tends to generate perceptions concerning the organisation's demands upon its employees. Hence, it may also relate to one's feelings of self-worth and assessment of organisational worth. In order to use this dimension in our typology, we dichotomised individual responses into two categories, according to whether they adhered more to public personnel conceptions stressing a merit and achievement orientation with reliance on factors of intrinsic importance to the performance of administrative tasks, or whether they were more closely associated with patterns of ascriptive, patrimonial, or patronage-oriented patterns of recruitment making use of elements which are largely extrinsic to the accomplishment of administrative work. This dimension, therefore, not only differentiates between the types of perceptions bureaucrats have concerning personnel matters, it is also a major element distinguishing 'modern' from 'traditional'[58] public administration. Consequently it is of considerable importance to the development of both political and bureaucratic culture and implies much about the administrative world views of public bureaucrats. It is important to note in this context that this dimension is a subjective one and that responses were widely distributed. Education, job qualifications, and talents were considered to fit the 'achievement/intrinsic' category; and the remainder were grouped in the 'ascriptive/extrinsic' category.

The second dimension upon which our typology is based concerns the individual bureaucrat's personal motives in seeking public employment. Again, this is an element upon which Reissman, Downs, and Presthus place considerable importance. The categories here included desiring to obtain any job, job security, professional advancement, personal advancement, independence at work, an ability to serve the public, and an opportunity to advance the public welfare. It is apparent that all but the last two items are primarily inner-oriented.[59] These are egocentric in the sense that the individual seeks a bureaucratic position primarily for his/her own benefit, rather than for that of others. The remaining items, on the other hand, express a concern for the community at large and are somewhat altruistic in their orientation. They also imply that the bureaucrat has objectives which he/she would like to see advanced through bureaucratic action. Community-oriented bureaucrats, therefore, are more in keeping with a model of sophisticated, high-prestige civil servants with high morale and a strong sense of *esprit de corps*.

These two dimensions yield the typology contained in Table 1.3. Three of the four categories correspond roughly to types introduced by Reissman and Downs. Bureaucrats in the fourth category can be considered 'statesmen', although not all of Downs' elements are applicable. They are community-oriented and believe that they work in an organisation which is based on personnel conceptions which reward achievement, education, and talent rather than political and personal connections. These bureaucrats tend to have a more positive orientation towards the bureaucracy than do others and they believe it plays a more positive role in the life of the nation. Their polar opposite is the only type having no correspondent in the other typologies. Bureaucrats in category I are inner-oriented and believe that political and personal connections are most important in obtaining bureaucratic positions. We propose to call them 'politicos' because they play a political game for their own advancement and are not oriented towards the community as a whole. Politicos are more likely to view the bureaucracy as being highly politicised and unfair than are any of the other types. They are less likely to attribute an important impact on the daily life of citizens to it, and, in general, they view the bureaucracy in a negative fashion. Individuals of type II roughly fit Reissman's conception of 'service bureaucrats', although here again the parallels should not be overstated. They are oriented towards the public at large and while finding the bureaucracy a somewhat useful framework for their activities, they nevertheless do not believe it is fully rational and functional in its assignment of individuals to tasks. In some ways, they share the traits of 'ambivalents', especially with regard to the gap between their outward orientation and overall view of the bureaucracy, which often tends to be more negative than that of the other groups. For instance, service bureaucrats are least likely to believe that, on the whole, bureaucrats do their jobs properly. Finally, category III consists of the 'job bureaucrat' who is inner-oriented and primarily attuned to the demands of modern bureaucratic organisation. They are least likely to view the bureaucracy as being highly politicised and generally relate to it in a favourable way.

Table 1.3: Bureaucrats' Patterns of Orientations Towards Bureaucracy

	Personal motives	
	Inner-oriented	Community-oriented
Perception of Personnel procedures		
Ascriptive/extrinsic	I: Politicos	II: Service bureaucrats
Achievement/intrinsic	III: Job bureaucrats	IV: Statesmen

As in the case of types of orientation found among the general public, it will be shown throughout a large portion of this study that these types are associated with distinct patterns of cognition, affect, and evaluation concerning public bureaucracy. Moreover, although these orientations are affected by organisational variables such as rank, seniority, functional specialisation, and politicisation, bureaucrats of each type can be found in all ranks and units of bureaucracy. Where the independent effects of such factors are important, they will, of course, be entered into the analysis.

This chapter introduces a concept of bureaucratic culture. It has been argued that in the twentieth century bureaucratisation has been a central facet of political life in many nations. However, the broad consequences of this process for citizenship, administration, and political community have not been sufficiently investigated. It is in this context that knowledge of citizens' and bureaucrats' patterns of orientation towards bureaucracy are of greatest importance. The structural characteristics, norms, and political roles of public bureaucracy engender different patterns of cognition, affect, and evaluation among the members of a political community. Relying on wide-ranging theories concerning these phenomena, it is possible to construct typologies of citizens' and bureaucrats' reactions to bureaucracy which are associated with different sets of perceptions and divergent feelings of efficacy towards that form of organisation. Finally, it has been suggested that much can be learned about the general nature of public administration and political communities by assessing the degree of congruence between citizens' and bureaucrats' orientations towards public bureaucracy.

Notes

1. Brian Chapman, *The Profession of Government* (London: Unwin University

Books, 1959), p. 296.

2. See Erich Strauss, *The Ruling Servants* (New York: Praeger, 1960); Hans Rosenberg, *Bureaucracy, Aristocracy, and Autocracy* (Boston: Beacon Press, 1958); and Milovan Djilas, *The New Class* (New York: Praeger, 1957).

3. See Henry Jacoby, *The Bureaucratization of the World* (Berkeley: University of California Press, 1973).

4. See among many others, Jacoby, *Bureaucratization;* Robert Presthus, *The Organizational Society* (New York: Random House, 1962); and Max Weber, *From Max Weber: Essays in Sociology*, trans. and ed. H.H. Gerth and C.W. Mills (New York: Oxford University Press, 1958), ch. 8.

5. See among others, Chris Argyris, 'The Individual and Organization: Some Problems of Mutual Adjustment', *Administrative Science Quarterly*, II (June 1957), 1-24; and Robert Merton, 'Bureaucratic Structure and Personality', *Social Forces*, 18 (May 1940), 560-568.

6. The literature here is far too extensive to cite in its entirety. Among the better known are Paul P. Van Riper, *History of the United States Civil Service* (Evanston: Row, Peterson, 1958); Roger Gregorie, *The French Civil Service* (Brussels: International Institute of Administrative Sciences, 1964); R.A.A. Chapot De Saintogne, *Public Administration in Germany* (London: Weidenfeld & Nicolson, 1961); W.J.M. MacKenzie and J.W. Grove, *Central Administration in Britain* (London: Longman, 1957); R.O. Tilman, *Bureaucratic Transition in Malaya* (Durham: Duke University Press, 1964); N. Dang, *Viet-Nam* (Honolulu: East-West Center Press, 1966); William J. Siffin, *The Thai Bureaucracy* (Honolulu: East-West Center Press, 1966); Fred W. Riggs, *Thailand* (Honolulu: East-West Center Press, 1966); W.D.K. Kernaghan (ed.), *Bureaucracy in Canadian Government* (Toronto: Methuen, 1969); A. Adedeji (ed.), *Nigerian Administration and its Political Setting* (London: Hutchinson Educational, 1968); and Guthrie S. Birkhead (ed.), *Administrative Problems in Pakistan* (Syracuse: Syracuse University Press, 1966).

7. For a partial listing, see Ferrel Heady and Sybil Stokes, *Comparative Administration: A Selective Annotated Bibliography* (Ann Arbor: Institute of Public Administration, University of Michigan, 1960), 2nd edn.

8. See among others, V. Thompson, *Modern Organization* (New York: Knopf, 1961); Charles S. Hyneman, *Bureaucracy in a Democracy* (New York: Harper, 1950); and F. Mosher, *Democracy and the Public Service* (New York: Oxford University Press, 1968).

9. See Gordon Smith, 'A Model of the Bureaucratic Culture', *Political Studies*, 22 (March 1974), 31-43.

10. Gabriel A. Almond and Sidney Verba, *The Civic Culture* (Boston: Little, Brown, 1965), p. 13.

11. Ibid., p. 14.

12. Franklin P. Kilpatrick, Milton C. Cummings, Jr., and M. Kent Jennings, *The Image of the Federal Service* (Washington: Brookings Institution, 1964), p. 246.

13. Alvin Gouldner, 'Red Tape as a Social Problem', in R.K. Merton *et al.* (eds.), *Reader in Bureaucracy* (Glencoe: Free Press, 1952), pp. 410-18; Elihu Katz and S.N. Eisenstadt, 'Bureaucracy and its Clientele—A Case Study', in Amitai Etzioni (ed.), *Readings on Modern Organizations* (Englewood Cliffs: Prentice-Hall, 1969), pp. 231-40.

14. The term is used here as in Thompson, *Modern Organization*, ch. 8.

15. Martin Albrow, *Bureaucracy* (New York: Praeger, 1970), p. 125.

16. Weber, *Essays in Sociology*, ch. 8; and Talcott Parsons (ed.), *The Theory of Social and Economic Organization* (New York: Free Press, 1947), pp. 329-41.

17. Weber, *Essays in Sociology*, ch. 8; Albrow, *Bureaucracy*, pp. 44-5.

18. Anthony Downs, *Inside Bureaucracy* (Boston: Little, Brown, 1967), p. 24.

19. Ibid., p. 25.

20. Thompson, *Modern Organization*, pp. 3-4.

21. Bernard C. Reimann, 'On the Dimensions of Bureaucratic Structure: An Empirical Reappraisal', *Administrative Science Quarterly*, 18 (December 1973), 462-76.

22. See Roger Mansfield, 'Bureaucracy and Centralization', ibid., 477-88.

23. See Richard Hall, *Organizations: Structure and Process* (Englewood Cliffs: Prentice-Hall, 1972), chs. 4-6.

24. Ferrel Heady, *Public Administration: A Comparative Perspective* (Englewood Cliffs: Prentice-Hall, 1966), p. 20.

25. Weber, *Essays in Sociology*, p. 214.

26. Warren Bennis, 'Beyond Bureaucracy', *Transaction*, 2 (July-August 1965), 32.

27. Weber, *Essays in Sociology*, p. 216.

28. Peter Blau and Marshall Meyer, *Bureaucracy in Modern Society*, 2nd edn (New York: Random House, 1971), p. 9.

29. Argyris, *Administrative Science Quarterly*, 2, p. 18; Merton, *Social Forces*, 23, pp. 405-15.

30. Argyris, *Administrative Science Quarterly*, 2, pp. 1-24.

31. Gouldner, 'Red Tape', in Merton *et al.* (eds.), *Bureaucracy*, pp. 410-18; and Thompson, *Modern Organization*, ch. 8. These works are sources of support for the remaining statements in this paragraph.

32. See Mosher, *Democracy and the Public Service*, ch. 3.

33. Weber, *Essays in Sociology*, p. 232.

34. See R. Neustadt, *Presidential Power* (New York: Wiley, 1960), esp. ch. 1.

35. Samuel Krislov, *The Negro in Federal Employment* (Minneapolis: University of Minnesota Press, 1967), p. 64.

36. See David H. Rosenbloom, 'The Civil Service Commission's Decision to Authorize the Use of Goals and Timetables in the Federal Equal Employment Opportunity Program', *Western Political Quarterly*, 26 (June 1973), 236-51; and Marc Galanter, 'Compensatory Discrimination in Recruitment to the Indian Public Service', unpublished paper delivered at the Meeting of the American Society for Public Administration, Denver, Colorado, 19 April 1971.

37. H.M. Somers, 'The President, the Congress, and the Federal Government Service', in Wallace Sayre (ed.), *The Federal Government Service* (Englewood Cliffs: Prentice-Hall, 1965), p. 95.

38. Herbert J. Storing, 'Political Parties and the Bureaucracy', in Robert A. Goldwin (ed.), *Political Parties, USA* (Chicago: Rand McNally, 1964), pp. 152, 154.

39. Katz and Eisenstadt, 'Bureaucracy and its Clientele', in Etzioni (ed.), *Modern Organizations*, p. 236.

40. S.N. Eisenstadt, 'Problems of Emerging Bureaucracies in Developing Areas and New States', in Nimrod Raphaeli (ed.), *Readings in Comparative Public Administration* (Boston: Allyn & Bacon, 1967), p. 227.

41. L.D. White, *The Prestige Value of Public Employment in Chicago* (Chicago: University of Chicago Press, 1929); *Further Contributions to the Prestige Value of Public Employment* (Chicago: University of Chicago Press, 1932); Morris Janowitz and Deil Wright, 'The Prestige of Public Employment: 1929 and 1954', *Public Administration Review*, 16 (Winter 1956), 15-21; and Kilpatrick *et al.*, *Image of the Federal Service*, p. 96.

42. Gouldner, 'Red Tape', in Merton *et al.* (eds.), *Bureaucracy*, p. 413.

43. Ibid., p. 414.

44. Ibid., p. 415.

45. Ibid.

46. Ibid., p. 416.

47. Thompson, *Modern Organization*, p. 170.

48. Ibid.

49. Ibid., pp. 172, 173.

50. Ibid., p. 173.

51. Ibid.

52. Ibid., p. 174.

53. Leonard Reissman, 'A Study of Role Conceptions in Bureaucracy', *Social Forces*, 27 (March 1949), esp. pp. 308-9 from which the remainder of the quoted material in this paragraph is taken.

54. Downs, *Inside Bureaucracy*, ch. 9. The remainder of the quoted material in this paragraph is taken from this source.

55. Presthus, *Organizational Society*, p. 203.

56. Ibid., p. 218.

57. Ibid., pp. 285-6.

58. Although these terms are fraught with difficulties, it is almost impossible to avoid them. They are employed here with all the caveats expressed by Joseph LaPalombara (ed.), 'Bureaucracy and Political Development: Notes, Queries, and Dilemmas', in Joseph LaPalombara (ed.), *Bureaucracy and Political Development* (Princeton: Princeton University Press, 1963), pp. 34-61.

59. It should be noted that the concept of 'inner-oriented' is not linked to that of 'inner-directed'.

2 AN APPROACH TO THE STUDY OF BUREAUCRATIC CULTURE

The bureaucratic culture of a given political community consists of its members' cognitive, affective, and evaluative orientations towards public bureaucracy. These, in turn, are to a considerable extent related to the personnel and organisational features of public bureaucracies. For example, our typologies of citizens' and bureaucrats' reactions to bureaucracy involve the dimensions of organisational complexity, fairness, and the nature of personnel processes. But national bureaucracies are organised along different lines and their operative characteristics can be quite divergent. One would expect, therefore, that relatively distinct types of bureaucratic culture could be found in separate political communities. However, rather than be entirely idiosyncratic, types of bureaucratic culture might vary with some overriding systemic factors. It has been argued forcefully in the literature of public administration and political science that the level of political development is such an element.

Bureaucracy and Political Development

'Political development', like 'bureaucracy', is a term fraught with difficulties and rife with differing interpretations. Yet, as in the case of bureaucracy, it is one which is so deeply ingrained in contemporary social science that it cannot be ignored. Perhaps here, as in other areas, an 'important source of confusion is the implicit or explicit free substitution of society, economic system, or social system for political system'.[1] However, most would probably agree with LaPalombara that political development is related to political change along at least four dimensions. The first of these is the 'degree of structural differentiation that exists for those institutions involved in the performance of political functions'.[2] Such differentiation 'involves the creation of new structures and roles for the performance of political functions; it implies an increased specialization or division of labor among those who are responsible for the performance of political functions'.[3] 'Magnitude' is a second dimension. It refers to 'the ratio of political activity, however institutionalized, to all of the other activity that takes place in society'.[4] Third is the 'degree of achievement orientation' that 'applies to political recruitment and role differentiation'.[5] In LaPalombara's view, 'maximum achievement orientation in political recruitment may be critical for a society that deeply and directly involves the government in economic development while only optimum achievement orientation may be necessary for democratization'.[6] Finally, there is the 'degree of secularization that persists in performing all of the political functions'.[7] 'Maximum secularization would require that the political process proceed primarily on the basis of a rationality of the ends of government and of the means utilized to achieve these ends.'[8]

LaPalombara suggests that there is co-variation along these dimensions and that the greater the amount of each found in a political community, the more developed is its political system. The primary utility of this approach is that it can move conceptions concerning political development away from culture-bound ideas involving 'Anglo-American' models of modernisation. In LaPalombara's words,

> It should be reasonably clear that development along these dimensions can occur irrespective of whether the population participates in the political process, whether one or more political parties exists, whether civil liberties are institutionalized, whether public policy is responsive to the wishes or demands of the people, whether a high degree of political pluralism is present, and so on. From the standpoint of possible change, there is nothing magical about the relationship of any of these dimensions and the particular institutional and behavioral characteristics we have come to associate with the United States or Great Britain. A particular combination of attributes along these dimensions might still evolve in either a democratic or a non-democratic framework. In other words, if *democratic* political development is the end in view, it must be analyzed in terms of variables that are additional to those we have been discussing.[9]

This is a point to which we shall soon return.

It is obvious that political development in this sense has important ramifications for public administrative systems. Although there may be considerable variation in institutional forms in this area, there also appear to be some general overriding patterns. For example, in a synthesis of much of the literature on comparative public administration, Ferrel Heady was able to identify the major characteristics of national bureaucracies in more and less politically developed nations. Taking the latter first, he found that their public bureaucracies are characterised by the following traits:

1. The basic pattern of public administration is imitative rather

than indigenous.

2. The bureaucracies are deficient in skilled manpower necessary for developmental programs.

3. . . . These bureaucracies . . . emphasize orientations that are other than production-directed. That is, much bureaucratic activity is channeled toward the realization of goals other than the achievement of program objectives.

4. . . . widespread discrepancy between form and reality . . .

5. . . . the bureaucracy in a developing country is apt to have a generous measure of operational autonomy.[10]

These features tend to combine and militate against bureaucratic legitimacy, efficiency, and political responsiveness. Such bureaucracies tend to be very hierarchical and dominated by a group which is culturally and socially unrepresentative of the population at large. Rule application is often personalised and, in general, administrative penetration of the society is resisted by the bulk of the citizenry.

In Heady's view, bureaucracies in more politically developed nations manifest considerably different characteristics. Among these are:

1. The public service of a modernized political system will be large-scale, complex, and instrumental in the sense that its mission is understood to be that of carrying out the policies of the political decision-makers.

2. The bureaucracy will be highly specialized and will require in its ranks most of the occupational and professional categories represented in the society.

3. The bureaucracy will exhibit to a marked degree a sense of professionalization, both in the sense of identification with the public service as a profession and in the sense of belonging to a narrower field of professional or technical specialization within the service . . .

4. Because the political system as a whole is relatively stable and mature, and the bureaucracy is more fully developed, the role of the bureaucracy in the political process is fairly clear, and the line of demarcation between the bureaucracy and other political institutions is generally definite and accepted.

5. The bureaucracy in a modernized polity will be subject to effective policy control by other functionally specific political institutions.[11]

These bureaucracies are therefore perceived as more legitimate, efficient, and politically responsive. They fulfil a greater number and variety of functions and consequently their penetration of the society is more extensive. They are also more impersonal in their interactions with clients. Recruitment patterns here are more achievement-oriented, and although bureaucratic representation is far from perfect, it is generally greater than in the bureaucracies of less developed political communities.[12]

A somewhat different way of classifying and conceptualising the relationship between levels of political development and the nature of bureaucratic structures and processes has been adopted by Banks and Textor, and Forward:

Modern: generally effective and responsible civil service, performing in a functionally specific, non-ascriptive social context;

Semi-modern: largely rationalized bureaucratic structure of limited efficiency because of shortage of skilled personnel, inadequate recruitment criteria, excessive intrusion on non-administrative organs, or partially non-congruent social institutions;

Transitional: largely rationalized ex-colonial bureaucratic structure in the process of personnel nationalization and adaption to the servicing or restructuring of autochthonous [i.e. 'indigenous'] social institutions;

Traditional: largely non-rationalized bureaucratic structure performing in the context of ascriptive or deferential stratification system.[13]

Differences of this magnitude in the nature of public bureaucracies in more or less developed polities would almost inevitably be reflected in their patterns of bureaucratic culture. They relate to several structural and behavioural characteristics, including complexity, roles, styles, political integration, and general performance, which could be expected to engender differential orientations towards bureaucracy among the members of a political community. However, these developmental tendencies are not closely associated with the type of regime or other political structures. Therefore, because the latter could also be expected to have a significant impact on bureaucratic culture, they too|must also be taken into account. It is useful in this connection to follow an approach developed by Janowitz and subsequently adopted by Eldersveld and associates[14] which dichotomises between democratically and non-democratically oriented political communities and specifies the administrative needs of the former. In terms of these formulations, in order for a public bureaucracy to be integrated fully and effectively into a democratic regime, it must be in a state of 'balance'. 'A bureaucracy is in imbalance when it fails to operate on the basis of democratic consent . . . Bureaucratic imbalance may be either *despotic* or *subservient. Despotic* implies that the bureaucracy is too much the master while *subservient* implies that it is too much the servant.'[15] Balance requires four elements:

1. Knowledge. The public must have an adequate level of knowledge about the operations of the public bureaucracy . . .

2. Self-interest. The public must consider that its self-interest is being served by the public bureaucracy. As a check on the disruptive consequences of self-interested demands on the bureaucracy, the public must be aware simultaneously of the bureaucracy's capacity to act as a neutral and impartial agent in resolving social conflicts.

3. Principle-mindedness. The public must be of the general opinion that the public bureaucracy is guided in its actions by a set of principles guaranteeing equal and impersonal treatment. Administrative routines, however, must be sufficiently flexible to cope with individual differences in order to insure adequate dealings with clients.

4. Prestige. Public perspectives toward the public bureaucracy must include adequate prestige value toward public employment as compared with other types of careers. Very low and very high prestige values would interfere with the bureaucracy's ability to operate on the basis of democratic consent.[16]

In non-democratically-oriented polities these elements would be of minimal or no concern and administrative processes would have little reason to take them into account.

By now it is evident that at least two dimensions have to be considered in the selection of political communities for the study of bureaucratic culture. One is the level of political development and the other is the degree of democratic orientation. However, an additional problem is also involved: should bureaucratic culture be analysed within a single political community or across several polities? Either approach could be used and each has significant advantages and disadvantages in so far as theory construction is concerned.

Cross-national analysis can be referred to as the 'most similar' research design. It involves the selection of systems (be they social, political, bureaucratic, or otherwise) as similar as possible with respect to as many characteristics as feasible. It is then expected that any significant differences which may be discovered will be attributable to a small number of variables, rather than to an agglomeration of systemic factors. For example, a difference in feelings of efficacy towards bureaucracy found among citizens of the United States and Canada could be attributed to a smaller number of intrasystem factors than could a similar difference between the citizenry of either of these nations and those of India. This approach has become quite popular in political science during the past two decades. Alford's analysis of the social antecedents of voting, in *Party and Society*,[17] and Almond and Verba's five-nation study provide important examples of this trend. Alford describes the choice of countries for his study in the following way:

> The Anglo-American countries—Great Britain, Australia, New Zealand, The United States and Canada—are alike in the important respect that they may be termed 'pluralist' political systems . . . Each of the Anglo-American countries tends toward a two-party system . . . The electorate is not fragmented into supporters of one or another small party hoping to gain seats and voice in a coalition government.[18]

Relatedly, Almond and Verba selected countries that have a 'democratic political system' but which differ radically with regard to their levels of political and economic development.

However, notwithstanding the obvious advantages of the 'most similar' design, it has an inherent limitation in that the independent variables which allegedly produce concomitant variations cannot be singled out and are therefore only presumed to be of importance. Consequently, 'the efficiency of this strategy in providing knowledge that can be generalized is relatively limited'.[19] In addition, cross-national studies almost inevitably tend to play down the importance of variation within individual societies. Alford, for instance, pays relatively little attention to the roles of third parties in his analysis which centres on the two major parties in each of the Anglo-American political systems.

Studies of single political communities generally adopt a 'most different' research strategy. They take as a starting point variation in the phenomena under investigation at a level lower than that of the system as a whole. Usually, this is the level of individuals, groups, or social classes. Consequently, systemic factors are not given any particular consideration among the possible antecedents of the variations under analysis. For example, one may be interested in explaining differences in public bureaucrats' attitudes towards democracy, individuals' images of civil servants, or their perceptions concerning bureaucratic representation. The underlying assumption of the 'most different' design in such a case would be that systemic factors play an insignificant role in explaining these divergencies. Further investigation consists of evaluating this assumption in the course of cross-systemic research. As long as it is not refuted, the analysis can legitimately proceed at the intra-systemic level. If, on the other hand, the assumption is rejected, systemic variables must be introduced.[20] In practice, the first step in the 'most different' design is to delineate independent variables, observed within systems, that do not violate an assumption of homogeneity in the total population. This, in turn, helps to eliminate allegedly idiosyncratic systemic factors.

The 'most different' research strategy, like the 'most similar' design, has important limitations. Although it can be used successfully to investigate within-system variations in some cases, in others, where the population is not homogeneous in so far as the independent variables are concerned, it cannot be usefully employed. Yet the latter constitute an important area for analysis. For instance, it appears to some that many societies which

> we call semideveloped on the basis of a number of national indices are really a mixture of developed and underdeveloped sectors (or regions), and that their peculiar problems result from this imbalance . . . It would seem that in some cases, particularly in Latin America, much of the difficulty lies in the further diffusion of modern elements from some regions to others, the modernization of some sectors while others are already highly modernized but suffer under strain created by the lag of others.[21]

The 'most different' design may be inappropriate for the study of such societies, depending on the degree of difference among various sectors, and therefore it may become necessary to consider systemic variables. Moreover, this approach tends to over-emphasise the importance of within-system variations and fails to provide an adequate perspective *vis-à-vis* other systems. For example, it would sometimes be useful to compare differences between the wealth of the richest and poorest deciles of a nation's population with similar differences in other political communities in order better to assess their magnitude.

In view of the limitations inherent in both the 'most similar' and 'most different' research designs and the systemic dimensions which have a significant bearing on patterns of bureaucratic culture, we have opted for a compromise, more or less middle-of-the-road strategy. It entails the selection, as the focus of our analysis, of a single political community, which is unevenly politically developed and could be placed in an intermediate position on a global continuum of such development. At the same time, however, in order to place our findings in a better perspective, we will compare them with related observations made with reference to other political systems. This approach has several advantages and there are significant theoretical reasons and precedents in the literature for it. Fred Riggs, for example, is one who argues forcefully for studying administration in intermediately and unevenly developed societies. His formulations are in terms of the physics of light:

> Whenever a structure performs a large number of functions, we may say it is 'functionally diffuse'; when it performs a limited number, it is 'functionally specific.' . . We can now create two models for social systems of a purely hypothetical type: in the first, all structures are highly diffuse; in the second, very specific. We . . . call the first model *diffracted*, and the second, *fused*.[22]

Highly 'diffracted' societies tend to be, but are not entirely identical to, highly industrialised societies, and 'fused' societies bear a similar relationship to those which are based on traditional agriculture. 'Prismatic models' combine 'quite traditional, relatively fused traits, . . . as well as relatively diffracted traits.'[23] Riggs argues that 'the "prismatic" concept helps us see why the models devised to study both ends of this continuum are inadequate for intermediate situations',[24] but throughout his development of 'the theory of prismatic society', he is able to use the concept to shed light on political communities at almost all levels of development. Moreover, the model is extremely useful in providing a deeper understanding of development *processes* themselves.

Although the adoption of this strategy more or less resolves our dilemmas with regard to cross-national, single polity, and developmental matters, it offers no help concerning the dimension of democratic orientation. Here, we have opted for the study of bureaucratic culture in a democratic political community for three major reasons. First, and most pragmatically, the kind of research necessary for this endeavour cannot ordinarily be conducted in non-democratic nations. Second, and more theoretically, as Janowitz, Eldersveld, and others suggest, public administration in democratically-oriented nations involves complexities that are present to a greater degree than elsewhere and it is therefore more interesting in many respects. Largely as a result of the incongruence and tension between democracy and bureaucracy, the building of an effective, democratically 'balanced' public administrative system is more difficult than the creation of non-democratic systems. Finally, and in a normative vein, we would like to see democratically-oriented developing nations succeed and hope that social science will be able to make significant contributions to their efforts.

The single political community that we have chosen as the focus of our analysis of bureaucratic culture is Israel. There are several reasons why we believe it is almost singularly well suited for such an approach. Although it is sometimes portrayed as a Europeanised, developed salient in the Middle East, in reality it is neither European nor Levantine, and its development, both political and economic, is uneven. Economically, it lies somewhere between what might be called the 'hard-core' under-developed nations and those which are thoroughly modernised. It fits neither model with ease, but nevertheless facilitates an understanding of both, and of development processes themselves. Its population in-cludes many highly educated and technically or professionally trained individuals whose skills would be an asset to any modern technological society. Yet there are also a good many who would certainly rank low on any kind of index of 'individual modernity'.[25] The technology of some of its sectors, such as the military, is among the most advanced in the world. In some sectors, though, economic life is far more primitive. At the same time that Israel is highly urbanised, agriculture continues to be a leading sector and a major source of foreign exchange. Yet even here development is uneven. Mechanised, sophisticated, irrigated farm-ing coexists alongside of age-old agricultural techniques. Similarly, retail-ing ranges from modern department stores to open markets in the trad-itional style. And so it goes, virtually throughout the entire economy— although it is important to note that Israel, unlike many less developed nations, has successfully launched itself upon a course of rapid techno-logical development and economic growth.

Similarly, Israel is politically both a new nation and an old one. Although the Jewish state has existed for only three decades in modern times, the Jewish 'nation' can be traced back several millennia. Its pol-itical institutions are new and continually developing. The degree of their structural differentiation is far greater than that of many nations which emerged during the post World War II period, yet until recently one political party dominated its institutions and political life and specialisation within the government is not as great as in many western political systems. Its political 'magnitude' is also mid-range. Much of its political development has consisted of the state's absorption of functions from the political parties. At one time, for example, the military, education, and some welfare functions were not fully conceived of as state activities. Even today, immigration is not a matter given entirely to state control. The degree of achievement orientation found in its political institutions also varies widely. The military has long been 'depoliticised' in this sense, but segments of the bureaucracy and local governments are still very much patronage-ridden. In terms of secularisation, the picture is also mixed. Israel has engaged in long-term planning in some sectors while others have been treated in a haphazard fashion. Again, the military provides an example of relative success; inability to achieve a desired population dispersal and to maintain the importance of collective farming (*kibbutzim*) in the economic, social, and political life of the nation represent examples of the latter. Its mixed political development is also manifested in its international political orientation. Although now closely aligned with the United States, it has at times been neutral and has had effective interactions with 'hard-core' third-world underdeveloped nations in Africa, Asia, and Latin America. Finally, while establishing political legitimacy has not been a serious internal problem, there are nevertheless some groups in the population that reject the state itself.

Socially, Israel also presents a highly diversified pattern. About 10 per cent of the population are Moslem and Christian Arabs. Although stringent regulations to control the movement and activities of these citizens have been almost entirely abandoned and flagrant discrimination is not as rife as it once was, this group is almost entirely unintegrated into the economic, social, and political mainstream of the nation. By and large they are spatially and culturally segregated, though they can vote and have token representation in the political system. They are only slightly more within the political community than are the Arab populations which fell under Israeli control in 1967. There are also important cultural and social distinctions within the Jewish population. Here the basic divisions are between those of Asian-African origins and those of European background, with native Israelis forming a less separate group. Among the former are large numbers of Middle Eastern and North African Jews. Their traditions, native languages, and cultures are radically different from those of Eastern and Western Europeans. The Asian-African group has done less well in Israel than the others and forms a kind of 'under-class' within the Jewish population. Leonard Fein described their situation in the following fashion:

> In almost every sphere, the positions of power and prestige are the domain of Westerners. The Easterner, relegated by his training to low status and low-income positions, and frustrated by the demands of modernization, is distressed. Some respond with bitterness, accusing the dominant majority of conscious discrimination. Others move toward Levantinism, imitating Western behavior but ignoring Western

values. Still others become cynical or apathetic. For most, however, there is no clear reaction but rather a general malaise.

In countless ways, the Easterner is reminded of his lower status. His employment is less regular, he works in less valued capacities, his income is lower, and his housing is less adequate. Nor can he console himself that these are the results of his relative newness in the country, for as the data show, even the pre-1948 Easterner fares less well than the European of whatever vintage . . . It is he who is the problem, the case, the irritant.[26]

The Israeli Bureaucracy

Our research design involves an in-depth analysis of bureaucratic culture in Israel and the comparison of our findings and application of our theoretical explanations to appropriate aspects of bureaucratic culture in other political communities. Therefore, while we are in no way attempting to undertake a comprehensive study of the Israeli bureaucracy as a political, administrative, or organisational entity, it nevertheless behoves us to provide a brief description of its most salient features. At the outset, it is desirable to address its most visible characteristics.

In 1973, the year of our study, the Israeli bureaucracy consisted of twenty-one ministries. The most politically central of these included the Ministries of Defence, Foreign Affairs, Finance, Education, and Labour. Together these ministries have controlled about 90 per cent of the national budget. Most of the remaining ministries have parallels in other democratic nations and deal with such functions as transportation, welfare, housing, communication, and the like. However, Israel also has some bureaucratic units which are largely a function of its distinct political circumstances. These include the Ministry of Absorption, which deals with the settlement of immigrants, the Ministry of Police, which not only has normal police functions but also has a heavy responsibility for maintaining security along the nation's permeable borders, and the Ministry of Religious Affairs, which has no parallel in more secular states. In terms of size, the bureaucracy consists of some 57,000 regular employees. This represents almost a four-fold increase in its numbers since Israel emerged as an independent state in 1948. For the most part, growth has been greatest in the Ministries of Finance, Labour, Health, Commerce and Industry, and Communication. Although there are several separate personnel systems, about 85 per cent of all *administrative* employees are grouped under a Uniform Schedule of twenty grades. Approximately half of all these employees are in the lowest ten grades

(1—10), whereas about 8 per cent are in the top five levels. The latter bear a great deal of responsibility for the initiation and implementation of policy. Occupationally, about 40 per cent are engaged in clerical work, 25 per cent are technicians, 10 per cent are employed in social welfare and health positions such as social workers and nurses, 15 per cent are maintenance and lower-level service workers, and the remaining 10 per cent are supervisors and professionals.[27] The average civil servant has attended high school; about 15 per cent have had only primary education or less, and another 14 per cent have completed a higher education.[28]

Salaries and other personnel arrangements are largely determined by agreement between the Israeli Civil Service Commission, employee unions, and the *Histadrut* (General Federation of Labour). Unionisation is almost complete and labour relations in the bureaucracy tend to follow the 'syndicalist' pattern of Western Europe[29] rather than the more amorphous and pluralist collective bargaining processes found in the United States. Generally, salary scales in the bureaucracy are not competitive with those in either private employment or other public institutions, such as the *Histadrut* and local administration. This is a major contributor to strikes and other work 'sanctions' (job actions) which often disrupt the course of public administration. Personnel turnover rates have also been a problem, although they are currently running at about 12 per cent a year in the Uniform Schedule. Turnover is highest in the lowest ranks and among those with relatively short seniority in the ministries dealing with social welfare.[30]

Despite considerable efforts at its establishment, a high degree of administrative professionalism has remained elusive. Only at the uppermost reaches of the civil service is there a strong tendency towards a career service. About 70 per cent of all those in the top five grades worked their way up through the ranks. On the other hand, the typical middle- and lower-level civil servant does not feel that there is much chance for professional development and career advancement. The lack of professionalism in the Israeli civil service flows from many sources. First, throughout the state's existence, there has been a shortage of administrative talent. This was especially acute in the early days of statehood. As Israel's first Prime Minister, David Ben-Gurion once remarked, 'Let us be frank. This is a trade we knew not formerly or, at least, have not followed for centuries past. We have to practise a new craft, and almost create something out of nothing.'[31] Moreover, Israel's early leaders contributed heavily to an anti-professional strain of thought which still has ramifications throughout the society. As Fein observes,

By and large, Israel's founding fathers were schooled in the doctrine of agrarian socialism, they were ideologically opposed to the hierarchic implications of professionalism, they believed that good will and hard work could conquer all. They themselves had successfully practiced egalitarian voluntarism.[32]

Partly as a result of this outlook, at the beginning,

> Above all, the State lacked good civilian organizers . . . Many of the leading businessmen, soldiers and politicians were muddlers when it came to organizing an office or a staff . . . The old guard that did yeoman service as Zionist organization emissaries, as presidents of local Zionist groups, and collectors of funds and propagators of propaganda, were seen to have outgrown their usefulness. As in all revolutions, the old revolutionaries, the born rebels and propagandists, became a liability once their cause had triumphed.[33]

Partly as a consequence of this outlook and early leadership crises and partly as a result of other pressing needs, the establishment of a modernised professional bureaucracy was given a low priority during the early years of statehood. Politicisation, which at one time was rife, also played a role in limiting the development of a professional civil service. Finally, by the time professionalisation became significantly stressed, the Israeli bureaucracy had developed a relatively low prestige and had considerable difficulty in competing for the scarce first-rate administrative talent available. As one such individual expressed it, 'We did not come to Palestine to be clerks.'[34] The problem is especially acute for recruitment to positions in outlying districts.

Another major characteristic of the Israeli bureaucracy is that the centralised nature of the political system makes the citizen highly dependent upon it for many services and necessities. These range from securing housing, education, and employment to obtaining drivers' licences and telephones. Consequently there is a great deal of interaction between Israeli citizens and their public bureaucrats, much of it face to face. In the view of the many, and especially Westerners, this interaction is characterised by inefficiency and disorder. As late as 1956, it was observed that:

> The Civil Service exhibited much of the malaise common to new or inexperienced Administrations; a concentration of work at the top levels and a lack of proper delegation and decentralization, poor

organization with responsibilities badly allocated or ill-defined, a general lack of adequate directives and instructions for the execution of the work, indifferent supervision, poor office methods and physical working conditions, a tendency to start projects before previous ones had been properly carried through and consolidated; indifferent treatment of the public and a lack of leadership and esprit de corps.[35]

Although the civil service has undoubtedly improved in the intervening years, many of these traits are still present. For instance, one keen observer of the Israeli bureaucratic scene, Gerald Caiden, likens it to an 'oriental bazaar', where everything is open to bargaining.[36] In many ways, client-bureaucrat interaction in high public contact positions and agencies underscores the transitional nature of Israeli administration. Here, the technological sophistication of the scientific and military sectors is almost entirely absent. Little is computerised and almost all interaction tends to be very time-consuming. Undoubtedly, the nature of these bureaucratic interactions has had an important impact on the Israeli bureaucratic culture and has contributed especially to the public's negative evaluation of both bureaucrats and the bureaucracy. Perhaps the overall character of public contact with the bureaucracy is best conveyed by the information in Table 2.1, which ascertains what the average Israeli citizen dislikes most about bureaucratic interaction. It is evident that wasted time and red tape, in the sense of having to find one's way through a myriad of officials, are an important fact of life when visiting bureaucratic agencies. Moreover, about one in every eight Israelis finds unsympathetic officials to be the worst feature of direct contact with the bureaucracy. Indeed, the nature of this kind of interaction is such that more than one outside observer has rhetorically asked, 'How did it get this way?'

Table 2.1: Elements the Israeli Public Finds Most Bothersome about Bureaucratic Interaction*

Item	Frequency	Percent
Wasted time	472	33
Long lines	186	13
'Non-understanding' civil servants	172	12
Being sent from one clerk to another	400	28
Other	100	7
NA, DK	100	7
Total	1,430	100

*Actual text of question: 'What disturbs you most when interacting with civil servants?'

A. Traditions

There is an answer, but of course it is not a simple one. As has already been noted, like other new nations Israel has lacked administrative talent. Moreover the bureaucracy has had trouble competing for that which is available. To further complicate matters, there was very little to build on when Israel became an independent nation and it has not yet been able to develop an administrative tradition stressing rationality, efficiency, and other modern organisational concepts. From the beginnings of the modern period of Jewish resettlement of Palestine in the 1880s until the emergence of Israel, the country was controlled by the Turks and then the British. Administration by the former was haphazard at best and almost totally ineffectual. Mandatory administration under the latter was a far cry from the kind of public administration generally associated with Great Britain during this century. Although each occupying nation allowed the Jewish community a considerable measure of self-governance, this experience was insufficient to provide anything more than the barest outlines of the shape public administration might take after independence. Indeed, one might conclude that Palestine was *never* well administered, at least since ancient times. Given that there was no single inherently successful or prized administrative tradition upon which the nation could build after independence, it was perhaps inevitable that a blending of different conceptions would occur. This was especially likely in view of the Israelis' early rejection of things and officials British. Even after a full decade of statehood, a member of the dominant political party announced to the legislature that 'it is still not clear to us what is the desirable image for our civil service. We cannot simply copy other countries'.[37]

Caiden argues cogently that contemporary public administration in Israel is the product of the mixing of four separate traditions. The first is the 'indigenous Middle Eastern style'.[38] Here, 'business is transacted at a regal pace, in a charmingly courteous, if exasperating, fashion'.[39] Deference to authority, status, and rank are combined with bureaucratic officiousness and the need for bargaining skills. By and large, 'It is a bargaining rather than a bureaucratic posture'.[40] The second legacy is from the British. It '. . . lingers in important areas of national government, despite attempts to reduce its influence in the early days of the state'.[41] Caiden views it as a 'no-nonsense, orderly, condescending, bureaucratic approach, with little room for bargaining, local initiative or disruption'.[42] It is most prevalent in the legal system and police organisation, although traces of this tradition can be found elsewhere as well.

In addition to these legacies are two traditions which are more closely related to Jewish circumstances. In Caiden's words,

> The third strand is composed of traditions brought by Jewish immigrants from their countries of origin, as varied as the contents of a spicery. Paranoiac ghetto attitudes mingle with dynamic, cosmopolitan, liberal entrepreneurship. Efficient, dogmatic, Central European bureaucrats work alongside contemplative philosophers unused to standardization and impersonal legal-rational authority. These variations are contained within a framework of bureaucratization, professionalism, functional requirements and clientele pressures. While in time they lose some of their sharpness, they do create a continuing problem in cooperation and coordination. Occasionally, under pressure, they explode into conflict.[43]

Finally, there is the tradition of the *vatiquim*, or old-timers and their offspring. This consists of a 'variety of styles related to position, experience, education, age, political ideology and personal ambitions'.[44] In general, however, this tradition relies on the 'pragmatic feel' of things, confidential and in-group decision-making, and personal or political connections. Here, bargaining is tolerated as a necessary evil and frequently relied upon, although with some distaste. Overlaying all of these traditions and their blending has been a high degree of politicisation of administrative matters.

B. Politics and Administration

Israel's administrative development parallels that of some other democratically inclined nations in that the bureaucracy has been used as an avenue for the distribution of patronage in connection with the creation of strong, mass political parties. For example, there is little doubt that patronage practices in Israel 'played an important part in galvanizing the parties into action', just as they did in the United States.[45] Moreover, these aspects of administration in Israel support the proposition that it may be only 'once political parties are strongly established, once the public is widely mobilized for political action, prepared to give volunteer support, and to contribute financially from a broad base of party membership, [that] it is possible to reduce or perhaps even eliminate spoils as an element of support for party activity'.[46] Furthermore, as in the United States, patronage was intertwined with the integration, settlement, and welfare of large immigrant populations.

In Israel, the most salient political factor affecting administrative matters has been the process of coalition formation. It is a parliamentary democracy which has had a dominant party system and a strong emphasis on centralised political operations. The legislature (*Knesset*) is elected through a nationwide system of proportional representation based on party lists. The ordering of candidates on these, and consequently a significant amount of the determination of who will be a member of the legislature, is done by the central committee of the political parties. The Cabinet consists of the Prime Minister, the heads of the various ministries, and ministers without portfolio. Its members do not have to be elected to the legislature. Although together these two bodies are the major institutions of formal political authority in Israel, the Cabinet has come to overshadow the legislature. It now exercises control over the formulation, initiation, and implementation of domestic and foreign policy. Its control, however, is dependent on majority support in the legislature, and so far the Israeli electorate has never provided this to a single political party. Hence, coalition governments have had to be formed.[47]

One of the central payoffs to coalition partners has been the distribution of public offices. Generally, each party entering into a governing coalition is awarded at least one of the ministry headships and/or significant lower posts in exchange for its agreement to throw its legislative support behind the dominant party. However, the distribution of positions to the various coalition partners has been disproportional to their electoral strength. The dominant party largely determines the conditions upon which others may enter into a coalition with it, and until recently the Labour Party has retained control of a majority of ministries which, together, account for an overwhelming share of the national budget. Moreover, ministries are viewed as a slack political resource which can be expanded to meet the needs of coalition formation. Thus, the expansion of ministries from twelve in 1949 to twenty-two in 1974 cannot be attributed strictly to a quest for administrative rationality and further political or economic development.

A major consequence of the politics of coalition formation has been politicisation of the bureaucracy. The smaller parties in control of the various ministries are in a position to dominate significant areas of public policy regardless of their overall strength in the electorate. For example, the policy strength of the National Religious Party, which has resisted secularisation of the state, has been many times greater than would be indicated by counting its followers in the general population. Moreover, these parties are also in a position to attempt to use 'their' ministries as an institutional base for the mobilisation and generation of greater political support. Largely as a result of this activity, personnel procedures and the distribution of services associated with the Israeli bureaucracy began to run along party lines.

Politicisation was greatest during the initial years of independence. At the outset, this was partly a product of Jewish community and Zionist politics in the pre-state period, as well as a result of the necessities of coalition building in the new state. Prior to independence,

> administration positions in the various organizations were functionally nearly identical with political positions because they were filled according to a key system . . . with some exceptions, the incumbents of the various administrative positions were also politicians and not professional civil servants.[48]

Although strict proportional representation was subsequently rejected, after independence this process was continued and facilitated greatly by the absence of stringent, or even any formal job qualifications. Indeed, a satisfactory war record, political connections, and knowledge of Hebrew, one of the two official languages, were perhaps the major prerequisites for public employment. As one observer wrote,

> In 1948, Ministers of the different coalition parties tended to fill their several Ministries with their own political supporters. There was a tremendous shortage of civil servants, each political party was very suspicious of the others and wanted to keep control of as many key posts as possible; there was no time to organize selection boards or to have competitive or even qualifying exams.[49]

Moreover, not only was the depth of patronage almost all-encompassing, bureaucratic outputs were themselves highly politicised. In Fein's words, 'services were performed chiefly for the party faithful',[50] and therefore, to some extent, one's housing and employment were related to one's political allegiance and connections. As these processes progressed, 'certain ministries became hardly distinguishable from party cells'.[51]

Although significant steps towards depoliticisation have been taken, it has not been fully achieved and many believe that party considerations still dominate Israeli administration. As one analyst of politics and administration in Israel expressed it,

> Politicians in Israel, especially members of the smaller political parties, believe that the Israeli civil service is the administrative arm of the Mapai party [Labour], that Mapai has taken advantage of its position as the largest political party to accept only political fellow-travellers

for important administrative posts, that it has blocked the advancement of qualified candidates who belong to other political parties, and that in essence, candidates are accepted into the civil service very often because of their political party affiliation and activity alone.[52]

Nevertheless, recruitment has been depoliticised to an extent, and some regulations for political neutrality have been adopted.

The development of a merit-based civil service became an overt goal of the political community in 1959. By that time, the state had been successfully established, the crush of new immigrants had abated, a more technological and less generalist outlook was emerging throughout several important segments of the society, the major political parties shared a greater degree of institutionalisation and were better able to mobilise popular support with less reliance on administrative patronage, and, finally, some of the earlier distaste for British methods had worn off. As in many other political systems, however, the process of civil service reform has been highly uneven. As Fein notes,

> In 1959, Israel began to move towards secularizing the civil service through competitive examinations and merit hiring. (Some agencies, including the army, had been depoliticized earlier. Others, such as the Ministry of the Interior, have been little touched by depoliticization.) The achievement of a full employment economy has aided in this process. But the effects of the older patterns have not yet been completely erased, nor has the new system touched the higher reaches of the bureaucracy very effectively.[53]

Briefly, the current recruitment procedure favours a closed civil service, but does not stress coherent career patterns. Under procedures ostensibly in effect since 1948, but having significant application for the first time only eleven years later, when a vacancy occurs in the upper levels of a ministry's hierarchy an 'internal tender' is circulated throughout the agency. This includes a job description, the position's rank, and a listing of the qualifications an applicant must have. In general, in order to apply for a vacancy, a civil servant must rank within two grades of it, unless it is in a field totally different from the one in which he or she is currently employed but may nevertheless qualify. Downward mobility is non-competitive. A number of positions are exempt from this process and can be filled solely on political grounds. These include the personal staff of ministers, ambassadors, directors general, advisors, accountants general, budget directors, and other high ranking officials. Those who apply for vacancies are examined by a committee which includes representatives of the Civil Service Commission, the ministry involved, and civil servants' union. Political affiliation is not a legitimate item for consideration. If no satisfactory candidate is found internally, the position may be opened for nation-wide competition. If this also fails to produce an acceptable candidate, the post may be filled by issuing a special contract to someone of the ministry's choosing.

As Heady notes, bureaucracies in less developed political systems are often characterised by a wide gap between form and reality. It is evident that these recruitment procedures allow for considerable flexibility in the process of determining who is the 'best' satisfactory candidate. As in the case of other matters-bureaucratic in Israel, formal requirements may sometimes be relaxed and applicants may be appointed despite their lack of some of the qualifications originally sought. Indeed, in the view of some the gap is so large that

> one must not lose sight of the fact that these rules are not applied in practice. Promotions are controlled at the top by the politicians and at the bottom by the unions. The experts who devised the system and who believe in it have no power at all to insure the operation.[54]

Nevertheless, in their somewhat haphazard application over a period of two decades, these procedures have contributed a measure to de-politicisation, and the civil service has become far more than an agglomeration of party cells.

Another factor militating against politicisation has been the adoption of regulations for political neutrality. Although far less stringent and comprehensive than those of nations such as the United States and Japan, these regulations, as similar ones found in Western European political systems, have taken a good part of the civil service out of active politics. Laws for this purpose were passed in 1959 and 1961. Together, they prohibit civil servants in the top three grades, and all other state employees who come into daily contact with the population, such as social workers, from participating in political organising, demonstration, and campaigning. Higher officials must resign their posts prior to running for political office and those in the lower grades must take a leave of absence for the duration of the campaign period.

In sum, the Israeli bureaucracy shares several similarities with those in other new nations. It has not been a dominant element in the political system, but rather its development has been largely a product of political arrangements beyond its boundaries. Politics has had an important impact on its size, scope, and personnel. As is true of other national bureaucracies created in the post World War II era, it displays a lack of professionalism and has had difficulty in acquiring the human resources it needs. In Israel's case, however, this condition stems both from the bureaucracy's relatively low prestige and inability to attract highly talented individuals, as well as their relative scarcity in the political community. As elsewhere, the bureaucracy has undergone rapid growth in an atmosphere of uncertain traditions and strong tendencies towards disorganisation. Although still considerably politicised, the values of merit and neutrality have taken hold to some extent, and are likely to be increasingly important in the future. Unlike those in several other nations, the Israeli bureaucracy has not generated an image of massive corruption, although few would argue that rule application is strictly impersonal. Finally, the bureaucracy has established a high degree of penetration of the life of the society, which is highly characteristic of more developed political systems and which, perhaps, is largely attributable to Israel's political centralisation. In any event, the bureaucracy has emerged as a potentially central force in the future life of the political community.

Research Procedure

The bulk of the data for this study were obtained in a series of interviews with Israeli citizens and public bureaucrats lasting from July to September 1973. Citizens selected for interviewing are a probability stratified sample. The twenty-two largest cities (those with populations over 15,000 in 1969) were all included in the sample, and then sub-sampled with probabilities proportional to their size. The sixty-eight cities with populations less than 15,000 were divided into two strata: those in 5,000 to 15,000 range and those under 5,000. These strata were sub-stratified, and cities were selected to represent the strata. The remainder of the Israeli population is located in rural areas; these were divided into strata by regions and type of settlements. The size of the populations in these settlements had to be estimated because they are not reported individually by the Israeli Bureau of Statistics. The estimates were derived by subtracting the population of cities from the total Jewish populations and assigning the remainder to rural settlements (the resulting fraction, 15 per cent, is a reasonably accurate estimate given the country's population distribution). Next, the number of settlements was divided into this remainder and each settlement was assumed to have the same number of adults (eighteen years and older).

The number of addresses issued to each interviewer was limited to twenty-five. The interviewers made the final respondent-selection within listed addresses on a random basis (with a random selection chart) after having sampled apartments within buildings to locate households. Two thousand sample addresses were selected from the 1973 electoral lists. The overall sampling fraction is 1/700, and applies to all strata and self-representing units. Allowance for persons not at home was made by a 'time-at-home' technique rather than by 'call-backs'. This procedure reduces the sample bias that would otherwise result from an under-representation of those who are difficult to find at home. A total of 1,600 citizens were interviewed. The correspondence between the final sample of respondents who completed interviews and the national census figures is shown in Table 2.2.

Table 2.2: Representativeness of the National Sample

	Israeli adult population (latest estimates from census data)*	Completed interviews in the sample
By sex		
Female	51%	49%
Male	49	51
Total	100%	100%
	(2,723.6)**	(1,571)
By education		
Primary or less	45%	48%
Secondary	40	33
High	15	19
Total	100%	100%
	(2,723.6)**	(1,575)

*Statistical Abstracts of Israel 1973, Jerusalem: Central Bureau of Statistics, 1973, pp. 45-6 and p. 125.
**In thousands.

A total of 850 potential interviewees holding positions in the Uniform Schedule of the Israeli bureaucracy was also selected with a probability proportional stratified sample. The sampling frame was restricted to the nation's three largest cities because almost 90 per cent of all civil servants in the Uniform Schedule are employed in them. The two strata were the size of the ministry and the proportions of civil servants in the various grades. To supplement the information gathered on the largely pre-coded questionnaires, thirty-five high-ranking public bureaucrats were interviewed in depth. Furthermore, to meet the criteria of comparability, identical questions pertaining to cognition, affect, evaluation, and politicisation were used for both the citizen and public servant groups. A total of 630 of the latter completed the interviews: 141 of these were from Haifa, 312 from Tel Aviv, and 177 from Jerusalem. Their distributions by rank and the nature of their ministries' missions are presented in Table 2.3.

Table 2.3: Organisational Characteristics of the Bureaucrat Respondents

Organisational characteristics	Percentage interviewed
Rank	
1 to 10	55%
11 to 15	36
16 to 20	9
Total	100%
	(630)
Mission	
Economic	10%
Social welfare	50
Other	40
Total	100%
	(630)

Our approach to the study of bureaucratic culture involves surveying the general population and public bureaucratic component of a single political community. This enables us to ascertain patterns of cognition, affect, and evaluation concerning bureaucratic objects, and to compare these both within and among the groups. The single polity that we have selected as the environment for the focus of our study is Israel. Because patterns of political development and democratic orientations are of considerable relevance to bureaucratic culture, we believe Israel is well suited for such a study. It emerged as an independent nation in the post World War II period and has an intermediate and uneven pattern of political and economic development. Its bureaucracy bears many similarities to those of both more and less politically developed nations. It roughly fits the model of a 'prismatic society', and therefore can serve to elucidate the nature of processes associated with bureaucratic culture in many other political communities as well. In this connection, we will endeavour to compare our findings and test our theoretical conclusions with relevant information and interpretations pertaining to other polities.

Notes

1. Joseph LaPalombara, 'Bureaucracy and Political Development: Notes, Queries, and Dilemmas', in Joseph LaPalombara (ed.), *Bureaucracy and Political Development* (Princeton: Princeton University Press, 1962), p. 36.

2. Ibid., p. 39.

3. Ibid., p. 40.

4. Ibid., p. 42.

5. Ibid., p. 44.

6. Ibid., pp. 45-6.

7. Ibid., p. 46.

8. Ibid.

9. Ibid., p. 47.

10. Ferrel Heady, *Public Administration: A Comparative Perspective* (Englewood Cliffs: Prentice-Hall, 1966), pp. 69-72.

11. Ibid., p. 39.

12. See K.J. Meier, 'Representative Bureaucracy: An Empirical Analysis', *American Political Science Review*, 69 (June 1975), 526-42.

13. John Forward, 'Toward an Empirical Framework for Ecological Studies in Comparative Public Administration', in Nimrod Raphaeli (ed.), *Readings in Comparative Public Administration* (Boston: Allyn & Bacon, 1967), pp. 454-5.

14. Samuel J. Eldersveld, V. Jagannadham, and A.P. Barnabas, *The Citizen and the Administrator in a Developing Democracy* (Glenview: Scott, Foresman, 1968), pp. 4-6; see also Morris Janowitz, Deil Wright, and William Delany, *Public Administration and the Public* (Ann Arbor: Institute of Public Administration, University of Michigan, 1958), pp. 6-8.

15. Quoted in Eldersveld *et al.*, *Citizen and Administrator*, p. 5.

16. Ibid., pp. 5-6.

17. Robert Alford, 'Party and Society', in F. Munger (ed.), *Studies in Comparative Politics* (New York: Thomas Y. Crowell, 1967).

18. Ibid., pp. 66-7.

19. A. Przeworski and Henry Tune, *The Logic of Comparative Social Inquiry* (New York: Wiley-Interscience, 1970), p. 34.

20. Ibid., pp. 36-9.

21. J. Linz and A. de Miguel, 'Within-Nations Differences and Comparisons', in R. Merrit and S. Rokkan (eds.), *Comparing Nations* (New Haven: Yale University Press, 1966).

22. Fred W. Riggs, *Administration in Developing Countries: The Theory of Prismatic Society* (Boston: Houghton, Mifflin, 1964), pp. 22-3.

23. Ibid., p. 29.

24. Ibid., p. 27.

25. See Alex Inkeles and David H. Smith, *Becoming Modern* (Cambridge: Harvard University Press, 1974), esp. part II.

26. Leonard Fein, *Politics in Israel* (Boston: Little, Brown, 1967), p. 46.

27. *Twenty Years of Service* (Jerusalem: Civil Service Commission, 1969); and D. Haniel, *The Civil Servant and the Service* (Jerusalem: Civil Service Commission, 1972 [Hebrew]).

28. Haniel, *Civil Servant*, p. 37.

29. Brian Chapman, *The Profession of Government* (London: Unwin University Books, 1959), pp. 37-8, 296-8.

30. David Haniel, *Levels of Pay and Turnover Rates in The Civil Service* (Jerusalem: Civil Service Comm., 1971 [Hebrew]).

31. Marver H. Bernstein, *The Politics of Israel* (Princeton: Princeton University Press, 1957), p. 153.

32. Fein, *Politics in Israel*, p. 190.

33. Jon Kimche, 'Tel Aviv: Messiah in a Business Suit', *Commentary*, 6 (December 1948), p. 531.

34. Donna Robinson, 'Patrons and Saints: A Study of the Career Patterns of Higher Civil Servants in Israel' (Ph.D Dissertation, Department of Political Science, Columbia University, 1970), p. 51. This is an excellent source for a discussion of the history of Israeli public administration.

35. United Nations, Technical Assistance Programme, *The Training of the Israel Civil Service*, prepared by F.B. Hindmarsh, 1956, p. 3; quoted, ibid., p. 248.

36. Gerald Caiden, 'The Political Penetration of Israeli Bureaucracy', monograph, Haifa University, 1974, p. 10.

37. Quoted in Robinson, 'Patrons and Saints', p. 234.

38. Gerald Caiden, *Israel's Administrative Culture* (Berkeley: Institute of Governmental Studies, University of California, 1970), p. 17.

39. Ibid.

40. Ibid., p. 18.

41. Ibid.

42. Ibid.

43. Ibid.

44. Ibid.

45. Fred W. Riggs, 'Bureaucrats and Political Development: A Paradoxical View', in LaPalombara (ed.), *Bureaucracy and Political Development*, p. 128. The statement is made with specific reference to the United States.

46. Ibid.

47. See David Nachmias, 'Coalition Politics in Israel', *Comparative Political Studies*, 7 (October 1974), 316-33.

48. Yehezkel Dror, 'Public Policy-Making in Israel', *Public Administration in Israel and Abroad*, 2 (1962), 7.

49. Edwin Samuel, *British Traditions in the Administration of Israel* (London: Vallentine, Mitchell, 1956), p. 25.

50. Fein, *Politics in Israel*, p. 189.

51. Ibid.

52. Robinson, 'Patrons and Saints', pp. 204-5. Robinson argues that, at least with regard to the second highest grade in the general administrative schedule, politicisation is far less prevalent than is generally believed. However, the nature of her methodology, which involved directly asking civil servants in this grade whether they thought that they obtained their positions as a result of politics, and similar questions, casts doubt on the validity of her conclusion concerning this point.

53. Fein, *Politics in Israel*, p. 189.

54. Quoted in Robinson, 'Patrons and Saints', p. 225.

3 PATTERNS OF COGNITION: THE PENETRATION OF BUREAUCRACY

It is desirable to begin an analysis of the nature of bureaucratic culture with an investigation of citizens' and public bureaucrats' patterns of cognition with regard to their national bureaucracy. This dimension refers to the extent to which members of the political community and those who staff its bureaucratic apparatus are knowledgeable about and attuned to the features and outputs of the bureaucracy. It is of crucial importance to the study of bureaucratic culture because it provides an indication of how salient different groups consider a public bureaucracy to be to their own lives and to that of the political community as a whole. In this sense, an analysis of patterns of cognition is somewhat prior to the investigation of other aspects of bureaucratic culture because if, as might be the case in some developing polities, the citizenry were largely or almost entirely unattuned to the operations of the bureaucracy, this would colour the interpretation of information gathered concerning patterns of affect and evaluation. More specifically, the cognitive dimension concerns patterns of awareness and information about bureaucratic structures and processes, and their roles in a nation's political, social, and economic life. Analysis of patterns of cognition enables one to assess, albeit roughly, the knowledge and information concerning a national bureaucracy that is possessed by citizen and bureaucrat alike, and to compare patterns between and among these groups. This dimension, in fact, is sometimes used to characterise whole societies. For example, it is not uncommon to refer to the Soviet Union or Israel as a 'bureaucratic society'. In everyday speech, the term is intended to connote that much of the nation's life is controlled by bureaucratic organisations and that ordinary citizens must continually interact with these in the course of their day-to-day lives. 'Bureaucratic' is used in this sense because it is believed to provide a meaningful and useful description of important social phenomena. The study of the cognitive dimension of a bureaucratic culture, therefore, represents an attempt to systematise this interest by making it possible to observe variations in the degree to which public bureaucracy is seen as a central condition of life and politics in different societal settings. Moreover, it makes possible the analysis of the antecedents of these differences.

As in several other areas of interest to the study of bureaucratic culture, it could be anticipated that patterns of cognition would be broadly associated with the level of a political community's development. This is especially true, perhaps, towards the lower end of the political development scale. Here, the average citizen is likely to be largely unaware of the national bureaucracy's functions and outputs and most members of the political community may find them of little salience to their lives. In such political communities, knowledge concerning the bureaucracy's major units, roles, and processes is not widespread. A majority of citizens may come into contact with bureaucrats only relatively infrequently and they may almost never attribute events and circumstances to 'the bureaucracy'. In such political systems, the central government and its administrative component simply do not penetrate[1] large portions of the society as a whole. Social structure tends to be more pervasive than state; traditional tribal and kinship authority structures are unrivalled by those based on 'rational—legal' premises. Although most of the world has already embarked upon a journey towards self-sustaining political and economic development, parts of Asia, Africa, and to a lesser extent, Latin America still approach this pattern. Eisenstadt describes the nature and roots of this pattern in post-colonial societies in the following fashion:

> Within these societies, the initial emergence of bureaucracies had been rooted in the need of the colonial powers for various resources and for the maintenance of law and order. The bureaucracy was based on over-all political control by the metropolitan powers; the administratio participated minimally in the indigenous political and social life of the community. This necessarily limited its activities, confining them to the basic administrative services.[2]

As nations became more politically developed, patterns of cognition concerning bureaucracy become more complex, less generalisable, and more directly related to the nature of the regime. In highly techno-logical and bureaucratised political communities, it could be expected that the vast majority of citizens would be cognisant of their national bureaucracy and some of its influences on their lives. Yet, even within such nations, a good deal of variation may exist. Thus, for example, although the United States, Great Britain, France, Western Germany, and the Soviet Union are roughly similar in their levels of political development, at least in LaPalombara's terms, awareness and information about their national bureaucracies on the part of their citizens could be expected to vary considerably. In the United States, the average citizen

is aware of the federal bureaucracy and knows something about it, but
in part because of his/her relatively infrequent contacts with it and in
part due to its somewhat unarticulated role in national politics, one
could expect it to be considered less salient to the individual than would
be the national bureaucracies of the other countries by their citizens. In
The Civic Culture, for instance, Almond and Verba found that West
Germans possessed more information about their national bureaucracy
than did Britons, and that Americans possessed somewhat less than
either.[3] Although no surveys are available on the USSR, we would
expect the average citizen to have more contact with the national bureaucracy and, given its level of penetration of the society, to attribute
greater salience to it. Indeed, in a passage worth quoting at length, Alfred
Meyer writes:

> the USSR is best understood as a large, complex bureaucracy com-
> parable in its structure and functioning to giant corporations, armies,
> government agencies, and similar institutions—some people might
> wish to add various churches—in the West. It shares with such bureau-
> cracies many principles of organization and patterns of management.
> It is similar to them also in its typical successes and inefficiencies, in
> the gratifications and frustrations it offers its constituents, in its
> socialization and recruitment policies, communications problems,
> and many other features. The Soviet Union shares with giant organ-
> izations everywhere the urge to organize all human activities ration-
> ally, from professional life to consumption patterns and leisure
> activities. It has in common with them a thoroughly authoritarian
> political structure, in which the elite is independent of control by
> the lower-ranking members of the organization, even though all or
> most giant bureaucracies in the modern world insist that their rank-
> and-file constituents participate in the organization's public life. Both
> in the USSR and in large organizations elsewhere, the individual finds
> himself thrown into a situation in which unseen and uncontrollable
> authorities ceaselessly impose social change unwanted by the con-
> stituents. All human beings must live in a world they themselves did
> not make; but in modern bureaucracies, they live in worlds someone
> is constantly seeking to remake.[4]

In the broad middle of the political development spectrum, we would
expect to find mixed patterns of cognition overall, and, perhaps more
significantly, very wide variations within the populations of individual
political communities. This assumption is enhanced by Almond and

Verba's findings that:

> the American and British respondents tend, on the whole, to have
> relatively favorable expectations of government; and educational
> differences have a relatively small effect on such expectations. In
> Germany overall expectations proved to be relatively high, but class
> differences in expectations . . . are also relatively large. In Mexico and
> Italy, and particularly in the former, overall expectations of favor-
> able treatment are relatively low, and educational differences in expect-
> ations tend to be relatively extreme.[5]

Thus, in the United States the percentage difference between those with
primary education only and those with some university training who
expected equal treatment in government offices was 8 per cent, in the
United Kingdom, it was 7 per cent, and in Germany 13 per cent, whereas in Italy it was 29 per cent and in Mexico it was almost a full 50 per
cent.[6] It is to this type of within-nation type of variation that we now
turn our attention.

The Impact of the National Bureaucracy

Analysis of within-nation patterns of cognition with regard to public
bureaucracy enables us to learn more about the interface between government and citizen in an area of almost universal growth. As noted in
the first chapter, government is increasingly becoming bureaucratised
and the interaction between citizen and state is more and more trans-
piring in the roles of client and bureaucrat. Different patterns of cognition, therefore, provide clues as to which groups of citizens are best
able to cope with contemporary government, and which are least able
to understand and deal with their political system. Moreover, such
patterns may give rise to significant tensions between bureaucrats and
clients which may militate against effective administration and are almost
certain to make the possibility of 'democratic balance' less likely. Incongruence between bureaucrats' and citizens' perceptions concerning the
nature of the bureaucracy's structural features, processes, and outputs
can lead to an ever-widening gap between the two groups which could
hamper both administrative action and the development of what might
be called 'participatory' citizenship. Bendix hints at the nature of the
complexities involved here:

> Access to influence upon the administrative process is a problem of
> increasing importance . . . As rights are universalized and govern-

mental activities proliferate, it is less problematic that the uneducated citizen is barred from public employment because he cannot qualify, than that he may not possess the aptitudes and attitudes needed to obtain reasoned consideration of his case by the public authorities. Such individuals are aided in their dealings with the government when their disadvantages are recognized. We should not gloss over the tragic incongruities between human concerns and administrative procedure, but the direct confrontation between individuals and officials characterizes only a fraction of the relations between administrators and the public. . . . When citizens desire to influence policy at any level, . . . they often combine their demands with those of others, whether the object is to have a party win an election, intercede with individual representatives, or modify the implementation of policy through contact with an administrative agency.[7]

However, it may be that those citizens who least understand their national bureaucracy are also least likely to form pressure groups or be mobilised by political parties. Hence, they may remain relatively unprotected in their dealings with bureaucrats. Furthermore, as McConnell and Lowi have pointed out with reference to the United States, the entrance of pressure groups into the administrative sphere often destroys the latters' independence, initiative, and original purpose.[8] Consequently, when bureaucrats believe their work is having a considerable impact on some aspect of national politics such as social integration, but the relevant clientele groups disagree, serious conflict may develop over desirable structures, processes, and policies. Perhaps this is best exemplified in the realm of social welfare and social work, in which strikes and even violent action are not uncommon means for bureaucrat and client to deal with one another.

In order to obtain a better understanding of the nature of the cognitive dimension, it is useful to subdivide it into three separate, but nevertheless interrelated elements. The first of these is the degree of impact which is attributed to a national bureaucracy, the second concerns its areas of impact, and the third involves the character of impact.

Taking these in their respective order, the first element to be investigated is the extent to which citizens and public bureaucrats believe that the national bureaucracy influences the daily lives of the members of the political community. To what extent do people in an unevenly and intermediately developed nation, such as Israel, find their national bureaucracy to be relevant to their lives and what patterns does this perception follow? An indication is provided by Table 3.1, which enables one to assess the bureaucracy's impact relative to that of Israel's other leading institutions. It shows that levels of cognition are generally high. Only a small proportion of both the public and the bureaucrats are unable or unwilling to assess the impacts of the institutions which together dominate much of the nation's political, economic, and social life. It is also apparent that Israelis find their bureaucracy to be of great importance. Thus, 41 per cent of the public believe it has a great effect on their lives. In fact, only the Cabinet, which, as noted in the previous chapter, is by far the most important central political institution in Israel, and local governments are perceived to have a greater impact. The bureaucracy, therefore, is perceived as the *national* institution with the second greatest impact on the average citizen's daily life. In some respect this finding is surprising and is indicative of what contributes to the making of a 'bureaucratic society'. The courts are viewed as relatively insignificant, whereas the legislature and the General Labour Federation (*Histadrut*) are thought to have a somewhat lesser impact than the bureaucracy. This interpretation is reinforced by the 'no effect' responses. Considerably fewer people consider the bureaucracy to be less central to their daily lives than perceive the legislature and dominant labour organisation to be unimportant. From this perspective, it is interesting to note that the same proportion believe that the Cabinet and the bureaucracy have no impact on their day-to-day lives.

Table 3.1 demonstrates further that not only is the bureaucracy of considerable salience to the average Israeli, those who staff it express a markedly different pattern of cognition from that of the general public. As might be expected in view of their association with, and knowledge of the bureaucracy, the public bureaucrats attribute greater importance to it than does the remainder of the political community. The bureaucrats however, differ from the public in another way as well. With the exception of the courts, they believe that all the central governmental institutions are considerably more important in the daily life of the Israeli citizen than does the public. If the establishment of 'a mature and well-organized civil service is one of the items high on almost any list of the needs of developing countries',[9] then the Israeli political system seems to have taken at least one major step by having created a bureaucracy which sees the national government as crucial in the life of the nation. Although mobilisation of civil servants' support for and identification with a central government is often taken for granted, it nevertheless may be one among several prerequisites for an effective implementation of national goals. Thus, in terms of policy-making and administration the bureaucrats' perception of governmental importance could reinforce

Table 3.1: Degree of Impact of Central Institutions on Daily Life: Public and Bureaucrats*

Institutions		Great effect	Some effect	No effect	Don't know	Total
Legislature	Public (N=1,506)	38%	25%	29%	8%	100%
	Bureaucrats (N=598)	46	31	20	3	100%
		D=-.14	df=3	p<.001		
General Labour Federation	Public (N=1,506)	36	23	36	5	100%
	Bureaucrats (N=596)	28	35	34	3	100%
		D=-.37	df=3	p<.02		
Courts	Public (N=1,501)	21	19	52	8	100%
	Bureaucrats (N=592)	19	25	52	4	100%
		D=-.040	df=3	p<.05		
Public bureaucracy	Public (N=1,499)	41	29	23	7	100%
	Bureaucrats (N=594)	48	34	16	2	100%
		D=-.12	df=3	p<.001		
Cabinet	Public (N=1,506)	51	20	23	6	100%
	Bureaucrats (N=597)	57	25	15	3	100%
		D=-.11	df=3	p<.001		
Local governments	Public (N=1,500)	49	24	19	8	100%
	Bureaucrats (N=593)	50	29	19	2	100%
		D=-.060	df=3	p<.05		

*The question read: 'Thinking about the country's important institutions, about how much effect do you think the following institutions have on your daily life?'

centralising tendencies and the drive towards self-sustained development. On the other hand, the gap between the public's and the bureaucrats' perceptions could be the source of differences between official and client, both singularly and collectively, with regard to further support for central governmental penetration of the life of the society.

The information contained in Table 3.1 leads to the conclusion that, overall, the Israeli bureaucracy is of high salience to both bureaucrat and citizen alike. To the extent that the establishment of a high level of bureaucratic penetration of the political community is a prerequisite to self-

sustained political and economic development, then, Israel has overcome this hurdle within a relatively short period of time. Yet, Almond
and Verba's analysis of Italy and Mexico, and to a lesser extent Western
Germany, suggests that the perceived impact of a public bureaucracy
might vary widely within a given society. Similarly, it could vary among
the public bureaucrats themselves. Taking the latter first, it is clear that
different patterns of cognition among bureaucrats could have important
effects on the development of a successful civil service. Perceptions concerning the impact of the institution in which one is employed, its units
and policies, are likely to affect one's orientations and motivation, and
hence the performance of the organisation as a whole. Wide perceptual
gaps among different types of bureaucrats make the process of organisational integration all the more difficult. Moreover, significant differences in the outlooks of higher and lower organisational members can
be especially debilitating. In terms of Etzioni's formulations, for
example, 'Organizations must continually recruit means if they are to
realize their goals. One of the most important of these means is the positive orientation of the participants to the organizational power';[10] and,
'From the viewpoint of the organization, pure normative power' is
often most useful because 'it can be exercised directly down the hierarchy'.[11] Power of this kind, however, involves the 'internalization of
[organizational] norms and identification with authority',[12] which is
likely to develop most readily where there is a high degree of congruence
between the higher and lower participants' attitudes and beliefs concerning the organisation's structures, roles, and procedures. It is desirable,
therefore, to investigate the patterns of cognition of the different types
of bureaucrats while controlling on rank.

Table 3.2 provides an indication of the effect of these two factors on
the bureaucrats' perceptions of the impact of the bureaucracy on the
daily life of the average citizen. It is evident that 'statesmen' believe
that it has the greatest impact, whereas their polar opposites, 'politicos',
perceive it to have the least. Thus, 55 per cent of the former compared
to only 44 per cent of the latter believe the bureaucracy has a 'great'
impact. Furthermore, there is substantial variation between the responses of 'service bureaucrats' and 'job bureaucrats', with the former
being somewhat more attuned to the bureaucracy's impact. These differences suggest that there are, indeed, significant divergencies within the
civil service and that different types of bureaucrats start out from different premises with regard to the basic matter of the scope of the bureaucracy's centrality in the day-to-day life of the society. It is hard to
imagine that the differences between statesmen and politicos would not

affect their policy orientations and role conceptions.

Table 3.2: The Bureaucracy's Impact on Daily Life by Bureaucratic
Types, Controlling for Rank

Type	Rank	Degree of impact			Total	
		None	Some	Great		
	Low	18%	35%	47%	100%	(72)
Statesmen	Middle	13	25	62	100%	(52)
	High	10	25	65	100%	(20)
Total		15	30	55	100%	(144)
		Gamma= .23 (p $<$.05)				
	Low	24	29	47	100%	(34)
Service	Middle	8	42	50	100%	(26)
bureaucrats	High	—	29	71	100%	(7)
Total		15	34	51	100%	(67)
		Gamma = .35 (p $<$.05)				
	Low	18	34	48	100%	(124)
Job	Middle	14	37	49	100%	(59)
bureaucrats	High	6	30	64	100%	(13)
Total		16	35	49	100%	(196)
		Gamma = .10 (p $<$.05)				
	Low	18	37	45	100%	(77)
Politicos	Middle	21	41	38	100%	(42)
	High	15	14	71	100%	(11)
Total		19	37	44	100%	(130)
		Gamma = .13 (p $<$.05)				

However, the organisational problems which might stem from such gaps are mitigated to a certain extent by the effect of rank on the bureaucrats' perceptions of the bureaucracy's impact. The information in Table 3.2 indicates that higher-ranking civil servants of all types attribute a considerably greater impact to the bureaucracy on the daily life of the average Israeli than do their counterparts in the lower ranks. For example, whereas 65 per cent of the statesmen in the top grades believe that the bureaucracy exerts a strong influence, only 47 per cent of those statesmen in the lowest ranks share this perception. Hence, a greater sense of the bureaucracy's importance exists among those who are in its major policy-making positions and this may act as an impetus for further bureaucratic action and its engagement in additional activities. Nevertheless, there are significant differences among the individual types within the higher ranks as well, and these could affect organisational integration and orientations. For example, at this level, politicos differ from job bureaucrats, which may be a reflection of more generalist versus more specialist outlooks. Thus, the basic importance of the types remains despite the relative influence of rank.

Significant variations also exist in the patterns of cognition of the public. As can be seen in Table 3.3, bureauphiles are most likely to believe that the bureaucracy has a considerable impact on their daily lives, and bureautics are the least likely. Indeed, 30 per cent of the latter attribute no influence to it, as compared to only 15 per cent of the former who view the bureaucracy's impact in this fashion. As could be expected, bureautolerants fall between these two polar types, although they are somewhat closer to the bureautics. These patterns are best explained, perhaps, in terms of the fact that perceptions are subjective and, therefore, the extent of perceived impact may be exaggerated or minimised in accordance with one's predispositions. Consequently, as a kind of defence mechanism, bureautics, who find the bureaucracy to be both complex and unfair, may subjectively tend to reduce the extent to which it affects their day-to-day lives. Bureauphiles, on the other hand, find the bureaucracy relatively easy to deal with, and consequently have no need for such a defensive posture, and may even exaggerate its importance. It is also evident, however, as would be suggested by Almond and Verba's study,[13] that such patterns are affected in a consistent direction by education. The higher one's education, the more likely one is to believe that the bureaucracy has a considerable impact on one's life. Nevertheless, differences remain between highly educated bureauphiles, bureautolerants, and bureautics, thereby re-emphasising the basic importance of individuals' predispositions towards public bureaucracy.

From the foregoing analysis, it is clear that for the most part, Israelis are cognitively oriented towards the impact of the bureaucracy on their daily lives. Among the general public, assessments of its impact are quite strong, and, indeed, place the bureaucracy among the most important central institutions in Israel in terms of the extent to which it affects their lives. Nevertheless, there is considerable variation in patterns of cognition in accordance with whether one is a bureauphile, bureautolerant, or bureautic. Hence, some citizens are far more attuned to the bureaucracy's impact than others. Bureaucrats tend to attribute a greater impact to the bureaucracy than does the public, and here, too, there are important patterns of variation. Bureaucratic type and rank exert a strong influence upon individual bureaucrats' perceptions. The higher one's rank, the more central one believes the bureaucracy is to the average citizen's daily life; and statesmen are far more likely to view it

Table 3.3: Public's Perception of the Impact of Bureaucracy on Daily Life by Types, Controlling for Rank

Types	Education	Degree of impact			Total	
		None	Some	Great		
	Primary	20%	20%	60%	100%	(126)
Bureauphiles	Secondary	16	19	65	100%	(112)
	High	6	10	84	100%	(78)
Total		15	17	68	100%	(316)
		Gamma = .30 (p<.01)				
	Primary	33	23	44	100%	(235)
Bureautolerants	Secondary	23	24	53	100%	(141)
	High	13	28	59	100%	(110)
Total		26	24	50	100%	(486)
		Gamma = .24 (p<.001)				
	Primary	36	25	39	100%	(250)
Bureautics	Secondary	26	23	51	100%	(149)
	High	20	24	56	100%	(93)
Total		30	24	46	100%	(492)
		Gamma = .23 (p<.001)				

as having a great impact than are politicos. The remaining types also differ and are located between these two polar opposites.

These findings strengthen our belief that there is much to be learned from the study of bureaucratic culture in societies which are unevenly developed and occupy intermediate positions on political and economic development spectra. In such societies, as in Israel, cognitive orientations may be at a relatively high level, however, and some groups are likely to be considerably less attuned to the bureaucracy's impact on their lives than others. This is especially true of those that find it difficult to internalise bureaucratic norms and relate to complex organisational structures. Within democratic political communities, the process of developing a 'participant' or even a 'parochial' political culture is a difficult and time-consuming one.[14] At the early stages of democratic political development, wide variations may exist in the extent to which different groups and types of individuals can be mobilised and socialised. Similarly, a central bureaucracy, while a major force in the life of a political community, is unlikely to have 'congealed' into an integrated, coherent, organisational whole. The public service in such countries may remain far from fully institutionalised and without a sense of distinctiveness.[15] This being the case, individual bureaucrats are likely to assess its impact differentially, and, overall, these assessments are likely to fall into patterns in accordance with how bureaucrats relate to bureaucratic norms, structures, procedures, outlooks, and outputs, as well as their vantage point in the hierarchy.

Areas of Impact

In political communities seeking to successfully undergo the processes of political and economic development, the most important functions of a public bureaucracy may be those which are directed towards nation-building and economic growth. Hence, it has been concluded that

> public administration turns out, increasingly, to be one of the first chapters of any rational theory of economic growth. While relevant for all of the developing countries, the importance of public administration in the emerging countries of Africa and Asia goes beyond directing the organizational process in economic and social fields. It has the immense task of creating a national unity and a national personality capable of surmounting the centrifugal force of tribal and regional rivalries and, on the other hand, instilling the ferment of change in traditional societies.[16]

Indeed, social integration may prove more difficult than economic development. The twentieth century is an age of nationalism and national liberation movements. Differences of race, ethnicity, language, and religion often threaten the dismemberment or collapse of political communities. Even some of the most politically developed nations, including the United States and the Soviet Union, have had great difficulty in dealing with such cleavages. Where the establishment of national institutions and central political authority is still problematical, social integration may be both crucial and highly elusive. Nations such as India, and to a lesser extent Israel, have only to look at developments in Pakistan and Nigeria to sense the urgency with which sub-cultural differences must be either eliminated or satisfactorily enmeshed.

An additional area in which a public bureaucracy may play a critical role in the process of nation-building concerns the establishment of democracy. Many, perhaps most, developing nations lack a genuine commitment to democratic values and processes, but almost all pay at least lip-service to them in the creation of national ideologies and attempts to establish political legitimacy. In some, such as Israel, India, and Mexico, democracy ranks with economic development as a major goal. Here, however, public bureaucracy's role is even more tenuous than in the areas of economic development and social integration. As noted in the first chapter, the relationship between bureaucracy and democracy is problematical. Bureaucratic organisation and processes are inherently undemocratic. To the extent that bureaucracy is a dominant political institution in any nation, it may militate against the establishment of effective democratic government. As Eisenstadt has observed, the basic dilemmas of bureaucracy revolve around the matter of whether it 'is master or servant, an independent body or a tool, and, if a tool, whose interests it can be made to serve'.[17] Increasingly, it has been argued that a non-democratically-oriented bureaucracy cannot adequately serve the needs of political communities stressing development within a democratic context:

> Underlying the concern for a democratic or effective public administration is, first, a belief that public administration must be based on public consent or support. The actions of public agencies and officials should reflect the aspirations, interests, demands, and support potential of the public it serves and directs. Official action should be responsible as well as rational, and above all, must command the respect and cooperation of citizens. Second is the concept of administration as a 'circular process', from the initial formulation of policy, to its implementation, to the modification of policy subsequent to its evaluation in the process of implementation, including feedback from the public at various steps in this process. This is a continuous, dynamic set of interactions. It conceives of citizens in a double role, as producers and consumers of goods and services, or as policy-makers and subjects. From both analytical and value premises, therefore, has come the emphasis on democratic responsiveness by officials and responsible citizen involvement as preconditions for an effective administrative process in the modern polity.[18]

How then, do citizens and bureaucrats in an unevenly developed political community such as Israel assess the impact of the central bureaucracy on the processes of national development, social integration, and establishing democracy?

Table 3.4 brings us closer to an answer to these questions. It reports the perceived degree of impact of the Israeli bureaucracy on national development, social integration, and democracy. In terms of domestic development goals, these areas have been of the greatest importance in Israel as well as elsewhere. Yet each has been problematical. Israelis enjoy a relatively high standard of living and economic development which has progressed at a very rapid rate. Nevertheless, inadequate housing and productivity remain central economic problems, the economy has been heavily dependent upon outside capital and aid, and growth appears to be far from self-sustained. Great efforts in the direction of social integration have been made, at least among the Jewish population. Hebrew, rather than a plethora of languages including Yiddish, Ladino, French, and Arabic, has become the overwhelmingly dominant national tongue. Nevertheless, a deep social cleavage between Israelis of Asian-African origins and those of European backgrounds remains and sometimes erupts into direct and violent confrontation.* Finally, although Israel has successfully established a democratic form of government, it has largely been a one-party dominant political system and has been controlled by a relatively compact and coherent 'establishment'[19] which reinforces its dominance through such practices as the maintenance of tight control over the machinery of political parties, news management, and even outright censorship.

Overall, as is evident from the information contained in Table 3.4, both the public and the bureaucrats believe that the Israeli bureaucracy has had a relatively strong impact on the developmental processes under consideration. However, there are also important differences between the two groups. Thus, the public bureaucrats perceive the bureaucracy to have a greater impact on national development than does the average citizen. Whereas 77 per cent of the former believe that the bureaucracy has a 'strong impact' or 'some impact' on these processes, only 64 per cent of the latter make this assessment. Furthermore, a higher percentage of the public reported 'other and don't know' with regard to the impact of the bureaucracy on national development. Even greater differences are observed concerning the perceived impact of the bureaucracy on social integration, which has been more problematical for the political community. Here, 83 per cent of the bureaucrats believe that the bureaucracy has had a significant impact, whereas only 63 per cent of the public make this judgement. In addition, there is a sizeable gap between the percentage of the bureaucrats and other members of the political community who attribute a 'great impact' to the bureaucracy's role in this area. The bureaucracy's activities in this regard are also less visible to the public at large as is evidenced by the number responding to the 'other and don't know' category.

A somewhat similar pattern is evident with regard to the bureaucracy* impact on the maintenance of democracy. In this area, however, the dif-

*Chapter 6 is devoted to an analysis of the impact of this cleavage on bureaucratic culture in Israel.

ferences between bureaucrat and public are less pronounced and a lesser impact is universally attributed to the bureaucracy. A little more than 30 per cent of the bureaucrats and a full 40 per cent of the public perceive the bureaucracy to have 'no impact' on democracy or responded in the 'other and don't know' category. Moreover, the responses of both the bureaucrats and the public in the 'great impact' category are the lowest for any of the three areas. This emphasises, once again, the difficult relationship between bureaucracy and democratic government.

Table 3.4: The Perceived Degree of Impact of the Israeli Bureaucracy on National Development, Social Integration, and Democracy*

Impact on		Great impact	Some impact	No impact	Other and DK	Total
National development	Public (N=1,590)	34%	30%	18%	18%	100%
	Bureaucrats (N=630)	35	42	15	8	100%
			D = - .13 df=3 p ⟨.001			
Social integration	Public (N=1,562)	39	24	17	20	100%
	Bureaucrats (N=625)	51	32	7	10	100%
			D = -.20 df=3 p⟨.001			
Democracy	Public (N=1,530)	31	29	17	23	100%
	Bureaucrats (N=590)	32	36	16	16	100%
			D = -.08 df=3 p ⟨.02			

*Actual text of questions: 'Thinking now about the public bureaucracy, about how much effect do you think its activities have on national development (social integration, democracy)?' The Hebrew equivalent used in the questionnaires for 'national development' was Hitpathut Leumit and for 'social integration'—Kibbutz Galuyot. The question on democracy pertains to the national political system. For the validity and comparability of these terms in the Israeli context, see for example Aaron Antonovsky and Alan Arian, *Hopes and Fears of Israelis: Consensus in a New Society* (Jerusalem: Academic Press, 1972), esp. pp. 197-221, and Schlomit Levy and Louis Guttman, 'Structure and Dynamics of Worries', *Sociometry*, vol. 38 (December 1975), pp. 445-73.

Taken together these findings are generally in accord with theoretical observations concerning development processes. There is greater agreement between the bureaucrats and the public with regard to the impact of the Israeli bureaucracy on national development than there is concerning social integration, which is less tangible, more problematical, and has remained more elusive. Perhaps the keys to these differences are visibility and salience. Economic development and nation-building in Israel have been rapid and largely successful. Economically, development has involved a great deal of building infra-structure, roads, highways, and housing developments. In terms of nation-building, the state has been fully established, tested in four wars, able to sustain an influx of immigrants which approximately tripled its population within a short period of time, and has created numerous new settlements and population centres. The salience of these areas for the population would be hard to overestimate. There is keen citizen interest in and support for a continually rising standard of living and strengthening of the polity, especially *vis-à-vis* Israel's neighbours. Social integration, on the other hand, is not a goal which is fully accepted by the population, the progress towards it is manifested in less visible ways, such as inter-communal marriage, equal opportunity, and a greater measure of equality itself. Consequently, bureaucrats are probably far more aware of efforts and activities concerning social integration, which involve whole ministries and agencies, than are the average citizens. This exemplifies the discrepancy between the producer and implementer of policy on the one hand, and the consumer of its application on the other, which often characterises administrative processes. Furthermore, it also indicates that such a division can be pronounced even with regard to the *level of impact*, rather than only with respect to its character. Finally, both citizen and bureaucrat are more sceptical of the bureaucracy's impact on democratic government. This is not because either group rejects the notion that Israel is in fact democratic, but rather because the bureaucracy's role in the political system remains somewhat ambiguous and its impact on democracy is not readily visible. Patronage and politicisation remain alongside merit and neutrality among its central features and it has yet to develop a strong institutional distinctiveness or set of coherent and dominant political roles. As Heady suggests, the latter condition is prevalent in almost all political systems undergoing rapid political and economic development.[20] Finally, the bureaucracy has not played a very significant role in the mobilisation of citizen support for the political system.

It is possible to learn more about these matters by investigating further the bureaucrats' and the public's perceptions concerning the bureaucracy's impact on each of the major developmental areas. Table 3.5 presents such information with regard to the bureaucrats. Again it can be seen that type and rank play an important role in ordering their perceptions. Here, however, rank affects the types differentially. Taking the area of national development first, statesmen, as might be expected,

Table 3.5: The Bureaucracy's Impact on National Development, Social Integration and Democracy by Bureaucratic Types, Controlling for Rank

		National development			Social integration			Democracy		
Type	Rank	Little impact	Considerable impact	Total	Little impact	Considerable impact	Total	Little impact	Considerable impact	Total
Statesmen	Low	55%	45%	100% (70)	29%	71%	100% (70)	59%	41%	100% (69)
	Middle	52	48	100% (51)	23	77	100% (52)	54	46	100% (50)
	High	38	62	100% (19)	19	81	100% (20)	49	51	100% (19)
		Gamma = .17 (p<.05)			Gamma = .15 (p<.05)			Gamma = .14 (p>.05)		
Service Bureaucrats	Low	67	33	100% (34)	37	63	100% (32)	67	33	100% (34)
	Middle	69	31	100% (26)	35	65	100% (26)	75	25	100% (25)
	High	84	16	100% (7)	43	57	100% (7)	90	10	100% (6)
		Gamma = -.16 (p<.05)			Gamma = -.01 (p>.05)			Gamma = .09 (p>.05)		
Job bureaucrats	Low	61	39	100% (123)	31	69	100% (122)	64	36	100% (121)
	Middle	53	47	100% (59)	39	61	100% (58)	55	45	100% (57)
	High	66	34	100% (13)	36	64	100% (11)	33	67	100% (11)
		Gamma = .07 (p>.05)			Gamma = -.19 (p<.05)			Gamma = .25 (p<.05)		
Politicos	Low	65	35	100% (72)	34	66	100% (71)	76	24	100% (70)
	Middle	65	35	100% (42)	44	56	100% (40)	61	39	100% (39)
	High	86	14	100% (7)	20	80	100% (7)	60	40	100% (6)
		Gamma = -.08 (p>.05)			Gamma = -.08 (p>.05)			Gamma = .28 (p<.05)		

believe the bureaucracy has contributed most, whereas politicos and service bureaucrats perceive it to have had the least impact. Furthermore, statesmen are the only type for whom higher rank is progressively associated with the perception that the bureaucracy has had a considerable impact. In other words, politicos, service bureaucrats, and job bureaucrats in the higher ranks believe that the bureaucracy has contributed less to national development than do their counterparts in the lower ranks. Indeed, notwithstanding the relatively few number of cases, the gap between high-ranking statesmen and high-ranking politicos is very large. Thus, whereas 62 per cent of the former attribute a considerable impact to the bureaucracy in this area, only 14 per cent of the latter view it in the same light. Somewhat similar patterns are found with regard to the other two areas as well. In both cases statesmen are the most positive in their assessment of the bureaucracy's contributions, and service bureaucrats are the least. The relative positions of job bureaucrats and politicos vary with the area, the latter being considerably less positive concerning the bureaucracy's contributions to democracy. Again rank affects each of the types in a different manner, sometimes increasing the assessment of impact, and sometimes decreasing it.

These findings reinforce the proposition concerning the heterogeneity of types in the public bureaucracy and the extent to which the civil service has not developed a uniform, integrated outlook concerning the three areas of critical importance to political and economic development. Indeed, in the higher ranks they are almost worlds apart in their perceptions of the bureaucracy's impact. Given that all of the types are found in all ranks and in all agencies, they must interact with one another if the bureaucracy is to utilise fully its human resources. Yet, one wonders how satisfactory such interaction can be with regard to policy-making and the direction of its implementation where such wide divergencies exist. For example, it is evident that with regard to the area of national development high-ranking statesmen's and politicos' basic perceptions pertaining to the contributions of the bureaucracy are so different that their co-ordination and consensus on policy matters would probably be extremely difficult to obtain. The same is true with regard to service bureaucrats and job bureaucrats in the area of democracy. Although pluralism within a public bureaucracy may be desirable, it is doubtful that the contributions of such dissensus outweigh their disadvantages. In any event, it is clear that the Israeli civil service lacks a coherence in outlook that is often associated with those which have achieved a greater degree of maturity and distinctiveness. Moreover, this condition is probably more typical than atypical of bureaucracies in less developed political communities.

Variations in patterns of cognition among the public regarding the bureaucracy's impact in each of the major developmental areas are also of interest. As is shown in Table 3.6, bureauphiles believe that the bureaucracy has contributed most to each of the areas, and bureautics perceive it to have had the least impact. The nature of these gaps strengthens the interpretation that, at least in unevenly developed nations, there is a consistency in the way in which different groups relate to the bureaucratisation of public life. These patterns, in turn, are related to individuals' ability to deal with bureaucratic structures and norms.

Overall, these patterns of cognition with regard to the bureaucracy's impact in the areas of national development, social integration, and the maintenance of democracy present a mixed picture which may be characteristic of many other political communities as well. Important

Table 3.6: The Public's Perception of the Bureaucracy's Impact on National Development, Social Integration and Democracy by Types

Types	National development			Social integration			Democracy		
	Consid-erable impact	Little impact	Total	Consid-erable impact	Little impact	Total	Consid-erable impact	Little impact	Total
Bureau-philes (N=309)	90%	10%	100%	84%	16%	100%	83%	17%	100%
Bureau-tolerants (N=457)	82	18	100%	74	26	100%	90	10	100%
Bureau-tics (N=442)	73	27	100%	67	33	100%	64	36	100%

Gamma = .35 (p .001)   Gamma = .28 (p .001)   Gamma = .34 (p .001)

differences exist both between and among the bureaucrats and the public. There are strong indications that the bureaucracy has yet to emerge as a coherent, not to mention integrated, force in the political system. Its activities are perceived differently by different groups of citizens and also by its own members. Its roles in nation-building are a matter of disagreement and even significant cleavage. Gaps between bureaucrat and citizen-consumer of bureaucratic processes and outputs are often considerable. In short, the bureaucracy has yet to establish a relatively clear and accepted role in the minds of the public and its own members, concerning its activities in the realm of political and economic development. Moreover, when we turn our attention to the character of its impact, it becomes readily apparent that the bureaucracy has yet to establish completely its legitimacy as a fully-fledged partner in the process of nation-building.

Character of Impact

Thus far, it has been observed that most Israelis believe that their national bureaucracy has a significant impact on their lives and on the political community's developmental processes. These findings leave no doubt that the bureaucracy has a high degree of salience in general. Salience, however, is a matter of impact, it does not provide an indication of whether bureaucratic performance is assessed[21] in a positive or negative fashion. When this question is analysed the difficulties of creating an effective, communicative, and democratically-oriented civil service in a new and unevenly developed nation become even more evident.

Table 3.7 presents the public's assessment of the bureaucracy's performance in each of the three developmental areas and the degree to which they perceive it to have an impact. It is clear that the more salient the bureaucracy is considered to be, the more positively it is evaluated by the public. The direction of this association is important because it indicates that a greater amount of support exists for the bureaucracy among those who are most cognisant of its activities. If those most attuned to its impacts had rated bureaucratic performance lowest, severe problems involving communication between the bureaucracy, as an institution, and the citizen-consumers of its performance might exist. Moreover, it would be extremely difficult for the bureaucracy to mobilise significant citizen support for its role in nation-building under such circumstances. On the other hand, although the general pattern of assessment suggests that difficulties of this nature may be avoided, the overall picture is nevertheless not encouraging. The public appears to be overwhelmingly dissatisfied with the bureaucracy's performance. At least 60 per cent of the public give its activities a negative rating in each of the developmental areas. Moreover, 'exteremly negative' ratings are several times more frequent than 'extremely positive' ones. Hence, the Israeli bureaucracy has a high salience overall, but lacks citizen support at the same time. Apparently it is viewed as a rather pervasive negative feature of political, economic, and social life in Israel.

This interpretation is reinforced by the information contained in Table 3.8. When the public is sub-divided into types, it becomes clear

Table 3.7: The Public's Assessment of Bureaucratic Performance by its Perceived Impact on National Development, Social Integration and Democracy

Degree of impact	Extremely positive	Positive	Negative	Extremely negative	Total
		National development			
Strong impact	6%	30%	40%	24%	100% (515)
Some impact	3	18	48	31	100% (387)
No impact	2	17	45	36	100% (130)
		Gamma = .23 (p<.001)			
		Social integration			
Strong impact	5%	31%	42%	22%	100% (514)
Some impact	3	20	47	30	100% (307)
No impact	3	19	42	35	99% (195)
		Gamma = .18 (p<.05)			
		Democracy			
Strong impact	4%	30%	43%	23%	100% (413)
Some impact	3	20	48	29	100% (384)
No impact	3	25	40	31	99% (188)
		Gamma = .12 (p<.01)			

that no group is strongly supportive of the bureaucracy's activities and roles in the three developmental areas. Indeed, two of the three groups rate its performance in a negative fashion. Thus, even among the bureauphiles, who are the group which is most positively oriented towards the bureaucracy in general, only 38 per cent give its performance a favourable evaluation, as compared to 22 per cent who rate it negatively. As might be expected, bureautics are the most negative in their evaluations, with almost 60 per cent giving the bureaucracy unfavourable ratings. Bureautolerants, while between these extremes, also tend to assess its performance negatively. Consequently, it can be concluded that, among the general public, the bureaucracy's appeal as an institutional force in political and economic development is weak in all quarters. This is all the more so in view of the fact that education exerts almost no impact on these groups' assessments.

As indicated in Table 3.9, the bureaucrats' assessments of the bureaucracy's performance in each of the three developmental areas under consideration present a considerably different pattern. Although, as in the case of the public, those who believe that the bureaucracy has had the greatest impact also tend to evaluate it more positively, there is a striking overall gap between the bureaucrats' and the public's ratings. Thus, the

Table 3.8: The Public's Assessment of Bureaucratic Performance by
          Types

Types	Assessment			
	Positive	Neutral	Negative	Total
Bureauphiles (N=320)	38%	40%	22%	100%
Bureautolerants (N=510)	24	41	35	100%
Bureautics (N=504)	12	29	59	100%

Gamma = .46 (p $<$ .001)

bureaucrats tend to be far more positive in their ratings of the bureaucracy's performance. This division could have important administrative
consequences. Almost inevitably, it would lead to frustration and
animosity. The bureaucrats believe that the bureaucracy's performance
has been helpful to political and economic development; the public
largely disagrees. A lack of public support is likely to constrain administrative action and to hamper its effectiveness. Administrators' inability
to gain public acceptance and support for their programmes and pro-
posals tends to generate frustration and unfavourable attitudes towards
the public. Moreover, there is a self-sustaining cycle involved here. The
less public support, the less administrative action, the less the perceived
impact of the bureaucracy, the greater the public's negative evaluation
of it. In addition, the less positive the bureaucracy's image, the harder
the recruitment of capable officials may be.[22] This situation is not, of
course, unique to Israel. Differences between citizens' and bureaucrats'
assessments of the features of a national bureaucracy exist elsewhere as
well,[23] and these appear to be a major problem in the establishment of
a fully effective public service. Fortunately for Israel, however, at least
those groups which attribute greatest relevance to the bureaucracy are
the most sanguine in their views of its performance.

   Finally, it is necessary to round out this discussion by examining
further the nature of the bureaucrats' assessments of the bureaucracy's
performance concerning developmental processes. This can be accomplished with the aid of Table 3.10 which reports their ratings by type
and rank. It is evident that there is considerable variation among the different types in general, with statesmen being the most positive in their
assessments, and service bureaucrats and politicos least. More striking
perhaps, is that here, unlike in the previous areas investigated, rank

Table 3.9: Bureaucrats' Assessment of the Bureaucracy's Performance, by its Perceived Impact on National Development, Social Integration and Democracy

Degree of impact	Assessment				Total
	Extremely positive	Positive	Negative	Extremely negative	
National development					
Strong impact	7%	46%	36%	11%	100% (207)
Some impact	3	38	47	12	100% (242)
No impact	2	36	42	20	100% (82)
			Gamma = .23 (p<.001)		
Social integration					
Strong impact	5%	44%	41%	10%	100% (346)
Some impact	2	39	40	19	100% (133)
No impact	2	29	48	21	100% (38)
			Gamma = .21 (p<.01)		
Democracy					
Strong impact	9%	48%	30%	13%	100% (185)
Some impact	2	37	48	13	100% (231)
No impact	4	36	46	14	100% (93)
			Gamma = .04 (p<.01)		

affects all four types in a similar fashion. Thus, throughout the bureaucracy, the higher one's rank, the more positively one rates its activities and roles concerning political and economic development. This finding does little to mitigate the earlier interpretation that large gaps in the different types' perceptions concerning the impact of the bureaucracy are likely to hamper its effectiveness as a policy-maker and implementer. However, it does indicate that there is considerable support for the bureaucracy's activities among those in the top ranks. In other words, although top-ranking bureaucrats differ radically in their views as to what the role of the bureaucracy has been in each of the three developmental areas, they nevertheless agree that its performance should be rated positively.

In sum, in the first chapter it was argued that the nature of public bureaucracy and the bureaucratisation of public life could be expected to engender different reactions among individual citizens and those who staff such organisations. It was maintained further that these reactions were likely to be broadly associated with social, psychological, and experiential characteristics. Typologies were constructed in an effort to

Table 3.10: Bureaucrats' Assessment of the Character of the Bureaucracy's
Impact by Types, Controlling for Rank

| Types | Rank | Assessment | | Total | |
		Negative	Positive		
Statesmen	Low	15%	85%	100%	(72)
	Middle	17	83	100%	(48)
	High	5	95	100%	(19)
		Gamma = .14 (p<.05)			
Service bureaucrats	Low	31	69	100%	(85)
	Middle	26	74	100%	(27)
	High	14	86	100%	(17)
		Gamma = .21 (p<.05)			
Job bureaucrats	Low	18	82	100%	(129)
	Middle	13	87	100%	(61)
	High	9	91	100%	(14)
		Gamma = .21 (p>.05)			
Politicos	Low	21	79	100%	(79)
	Middle	17	83	100%	(41)
	High	14	86	100%	(16)
		Gamma = .15 (p<.05)			

tap the latter two, and the relationship between social background and
bureaucratic culture is investigated separately in chapter 6. Analysis of
the cognitive orientations towards the Israeli bureaucracy of public
bureaucrats and citizens lends considerable support to these interpretations. It is evident that different types of bureaucrats and citizens do
in fact perceive large differences in the impact of the public bureaucracy
on their daily lives and on the nation's developmental processes. Although
these patterns are sometimes affected by other factors, such as rank and
education, they nevertheless retain their central predominance. Thus,
statesmen differ consistently from politicos, and bureauphiles similarly
from bureautics. These differences pertain not only to the salience of
the bureaucracy but also to the fashion in which its performance is assessed.

In addition, the nature of these patterns of cognition is of considerable importance to politics and administration. There are considerable
gaps between and among the bureaucrats and public. These must
inevitably affect the course of bureaucratic policy-making and the bureaucracy's role in the nation's development and politics. It is clear that
the civil service lacks anything resembling a unified outlook with regard
to the central areas of national development, social integration, and the

bureaucracy's interface with democracy. Indeed, the outlooks of different types of high-ranking bureaucrats are such that co-ordination with regard to policy-making may be extremely difficult, if not almost entirely infeasible. Moreover, the gaps between the bureaucrats and the citizen-consumers of their performance are also large and there is little citizen support for the bureaucracy's activities. Finally differences among the members of the political community in general suggest that not all citizens are able to be full participants in the public life of the bureaucratised polity. This, then, constitutes a large part of the subject matter of the following chapter.

Notes

1. The word 'penetration' is not intended to connote any degree of totalitarianism or authoritarianism, but rather is used in the sense of 'permeation' or 'outreach'. This follows the usage in Eldersveld *et al., The Citizen and the Administrator in a Developing Democracy* (Glenview: Scott, Foresman, 1968), pp. 100-3. As Eisenstadt states, 'The difference between modern democratic, semi-democratic, and totalitarian political systems does not lie in the spread of power, for this is common to all of them. The difference lies in the ways in which the rulers react to this power. The spread of potential political power is a characteristic of all modern political systems, including the totalitarian as distinct from pre-modern or traditional.' S.N. Eisenstadt, 'Bureaucracy and Political Development', in J. LaPalombara (ed.), *Bureaucracy and Political Development* (Princeton: Princeton University Press, 1967), p. 99.

2. S.N. Eisenstadt, 'Problems of Emerging Bureaucracies in Developing Areas and New States', in Nimrod Raphaeli (ed.), *Readings in Comparative Public Administration* (Boston: Allyn & Bacon, 1967), p. 221.

3. Gabriel Almond and Sidney Verba, *The Civic Culture* (Boston: Little, Brown, 1965), p. 59.

4. Alfred Meyer, *The Soviet Political System* (New York: Random House, 1965), pp. 467-8.

5. Almond and Verba, *The Civic Culture*, p. 75.

6. Ibid.

7. Reinhard Bendix, *Nation-Building and Citizenship* (New York: Wiley, 1964), pp. 129-30.

8. Grant McConnell, *Private Power and American Democracy* (New York: Knopf, 1966), esp. part II; and Theodore J. Lowi, *The End of Liberalism* (New York: W.W. Norton, 1969), esp. ch. 3.

9. Richard B. Taub, *Bureaucrats Under Stress* (Berkeley: University of California Press, 1969), p. 3.

10. Amitai Etzioni, 'Leaders' Control and Members' Compliance', in Gerald D. Bell (ed.), *Organizations and Human Behavior* (Englewood Cliffs: Prentice-Hall, 1967), p. 83.

11. Ibid., p. 82.

12. Ibid., p. 84.

13. See Almond and Verba, *The Civic Culture*, esp. pp. 315-24.

14. Ibid., esp. chs. 11 and 13.

15. For a discussion of this problem see Charles W. Anderson, *Politics and Economic Change in Latin America* (Princeton: Van Nostrand, 1967), ch. 6.

16. Roberto de Oliveira Campos, 'Public Administration in Latin America', in Raphaeli (ed.), *Readings in Comparative Public Administration*, p. 285.

17. S.N. Eisenstadt, *Essays on Comparative Institutions* (New York: Wiley, 1965), p. 179.

18. Eldersveld *et al.*, *Citizen and Administrator*, pp. 3-4.

19. See Yuval Elizur and Eliahu Salpeter, *Who Rules Israel?* (New York: Harper & Row, 1973).

20. See generally, Ferrel Heady, *Public Administration: A Comparative Perspective* (Englewood Cliffs: Prentice-Hall, 1966), esp. pp. 69-72. For a discussion in the context of Latin America, see Anderson, *Politics and Economic Change in Latin America*, ch. 6.

21. The evaluative dimension of bureaucratic culture is explored in depth in ch. 5.

22. See ch. 7 *infra.*, and more generally, F.P. Kilpatrick *et al.*, *The Image of the Federal Service* (Washington: Brookings Institution, 1964).

23. See ibid., esp. chs. 6-10, and Eldersveld *et al.*, *Citizen and Administrator*, p. 92ff.

4 PATTERNS OF AFFECT: EFFICACY AND CITIZEN COMPETENCE

The bureaucratisation of public life transforms the nature of citizenship and the relationship between political system and political community. This is especially true in democratic systems, but it applies elsewhere as well. A high degree of bureaucratic penetration of the political, economic, and social spheres of a nation places the bureaucracy in the position of what might be referred to as a 'double gatekeeper'. On the one side, public policies are formulated by political authorities and channelled through the bureaucracy for implementation. Inevitably, they are subject to modification through administrative process and interpretation. This is particularly true in developed political communities in which bureaucrats are generally highly specialised and possess an amount of expertise unmatched by politicians. The alteration of public policy in this fashion contributes to bureaucratic policy-making, but it does not circumscribe its limits. In some systems, the initiative for the formulation of public policy has been transferred from the legislative to the executive branch; in others, much legislation is confined to establishing the broad objectives of policy, while allowing administrators to choose the 'means' for their attainment; and at the very least, almost everywhere bureaucrats have an important role as advisors to those formally charged with responsibility for policy-making. Hence, to a large extent, public bureaucracy is at once a buffer between political authorities and citizens and to be numbered as a unit among the former. On the other side, therefore, citizen demands and supports may be channelled directly towards the bureaucracy, in an effort to maintain or change the nature of public policy and its application. One of the complexities of the process of bureaucratisation, however, is that it limits the relevance of other and more traditional avenues for political inputs and outputs. Consequently, bureaucratisation forces citizen participation in political life to focus more and more on the bureaucracy.

Bureaucratisation and Citizenship

The nature of this process is best explained, perhaps, with reference to political history and political culture. The development of the nation-state was associated with a centralisation of the means for the distribution of public goods and services. For example, welfare and educational functions were taken over from religious organisations, the regulation of labour standards and practices was divested from guilds, private armies were abolished, and the right to practise the 'free' professions became contingent upon state approval.[1] Eventually, even some of the distributive functions of political parties, such as aid to immigrant populations and the allocation of public jobs, were largely absorbed by the state. Yet, government has precious few means for the distribution of public goods and services which do not run through bureaucratic organisations. To a considerable extent, therefore, the development of contemporary political arrangements has been associated with the near monopolisation of political output channels by public bureaucracies. The converse of this process is the reduction of the channels through which citizens can exert influence over the direction of government.

Bureaucracy's aggregation of the means through which citizens can participate in government is largely a result of the breakdown of more traditional channels of influence, to which bureaucratisation itself has contributed. This is a question of political culture and dominant modes of political exchange. It is useful to follow Heidenheimer[2] in this regard by classifying the latter into four major types found in political communities with democratic orientations. First is the 'traditional familist (kinship) based system'. Its major characteristics are that 'loyalty to the nuclear family is the only loyalty that counts', 'upper-class inhabitants avoid entering into patron-client relationships with the poorer families', and 'there is not enough trust to support the kind of "political machine" characteristic of American cities, because the voters do not believe in the promises of potential bosses, and the latter have no faith that the bribed voters will stay bought'.[3] In such a society, political exchange tends to be a matter between individuals, rather than among individuals, interest groups, and/or political parties.[4] A second model of political culture and political exchange is the 'traditional patron–client based system'. It can be described in the following fashion:

> They exist in the twentieth century but are still the captives of belief and authority patterns rooted in the distant past. Protection is sought outside the family; but in the minds of the simpler peasants the powers of supernatural patron saints and of the upper-class patrons blur into one another... Through the patron-client relationships, which unlike the kinship relationship is based upon voluntary choice of both parties, a strong sense of reciprocal obligation develops. Friendship ties and those to the patron in particular are viewed as the 'throwing stick' that gives the extended family greater range when

dealing with established authority. Out of reciprocity the family head pledges his own voting support and that of his entire family to the patron's discretion. The client maintains this dependency tie to the patron because he senses a need for protection that neither the family nor the state is able to provide.[5]

Third is the 'modern boss—follower based system,' which differs from the patron—client pattern of exchange in that it occurs in highly differentiated economies. Although traditionally legitimated elites are largely out of place in this context, 'many aspects of the boss—follower relationship are modeled on that of the patron—client relationship in the traditional setting'.[6] However, this mode of exchange is far more fluid and flexible. Finally, there is the 'Civic-Culture-Based System'. Here,

The citizens do not feel they need to work through an influential intermediary in order to get the benefit of the laws and administrative programs. They have developed strong community-regarding norms, which are supported by viable voluntary associations who repay their volunteer activists in tokens of moral satisfaction rather than money or money's worth. Political exchange relations follow a model of diversified and indirect social exchange . . . Political obligations insofar as they are still undergirded by economic exchange techniques, assume sophisticated and respectable new forms, such as testimonial dinners, lawyer's fees, consultant contracts, and campaign funds. These communities are 'clean' because the political leaders are not bound by reciprocity agreements with lower-class followers, which the latter could utilize as channels for forcing their styles of competition on the more 'respectable' strata.[7]

It is evident that bureaucratisation, in the Weberian sense, tends to limit all but the latter mode of political exchange. The norm of impersonality renders ineffective familist (kinship) patterns of political influence. As discussed earlier, bureaucracy reacts without regard to persons,[8] and the bureaucratic official is constrained from giving preference to members of his or her family, or anyone else for that matter. The selection of bureaucrats on the basis of non-ascriptive criteria, coupled with impersonality, tends to negate channels of influence associated with patron—client systems. Put simply, patterns of legitimacy change and the traditional patrons are likely to be displaced by more 'ideal type' bureaucrats. Bureaucratisation not only limits the importance of boss-follower patterns of exchange by reducing the importance of political parties in the distribution of public goods and services, it actually tends towards the destruction of such systems by creating 'neutral' (non-partisan) administration and by denying political machines the widespread use of patronage. In all cases, bureaucratisation, in this sense, limits the importance of 'crude political reciprocity in economic terms, such as the bribe . . . '.[9] This, of course, is not to say that bureaucracies and bureaucrats may not be corrupt, but rather to suggest that such corruption represents a perversion of the principles behind such organisations and tends towards 'debureaucratization'.

How, then, can the members of a bureaucratised democratic political community exert influence on their political system? Traditional channels and political machines are rendered largely irrelevant by bureaucratisation. Even in the absence of boss—follower exchange relationships, political parties decline as effective channels for citizen influence as bureaucracies absorb more and more policy-making functions from legislatures and become less partisan and more expert. As Heidenheimer suggests, the exchange model of the 'civic culture' retains importance. Influence may be wielded through voluntary associations and pressure groups, especially those which ostensibly are dedicated to the promotion of the 'public interest' and can more or less successfully rationalise their activities in this fashion. In so far as their influence is projected towards a public bureaucracy, their legitimate functions are limited to supplying information, expert technical knowledge, and interpretation. As Eisenstadt notes, however, close interaction between bureaucrats and such groups can be destructive of bureaucratic administration, and, therefore, presumably may be restricted by administrators:

> Here there is subversion of the goals and activities of the bureaucracy in the interests of different groups with which it is in close interaction (clients, patrons, interested parties). In debureaucratization the specific characteristics of the bureaucracy in terms both of its autonomy and its specific rules and goals are minimized, even up to the point where its very functions and activities are taken over by other groups or organizations. Examples of this can be found in cases when some organization (i.e., a parents' association or a religious or political group) attempts to divert the rules and working of a bureaucratic organization . . . for its own use or according to its own values and goals.[10]

In any event, as McConnell has argued, the average citizen is not likely to be well represented by a pressure group, even if he or she is a member of one,[11] and consequently, even in 'civic cultures' opportunities for the exertion of citizen influence on public bureaucracy are generally limited.

It is evident from the foregoing discussion that the ways in which citizens relate to the monopolisation of political input and output channels by public bureaucracies is a matter of the utmost concern to the study of bureaucratic culture. Do citizens feel that they can have some influence on bureaucracy, and, if so, how strongly and in what ways? To what extent do they actually try to exercise influence? And with what are these matters associated? These questions can be studied through the use of two concepts, efficacy and citizen competence.

Efficacy and Citizen Competence

Political efficacy has been the focus of a considerable amount of research in recent years. Most generally, it refers to 'the extent to which the citizen believes himself to be effective in politics'.[12] For instance, how high does an individual citizen feel is the probability of his or her influencing the outcomes of political events? What are the feelings of the members of the political community as a whole in this regard? And, what are the channels through which citizens believe influence is best wrought? Hence, efficacy is a subjective matter; it concerns the perceived probability of influence, rather than the actual probability or influence itself. Nevertheless, the concept provides an insight into the nature of citizen influence in various political systems. Thus, where citizens feel highly inefficacious, elite dominance is likely to be more intense.

Citizen competence is a related concept. In a strict sense, it refers to the extent to which citizen involvement in political or administrative matters does, in fact, change the outcomes of events. Hence, it is a more objective approximation of citizen influence. In practice, however, the measurement of influence, in this sense, has remained difficult, if not impossible, and the concept is used more generally to 'relate primarily to the degree of initiative an act requires'.[13] In other words, those who are more involved in attempts to exert influence and to take other political action are deemed to be more competent even if they fail to achieve their objectives. Citizen competence, then, becomes a matter of citizen mobilisation and ability and willingness to find channels of possible influence. A high measure of citizen competence, in this sense, provides an indication of the extent to which citizens actually attempt to exert influence over political authorities. Consequently, it is of particular importance with reference to democratic political communities. Almond and Verba, for example, write:

Democracy is a political system in which ordinary citizens exercise control over elites; and such control is legitimate; that is, it is supported by norms that are accepted by elites and nonelites. In all societies, of course, the making of specific decisions is concentrated in the hands of very few people. Neither the ordinary citizen nor 'public opinion' can make policy. If this is the case, the problem of assessing the degree of democracy in a nation becomes one of measuring the degree to which ordinary citizens control those who make the significant decisions for a society—in most cases, governmental elites.[14]

Where citizens make little effort to exercise such control and where they feel that they are unable to have a significant impact on the course of political events, government is likely to be less democratic.

Because public bureaucracy is so pervasive in contemporary government, analysis of efficacy and citizen competence with regard to central administrative systems is necessary for gaining a greater understanding not only of bureaucratic culture, but of modern political life as well. If bureaucracy is to be 'democratically balanced', it must be responsive to the members of the political community, instil in them feelings of efficacy, and provide avenues through which they can exert influence over it. At the same time, however, it must remain impersonal, politically neutral in a partisan sense, and somewhat aloof from both citizens and political authorities. Such a balance, of course, is difficult to attain and tends to remain elusive.

For the most part, within basically democratic regimes, as in the case of cognition, it could be expected that patterns of efficacy and citizen competence with regard to public bureaucracy would vary cross-nationally with levels of political and economic development. For instance, in their five-nation study, Almond and Verba found considerable variation in the extent to which citizens of different countries expected public bureaucrats to consider seriously their point of view. This expectation was greatest in the United Kingdom where it was held by 59 per cent of the population and lowest in Mexico where only 14 per cent thought serious consideration would be forthcoming.[15] West Germany, the United States, and Italy ranked between these extremes with 53 per cent, 48 per cent, and 35 per cent respectively, of their populations expecting serious consideration.[16] Moreover, the size of the proportion of each national population that believed its point of view would be *totally* ignored by bureaucrats followed the same pattern.[17] Almond and Verba conclude that 'the divergences among the nations on this set of figures can hardly be overemphasized. Certainly the British live in an entirely different governmental world from that of the Mexicans or Italians'.[18] Relatedly, another study found that in India most people thought that 'political pull—knowing the right person —plays an important part in whether the government will help a private person with some problem he has'.[19] Moreover, this feeling was more prevalent among the rural (and presumably less developed) population than among urbanites.

The latter finding suggests that within a single political community there may also be considerable variations in the efficacy and citizen competence of different segments of the population. This condition is related to the 'citizen-building' component of political development and to the nature of social integration, as well as to the achievement of a 'democratically balanced' bureaucracy. Significant differences in feelings of efficacy and levels of citizen competence with regard to a public bureaucracy suggest a failure to mobilise and respond equally to all major groups found within a polity.

A final consideration in the analysis of patterns of efficacy and citizen competence concerns the prevalence of these feelings among public bureaucrats and the extent to which they are different from those of the general public. Our investigation of patterns of cognition demonstrates that significant gaps between bureaucrat and client can exist and suggests that these can present formidable barriers to communication and administrative action. Similarly, if, for example, in contrast to the general public, bureaucrats feel greatly more efficacious and possess considerably higher levels of citizen competence, it would suggest that they are more of the order of 'ruling servants' than 'public servants'. It would also imply that democracy is less than fully effective and might indicate that elite dominance is strong. Moreover, it would indicate that the public bureaucracy is not fully 'democratically balanced'.

Bureaucratic Efficacy

It has been argued that a citizen feels a high sense of bureaucratic efficacy when he or she believes that there is a considerable probabability that his or her actions could effectively influence the outcomes of bureaucratic decisions and processes. A bureaucratically efficacious citizenry is especially important in democratic political systems in which there is a high degree of penetration by the public bureaucracy of the political, economic, and social life of the nation. Low bureaucratic efficacy under such circumstances indicates that members of the political community feel unable to influence the political system through its major, and perhaps, even dominant input channels. It also makes bureaucratic responsiveness less likely and thereby militates against effective democracy.

In many ways, Israel is an ideal political community in which to study these matters. As is evident from the preceding chapter, Israeli citizens and bureaucrats perceive their bureaucracy to have a great impact on daily life, national development, and social integration. These subjective characterisations appear to comport well with objective reality. The centralised nature of the polity makes the average Israeli highly dependent upon the national bureaucracy. A majority of Israelis come into frequent contact with bureaucratic agencies, the range of whose activities extends from matters of vital importance to national survival to those of almost trivial consequence. Moreover, the Israeli bureaucracy manifests a considerable degree of flexibility. Although most bureaucratic outputs are determined by law and administrative regulation, in Israel others are a product of the interaction between bureaucrat and client. In the latter event, there is a good deal of ambiguity as to the final ruling or action. Neither the bureaucrat nor the client has a clear set of expectations. Each is vulnerable to the other and the outcome of their interaction may be largely the result of their relative bargaining skills and political resources. As Caiden observes, some aspects of the Israeli administrative process involve:

> the giving and taking of favors. Followers seek favors: leaders give or deny them. Superiors demand favors; subordinates give or deny them. Negotiators ask for mutual favors; protesters deny mutual favors. Co-operation is a favor to be returned. Service is a favor to be denied. Business is reciprocity in favors. In this environment, there is little respect for universality. Laws can be made and unmade, rules followed or ignored, commands executed or countermanded, decisions accepted or reversed, all as a matter of favor. What can be done can also be un-done very quickly. Everything is open to debate, negotiation, compromise on a person-to-person basis. Laws can be enforced or ignored; breaches can be exposed or covered up; loopholes can be denied or suggested; exemptions can be accepted or rejected; definitions can be interpreted one way or another.[20]

Moreover, 'the same transaction may be continually renegotiated and different deals struck at different points of time'.[21] Hence, neither the bureaucrat nor the client necessarily accepts immediate outcomes as final. The client may appeal to a higher authority or seek reversal by enlisting the aid of outsiders. If the bureaucrat thinks that the issue warrants it, he or she may mobilise resources as well. However, the mode of appeal is far from standardised. The citizen may attempt to bribe the bureaucrat, use *protekzia* (political pull) to by-pass or even injure the bureaucrat, or simply appeal to his or her sense of humanity. In any event, though, the client's success depends considerably upon his or her own skills and connections. In such a fluid process, feelings of bureaucratic efficacy are all the more important as indicators of the extent to which members of the political community believe they can exert influence over some of the major output channels of the political system.

The first aspect of bureaucratic efficacy to be investigated concerns the extent to which individuals feel that they could change an administrative regulation which they consider to be unfair or unjust. A second element involves the channels through which the efficacious members of the political community would actually attempt to change such a measure. We can begin our analysis of these elements with Table 4.1 which displays the distribution of responses of Israeli bureaucrats and citizens to the following question: 'Suppose a regulation were being considered by one of the various ministries that you considered unjust or unfair. What do you think you could do?'

It is evident that the Israeli public feels highly efficacious with regard to bureaucratic actions. About two-thirds of the respondents believe they could take some useful action to oppose the adoption of an undesirable bureaucratic regulation. This finding is somewhat surprising. For example, in the five nations they studied, Almond and Verba found the following population percentages that felt they could do something about an unjust *national* regulation: United States, 75 per cent; Britain, 62 per cent; Germany, 38 per cent; Italy, 28 per cent; Mexico, 38 per cent.[22] Relatedly, Eldersveld and associates found that in India, 41 per cent of rural inhabitants and only 21 per cent of urbanites felt confident that they could do something about a health official who was not performing his job properly.[23] Although in a strict sense, these data are not comparable, they nevertheless suggest that Israelis are indeed an efficacious lot. Perhaps this is largely a function of national size, for Almond and Verba found higher levels of efficacy with regard to *local* regulations. However, high efficacy might be a more central characteristic of the Israeli political and bureaucratic cultures. As might be expected, the public bureaucrats feel even more efficacious than the general citizenry, probably as a result of their greater familiarity with bureaucratic procedures, processes, and power centres.

The channels through which the public and the civil servants would

Table 4.1: What Citizens Could Do to Try to Influence the Public
         Bureaucracy*

What citizens could do	Public (N=1,500)	Public Bureaucrats (N=630)
Nothing	38%	32%
Appeal to a higher authority in the ministry in question	21	38
Legal means		
Consult a lawyer; appeal through courts	10	5
Appeal through Ombudsman	9	10
Enlist supportive audience		
Write to newspapers or magazines	16	11
Look for *protekzia*	4	2
Work through a political party	3	4
Take some violent action	2	—

D = -.12 df = 7 p <.001

*Totals do not add up to one hundred since some respondents gave more than one answer.

attempt to influence the bureaucracy are diverse, and they vary in emphasis. Both the public and the bureaucrats believe that appeal to a higher authority is the most effective strategy for forestalling the adoption of an undesirable regulation. However, the difference between the two groups is striking. Whereas 38 per cent of the public bureaucrats reported that they would use this strategy, only 21 per cent of the general citizenry believed that such a method would be effective. Obviously, the bureaucrats would tend to have greater access to higher authorities, but it appears that they are also much more reluctant to seek external assistance in such an endeavour. Although the Israeli bureaucracy is anything but unified it appears that, nevertheless, the norm of settling conflict among its members rather than between them and outsiders has taken hold to a considerable extent.

Conversely, the public is more willing to use outside channels. The most popular strategies here are writing to a newspaper, consulting a lawyer, and appealing to the Ombudsman. Several of the Israeli newspapers carry a daily section devoted precisely to citizen complaints concerning bureaucratic action. These are usually reported with a response solicited from the ministry involved, and are an effective avenue for seeking redress. For instance, during a randomly selected month (March 1974), 178 out of 319 complaints reported in the nation's two most popular newspapers (*Ma'ariv*, and *Yediot Aharonot*) were settled in the complainant's favour.

The Ombudsman is also viewed as an appropriate channel for exercising influence.[24] This institution has enjoyed an almost uniquely high respect among both the general public and government officals. Since its establishment in 1972,[25] it has taken a pivotal role in criticising misconduct by public bureaucrats of all ranks, including the heads of ministries. Furthermore, it has achieved an aura of political independence and impartiality when dealing with the public bureaucracy.[26] One indicator of its success is that the number of complaints registered through it increased by 300 per cent by 1974. However, its jurisdiction is limited and to some extent its effectiveness may be decreasing as time goes on. The popularity of both the newspapers and the Ombudsman as avenues for exercising influence suggest a relationship between high bureaucratic efficacy and the existence of institutionalised and accepted channels for challenging bureaucratic decisions. Indeed, it may be that such channels are prerequisites for the achievement of a 'democratic balance'.

The remaining channels for exerting influence share a relatively low popularity among the public and the bureaucrats. Perhaps the most striking finding here is that relatively few citizens and almost no bureaucrats reported a willingness to rely on *protekzia*. This stands in some contrast to Danet and Hartman's findings that, in 1968, 20 per cent of all Israelis, and almost 70 per cent of those having access to it, used *protekzia* in bureaucratic matters.[27] However, while they found that personalised treatment was common and perhaps becoming more so, they also concluded that 'bureaucratic norms were far more widespread than non-bureaucratic norms, and . . . that these (bureaucratic) norms are becoming increasingly institutionalized rather than extinguished over time'.[28] Our findings suggest that (1) either the norm of impersonality has become even stronger, or (2) that both the norm and the actual behaviour associated with it have become increasingly congruent and dominant.

A third aspect of bureaucratic efficacy concerns the extent to which it is believed that attempts to influence the public bureaucracy will be successful. Individuals who feel that their efforts to change an administrative outcome will be effective are considerably more likely to take some action than those who see no chance for success. Table 4.2 displays the frequency distributions of answers to the following question: 'If you made an effort to change an unjust regulation, how likely is it that you would succeed?' It is evident that whereas neither the general public nor the bureaucrats believe that they are 'very likely' to succeed in having a regulation changed, the latter share a greater degree of confidence. Thus, 34 per cent of the bureaucrats think that their chance of success is moderate in comparison to 25 per cent among the general public. A considerably higher proportion of the public (46 per cent) is also convinced that there is virtually no possibility of engaging in a successful attempt at influencing the bureaucracy. This tends to qualify the initial interpretation that Israelis are highly efficacious with regard to bureaucracy. Apparently, while most think they can take some action to alter an unjust regulation, a considerable majority also think that success is unlikely.

Table 4.2: The Perceived Probability of Successfully Influencing the Bureaucracy: Public and Bureaucrats

Percentage who said:	Public	Public bureaucrats
Very likely	5%	6%
Moderately likely	25	34
Somewhat unlikely	17	17
Not at all likely	46	35
Other, NA, DK	7	8
Total	100%	100%
	(1,420)	(595)
	D = -.10 df = 4 p $<$ .01	

More can be learned about the nature of bureaucratic efficacy by examining it with respect to types of individuals and bureaucrats. Table 4.3 indicates that, as might be expected, among the public it is the bureauphiles who feel most highly efficacious. Bureautics, on the other hand, tend to display a low sense of bureaucratic efficacy. Thus, whereas only 23 per cent of the former are inefficacious, over half of the latter are. Bureautolerants fall in between these two groups, and tend to be considerably more efficacious than inefficacious. Coupled with our findings in the previous chapter, therefore, it appears that those types of citizens who are most attuned to the bureaucracy's penetration of the life of the political community also feel better able to exercise a measure of control over it. This, in turn, suggests that there might be important differences among the types with regard to the channels through which they feel influence can be most effectively exerted on the bureaucracy. It is evident from Table 4.4 that this is indeed the case. Efficacious bureauphiles are much more likely than efficacious bureautics to use avenues of influence which are essentially bureaucratic in nature, such as 'appealing to a higher authority' or the Ombudsman. Those among the bureautics who are efficacious, on the other hand, in keeping with Thompson's and Gouldner's observations concerning them, are considerably more comfortable with extra-bureaucratic channels such as political pull, writing to newspapers, and working through political parties. This finding strongly suggests that if those citizens who find bureaucratic interaction

Table 4.3: The Public's Bureaucratic Efficacy by Types

Types	High efficacy	Low efficacy	Total
Bureauphiles	77%	23%	100% (306)
Bureautolerants	61	38	99% (415)
Bureautics	47	53	100% (343)
	Gamma = .40 (p <.001)		

Table 4.4: The Public's Means of Influencing Bureaucratic Decisions by Types

Types	Bureaucratic*	Non-bureaucratic**	Total
Bureauphiles	56%	44%	100% (236)
Bureautolerants	47	53	100% (253)
Bureautics	33	67	100% (161)
	Gamma = .28 (p <.001)		

*Bureaucratic means include 'appeal to a higher authority', and 'appeal to the Ombudsman'.
**Non-bureaucratic means include 'use of courts', 'complain in newspapers', 'seek *protekzia*', 'through a political party', and 'demonstrate and other violent means'.

most difficult are to be able to exert influence over many of the political system's major output channels, established, legitimate, and non-bureaucratic means must exist for this purpose. Among other possibilities, these could include complaint columns in newspapers, as in Israel, or direct intervention in bureaucratic matters by individual legislators, as is common in the United States.

Providing convenient channels through which citizens may attempt to exercise influence over the course of a public bureaucracy's activities is but one means of enhancing their efficacy. It is generally believed that widespread education is a functional prerequisite to a high degree of citizen participation in a political system and to popular control over political authorities. To some extent, then, democracy is dependent upon a formally educated citizenry. For example, Almond and Verba found that 'educational attainment appears to have the most important demographic effect on political attitudes'.[29] They reasoned that:

> The main reason for this is probably that education has so many different kinds of effects. For one thing, people do *learn* in schools: they learn specific subjects as well as skills useful for political participation. And they learn the norms of political participation as well. Much of this learning may be through direct teaching; some of it may be more indirect. Not only does education influence political perspectives, it also places the individual in social situations where he meets others of like educational attainment, and this tends to reinforce the effect of his own education.[30]

They also observed that one of 'the manifestations of this cross-national uniformity' concerning education was that the more educated individual 'is more likely to consider himself capable of influencing the government'.[31] The extent to which bureaucratic efficacy is associated with education among the types found in the Israeli general population is indicated by Table 4.5. It shows that among bureauphiles and bureautics there is a consistent tendency for increasing education to be associated with greater efficacy. Nevertheless, the basic importance of the types is evident from the fact that even highly-educated bureautics tend to be less efficacious than bureauphiles with little formal education. Among bureautolerants, however, the pattern is less clear. Those who have attained secondary education tend to be more efficacious than both those with high levels of education and those with lesser education. It may be concluded, nevertheless, that increasing the educational level of the members of a political community is one way of enhancing their feelings of efficacy with regard to the political system's major output channels and, perhaps, also fostering their control over it.

Important differences regarding feelings of efficacy pertaining to the public bureaucracy also exist among the types of Israeli bureaucrats. Table 4.6 indicates that statesmen, as might be expected, tend to be the most highly efficacious of the bureaucrats, and that service bureaucrats are the least likely to have a high sense of efficacy. The latter, it will be recalled, are community-oriented and, given this finding and those concerning their cognitive orientations reported in the previous chapter, they increasingly appear to be frustrated by the bureaucracy in their efforts to render public service. Job bureaucrats and politicos fall between these extremes. It is interesting to note that although, overall, the bureaucrats

Table 4.5: The Public's Bureaucratic Efficacy by Types, Controlling for Education

Types	Education	Low efficacy	High efficacy	Total	
Bureauphiles	Primary	27%	73%	100%	(96)
	Secondary	21	79	100%	(108)
	High	12	88	100%	(78)
		Gamma = .32 (p<.01)			
Bureautolerants	Primary	44	56	100%	(233)
	Secondary	28	72	100%	(157)
	High	32	68	100%	(121)
		Gamma = .22 (p<.05)			
Bureautics	Primary	60	40	100%	(252)
	Secondary	43	57	100%	(146)
	High	37	63	100%	(93)
		Gamma = .33 (p<.001)			

are more efficacious than is the public, bureauphiles among the general public actually have a higher sense of efficacy than any of the bureaucratic types. Bureautics, on the other hand, are less efficacious than any of these. Among the bureaucrats, as the table shows, those in the lowest and highest ranks tend to be more efficacious than those at the middle levels, and there is some tendency for those of high rank to have a greater sense of efficacy. The latter finding is not surprising as high-ranking bureaucrats have important policy-making responsibilities and must be in frequent contact with political authorities in order to perform their jobs. The lower efficacy of middle-ranking bureaucrats, however, calls for an explanation. It may be that this group finds itself at once more differentiated from the public at large and more constrained by bureaucratic organisation than those in the lower ranks. Middle-level bureaucrats are likely to have some contact with those at the top with regard to policy-making, but the hierarchical nature of the bureaucracy may limit both their impact and sense of efficacy. Those in the middle ranks, therefore, may tend to develop the belief that there is little that they can do to influence the course of bureaucratic activities. Like Presthus's 'ambivalents', they are to some extent 'in' the organisation, and considerably more so than those in the lower levels, but nevertheless unable to exercise much influence over it. This finding has important consequences for the prospects of developing a responsive and democratically balanced bureaucracy which are examined in chapter 8. Jumping ahead, though, it should be mentioned that decreasing the centrality of hierarchy in bureau-

Table 4.6:   Bureaucratic Efficacy by Types Controlling for Rank

Types	Rank	Low efficacy	High efficacy	Total	
	Low	25%	75%	100%	(56)
Statesmen	Middle	33	67	100%	(45)
	High	25	75	100%	(21)
Total		27	73	100%	(122)
		Gamma = .08 (p>.05)			
	Low	32	68	100%	(97)
Job bureaucrats	Middle	35	65	100%	(50)
	High	22	78	100%	(19)
Total		32	68	100%	(166)
		Gamma = .01 (p>.05)			
	Low	60	40	100%	(25)
Service	Middle	37	63	100%	(19)
bureaucrats	High	25	75	100%	(14)
Total		47	53	100%	(58)
		Gamma = .50 (p<.05)			
	Low	28	72	100%	(60)
Politicos	Middle	43	57	100%	(34)
	High	33	67	100%	(18)
Total		34	66	100%	(112)
		Gamma = -.26 (p<.05)			

cratic organisations and establishing more participatory internal decision-making processes may provide one key to resolving the tension between democracy and bureaucracy.

Citizen Competence

It has been observed that a majority of Israeli citizens and public bureaucrats believe that there is something that they could do to influence the course of bureaucratic activity. At the same time, however, they also maintain that their actions would be unlikely to succeed. Thus, Israelis believe that channels for exercising influence over the bureaucracy do exist, but also that these offer a relatively low prospect of yielding the desired objectives. An obvious question, therefore, is, to what extent do Israelis actually engage in such activities? In a broad sense, this question not only concerns efficacy and citizen competence, but it also involves the contrasting norms of bureaucratic impersonality and democratic participation.

Table 4.7 presents the responses of the public and the bureaucrats regarding actual attempts to influence the Israeli bureaucracy. The most striking finding regarding citizen competence, which can be viewed as a

Table 4.7: Percentage of Israelis who Attempted to Influence the Public Bureaucracy*

Percentage who attempted	Public	Public Bureaucrats
Often	4	7
A few times	13	24
Never	79	66
Other, DK, NA	4	3
Total	100%	100%
	(1,486)	(623)

$D = -.14$ df = 3 $p < .001$

*Actual text of question: 'Have you ever done anything to try to influence an administrative regulation?'

behavioural component of bureaucratic efficacy, is that almost 80 per cent of the general public and about two-thirds of the civil servants report that they have never attempted to influence the course of bureaucratic actions. Whether because they perceive their chances of success as being slim or because they tend to practise the norm of impersonality, it is evident that most Israeli citizens and public bureaucrats are willing to allow the bureaucracy to adopt its own course or to follow the dictates of political authorities. This interpretation is reinforced by the earlier findings that Israelis overwhelmingly give their national bureaucracy negative ratings for its performance in areas of critical importance to economic, social, and political change. Their lack of attempts to influence the bureaucracy, therefore, can hardly be attributed to their satisfaction with it. Nevertheless, there is a sizable minority, especially among the bureaucrats, who have, in fact, engaged in efforts to change the course of bureaucratic action at least a few times. It should also be noted that despite the overwhelming tendency of Israelis not to actually attempt to influence administrative regulations, the difference between the public and the bureaucrats is nevertheless important. The latter, as might be expected, display a far greater degree of citizen competence than the former. Thus, 31 per cent of the bureaucrats report having attempted to influence the bureaucracy, whereas only 17 per cent of the general public make the same claim.

These overall patterns are not surprising. It could be expected that there is more people 'could do' than they 'have done'. However, the gap between the two is very sizable for both the bureaucrats and the public. Apparently here, norms or attitudinal expressions do not comport well with behaviour. As Danet and Hartman suggested, this may be characteristic of transitional and developing nations, where modern practices and concepts exist as a thin veneer over more traditional ways. In any event, it is reasonable to conclude that although Israelis have developed feelings of efficacy, they have yet to effectively translate them into a high level of citizen competence. Channels for participation are perceived to exist, but they remain relatively unused.

This conclusion is reinforced by examining the citizen competence of the different types among the public and the bureaucrats. As noted above, 17 per cent of the general population reported having attempted to influence the bureaucracy 'often' or 'a few times'. None of the types among the public reported a strikingly greater propensity to engage in influence attempts. Although bureauphiles are more likely to engage in such efforts, only 22 per cent of them reported having done so. Bureautics are the least likely to display a high degree of citizen competence, and only 14 per cent of them claimed to have tried to influence the course of bureaucratic actions. Bureautolerants are close to the average for all citizens: 18 per cent of them have a high level of citizen competence. A similar pattern exists with regard to the types among the bureaucrats. Here, however, there is even less deviation from the overall average of 31 per cent who report having engaged in efforts to influence the bureaucracy at least a few times. Politicos and service bureaucrats are the most highly competent, in this sense, with 34 per cent and 33 per cent having sought to influence the course of bureaucratic actions. Statesmen's level of citizen competence is equal to the average for all bureaucrats, and job bureaucrats are the least competent with 27 per cent reporting having engaged in influence attempts. It is interesting to note that in contrast to the public, those types of bureaucrats which are least efficacious display the highest level of citizen competence. This is perhaps explained by politicos' and service bureaucrats' tendency to view the bureaucracy acting in a 'personalised' manner. To the extent that one believes an institution manifests the norm of impersonality, one may be more likely to view it as impervious to personal action and, therefore, to be less likely to attempt to influence the course of its actions. Finally, among the public, education is positively related to greater citizen competence, and among the bureaucrats the same is true of rank. In both cases, however, the basic patterns of dispositions towards bureaucracy associated with the different types retain their importance.

Analysis of patterns of bureaucratic efficacy and citizen competence indicates that bureaucratisation places important barriers in the path of political participation in democratically-oriented political communities. Although citizens' sense of efficacy may be relatively high, there is likely to be a considerable amount of variation among them, and their expectations of successfully influencing the course of bureaucratic action may be quite low. Moreover, it is possible, as in Israel, for a wide gap between feelings of efficacy and levels of citizen competence to exist. Patterns of efficacy and competence are affected by education, but increasing the educational levels of the population presents only a partial resolution of the conflict between bureaucratisation and democracy. In order to encourage greater participation and efforts to influence the major input and output channels of developed political systems, it may be necessary to provide legitimate and relatively non-bureaucratic avenues for so doing. Furthermore, this analysis suggests that it may be extremely difficult for national bureaucracies to mobilise popular participation. Incongruences between public bureaucrats and the rest of the members of a political community may also exist, as is true in Israel. It is to be expected that bureaucrats would be somewhat more efficacious and competent than the general population, but if the gap between the two is large it may signify that bureaucrats form a portion of a ruling establishment rather than a group that serves as a buffer between the citizenry and political authorities.

Notes

1. For a discussion of these developments, see Ernest Barker, *The Development of Public Services in Western Europe, 1660-1930* (Hamden, Conn.: Archon Books, 1966); and Karl Polanyi, *The Great Transformation* (Boston: Beacon Press, 1957).

2. Arnold J. Heidenheimer, 'The Context of Analysis', in Heidenheimer (ed.), *Political Corruption* (New York: Holt, Rinehart & Winston, 1970), pp. 3-28.

3. Ibid., p. 20.

4. See Edward C. Banfield, 'The Moral Basis of a Backward Society', ibid., pp. 129-37.

5. Heidenheimer, 'The Context of Analysis', ibid., pp. 20, 22.

6. Ibid., p. 22.

7. Ibid., pp. 22-3.

8. Max Weber, *From Max Weber: Essays in Sociology* (New York: Oxford University Press, 1958), p. 215.

9. Heidenheimer, 'The Context of Analysis', in Heidenheimer (ed.), *Political Corruption*, p. 23.

10. S.N. Eisenstadt, 'Bureaucracy, Bureaucratization, and Debureaucratization', in Nimrod Raphaeli (ed.), *Readings in Comparative Public Administration* (Boston: Allyn & Bacon, 1967), p. 364.

11. Grant McConnell, *Private Power and American Democracy* (New York:

Knopf, 1966), esp. ch. 10.

12. Sidney Verba and Norman Nie, *Participation in America* (New York: Harper & Row, 1972), p. 83.

13. Ibid.

14. Gabriel A. Almond and Sidney Verba, *The Civic Culture* (Boston: Little, Brown, 1965), p. 136.

15. Ibid., table 3.3, p. 72.

16. Ibid.

17. Ibid., p. 170.

18. Ibid., p. 171.

19. Samuel Eldersveld *et al.*, *The Citizen and the Administrator in a Developing Democracy* (Glenview, Ill.: Scott, Foresman, 1968), table 2.11, p. 25.

20. Gerald Caiden, 'The Political Penetration of Israeli Bureaucracy', unpublished monograph, Haifa University, 1974, pp. 9-10.

21. Ibid., p. 10.

22. Almond and Verba, *Civic Culture*, table 6.1, p. 142.

23. Eldersveld *et al.*, table 2.13, p. 26.

24. This is by no means unique to Israel. For a comparative analysis, see Larry B. Hill, 'Institutionalization, The Ombudsman, and Bureaucracy', *American Political Science Review*, 68 (September 1974), 1075-85.

25. Prior to this year, the State Controller was in charge of citizens' complaints.

26. Leon Boim, 'Ombudsmanship in Israel', *Edizone Dell'Instituto Di Studi Legislativi*, Rome, 1968.

27. B. Danet and H. Hartman, 'On "Proteksia"', *Journal of Comparative Administration*, 3 (February 1970), 432.

28. Ibid.

29. Almond and Verba, *Civic Culture*, p. 315.

30. Ibid., p. 316.

31. Ibid., pp. 317-18.

5 PATTERNS OF EVALUATION: THE IMAGE AND SELF-IMAGE OF PUBLIC BUREAUCRATS

Patterns of evaluation are an additional element of critical importance to both an understanding of the political consequences of the bureaucratisation of public life and to the analysis of bureaucratic culture. This follows from our analysis of patterns of cognition and affect. National bureaucracies may penetrate almost all aspects of the political, social, and economic life of developed polities. As they do so, not only do they and the political systems of which they are a part become more salient to the individual, but such bureaucracies tend to monopolise the political input and output channels available to citizens and political authorities alike. In 'bureaucratic societies' such as the Soviet Union, the importance of citizens' and bureaucrats' evaluations of bureaucratic personnel and their performance is largely self-evident. Bureaucrats constitute a major segment of the ruling group and the images citizens hold of them is of relevance to the nature of citizens' support for political authorities and the regime. However, even where the members of a political community are highly efficacious and demonstrate an extensive degree of citizen competence with regard to administrative matters, public bureaucrats may nevertheless resemble a group of 'ruling servants'. In any event, their political roles and power positions are such that citizens' evaluations of their performance and character is a central element of both political and bureaucratic culture, which can tell us much about the nature of political communities, citizenship and administration within them.

At the same time, however, analysis of patterns of evaluation should not be confined to the general population of a political community. The evaluations made by public bureaucrats themselves are also of great interest. Their outlook on such elements as the honesty and efficiency of their colleagues and the organisation in which they are employed is likely to provide important insights into the nature of the bureaucratic environment, as they perceive it, and into the bureaucracy's behaviour. Furthermore, the degree of congruence between citizens' and bureaucrats' evaluations provides additional information of considerable consequence. For instance, as Eldersveld and associates write with special reference to India:

A critical problem in the analysis of any administrative or organizational subsystem is the measurement of the extent of congruence in perspectives between different levels of the system. In the study of administrative organizations we must be concerned with the different images of political reality held by the official cadres and their publics or clienteles . . . [I] t is . . . important to know whether administrators see the system as functioning in the same manner as the public sees it. If great disparities exist in the two images it may not only be difficult to mobilize support, but, more importantly, it may be difficult to change the system. Disparities would suggest perceptual isolation and unreality or indifference, or both. The ideal objective . . . would be administrative cadres which could accurately predict and interpret public views and evaluations of the administrative system, whether or not there was congruence on personal preferences for policy goals. The greater the inability of administrators to predict and interpret, the greater the likelihood that misunderstanding, inappropriate expectations, and non-cooperation will develop.[1]

Differences in the public's and bureaucrats' patterns of evaluations are also of relevance to a national bureaucracy's attractiveness as an employer, as was demonstrated by Kilpatrick and associates.[2]

Assessing Image and Self-Image

One method of determining the nature of citizens' and civil servants' patterns of evaluation of public bureaucrats is to ascertain the character of the images that they hold of them. Rather than providing a simple index of support for public bureaucrats, such an approach makes it possible to develop a kind of 'composite picture' of how civil servants are viewed by various groups. This, in turn, yields important information concerning the interfaces between citizen and bureaucrat and among bureaucrats themselves. The ways in which citizens stereotype public bureaucrats will surely affect the fashion in which they relate to them. Furthermore, the nature of such images provides an indication of what transpires in the minds of citizens when they think about bureaucrats. Such information, of course, is central to our theory of bureaucratic culture. Knowledge of the bureaucrats' self-image, or perhaps more exactly, image of their colleagues, is also of great interest. Their views in this regard provide a picture of public bureaucrats from the inside, so to speak, that can tell us much about the nature of a public bureaucracy.

The semantic differential is one approach for describing such images.

It is a method of indexing individual experiences to referents of concepts, this being accomplished with respect to a series of dimensions denoting the generalised qualities of experiences. The method assumes that although different individuals see things somewhat differently, there is some core meaning to all concepts. For instance, the bureaucrat and the client may share the meaning of a concept such as 'service' even though their perceptions of what 'service' entails may be considerably different.[3]

The semantic differential is conceptualised in terms of 'semantic space'. This consists of three dominant dimensions: evaluation, potency, and activity. In other words, a person's image of civil servants, for example, can be ascertained by having the individual locate the concept 'civil servant' on an evaluative dimension, a potency dimension, and an activity dimension. These three dimensions correspond to fundamental psychological attributes of individuals, and to the organisation of their images. The dimensions of the semantic differential therefore represent fundamental dimensions of the individual's adjustment to the objects in his or her environment.

The first dimension of the semantic space, evaluation, corresponds to a person's tendency either to make an approach towards an object (or a concept that stands for an object) or to seek to avoid it. The evaluative dimension measures the extent to which the object has positively or negatively reinforced the individual's responses. Adjectives such as 'good—bad' and 'honest—dishonest' are used to compose this dimension. Potency, the second dominant dimension of the semantic space, measures either the amount of adjustment that a person makes or has to make to an object, or the amount of effort which an individual puts into the response to a stimulus (concept). Adjectives such as 'strong—weak', 'tenacious—yielding', and 'deep—shallow' refer to the extent of effort which an individual puts into the responses to concepts characterised by these terms. For example, more effort is exerted in adjusting to strong bureaucrats than to weak ones, to tenacious public servants than to yielding ones, and so on. The third dominant dimension, activity, refers to the necessity or non-necessity of making movements in adjusting to objects. Adjectives such as 'fast—slow', 'active—passive', and 'rush—cautious' refer to the necessity of making a more or less rapid adjustment to objects. It is assumed that it is a greater necessity to change one's adjustment to something which is 'fast', 'active', or 'rushing' than to something which is 'slow', 'passive', or 'cautious'.

Taken together, these three dimensions account for what happens when an individual is asked to relate to a concept such as 'public bureaucrat'* on a series of semantic differential scales. Presumably, the respondent will make a series of responses. The individual views the concept through a perceptual system, recalls examples of the concept, associates with it, and may be aware of some sort of image of it. The individual's responses or reactions to the concept depend upon the sum total of learnings and experiences that are available to him or her at the particular time. These learnings depend upon reinforcement through social interaction and individual experiences with the object (concept).

For the purposes of the present analysis of bureaucratic culture, ten bipolar, seven-point descriptive scales were administered to our interviewees. Four scales are evaluative. These consist of the following adjectives: 'good—bad', 'honest—dishonest', 'pleasant—unpleasant', and 'efficient—inefficient'. Three scales measure the potency dimension: 'strong—weak', 'brave—cowardly', and 'deep—shallow'. An additional three scales were used to tap down the activity dimension. These were 'active—passive', 'fast—slow', and 'stable—unstable'. The selection of these scales was made in conformity with three operational criteria: first, the relevance of each pair of adjectives for describing the connotative meaning of the concept 'public bureaucrat' within the context of the Israeli political community; second, the response rate to a set of twenty-two scales administered in a pilot study;[4] and, finally, the presumed relationship of each scale to one of the three dominant dimensions in the semantic space. In terms of the latter criterion, reliance was placed on previous cross-cultural findings and the factor loadings obtained in analysing the pilot data.[5]

The Image and Self-Image of Israeli Bureaucrats

Assessing and comparing the image and self-image of public bureaucrats involves several elements. One is the basic question of whether 'public bureaucrat' is a concept of sufficient salience and clarity to enable individuals to relate to it. Second, is the extent to which images and self-images are homogeneous or heterogeneous. Thirdly, it is desirable to summarise the character of images and to explore their antecedents and implications. An analysis of these facets of patterns of evaluation can begin conveniently with the formation presented in Table 5.1. It displays the distribution of responses of both the Israeli bureaucrats and general public on the ten scales employed. Overall, both groups were able to relate strongly to the concept of 'public bureaucrat' with

*In Hebrew, *Ovdai Hamedinah* (literally, workers of the state), which does not carry the pejorative connotation which some might attach to 'public bureaucrat' in English.

Table 5.1: The Image and Self-Image of Israeli Bureaucrats: Percentage Distribution, Means, and Variances on Ten Scales, Public (N=1,590) and Bureaucrats (N=630)

	1	2	3	4	5	6	7	NA	Mean	Variance
					Evaluative					
good—bad										
Public	7.7	8.4	14.4	36.3	16.1	7.2	4.6	5.2	3.9	2.8
Bureaucrats	8.4	16.3	22.4	34.4	10.5	4.4	1.4	2.2	3.1	1.9
honest—dishonest										
Public	10.4	18.6	17.7	30.1	8.9	4.9	4.1	5.7	3.3	2.7
Bureaucrats	15.1	23.8	24.4	22.2	7.3	5.2	1.1	2.9	2.7	2.0
pleasant—unpleasant										
Public	6.3	8.7	13.4	29.7	17.1	11.5	8.3	5.1	4.1	3.2
Bureaucrats	8.1	14.3	24.1	28.3	14.1	7.3	2.1	1.7	3.4	2.1
efficient—inefficient										
Public	7.4	7.5	14.2	31.1	14.0	9.6	10.3	6.0	4.2	3.5
Bureaucrats	8.9	15.4	20.3	29.5	12.4	7.8	3.2	2.5	3.3	2.4
					Potency					
strong—weak										
Public	10.2	10.0	15.2	32.6	10.9	7.5	6.8	6.7	3.5	3.4
Bureaucrats	6.7	10.3	17.6	33.0	13.9	10.0	5.1	3.3	3.8	2.6
brave—cowardly										
Public	9.5	8.5	16.2	36.5	9.6	6.1	6.0	7.6	3.5	3.1
Bureaucrats	7.1	12.5	19.8	34.3	10.5	6.5	5.6	3.7	3.6	2.5
deep—shallow										
Public	11.3	7.9	12.1	29.1	17.2	10.3	4.3	6.4	3.9	3.5
Bureaucrats	8.9	15.7	22.7	24.4	14.3	6.7	4.2	3.1	3.2	2.6
					Activity					
active—passive										
Public	8.3	6.8	9.2	26.4	15.3	15.2	12.3	6.3	4.4	4.1
Bureaucrats	6.7	11.7	18.0	25.4	14.0	13.7	8.4	2.4	3.6	2.9
fast—slow										
Public	5.0	4.5	8.2	22.1	15.0	15.1	24.3	6.0	4.8	4.2
Bureaucrats	4.6	8.4	13.1	33.2	17.9	10.8	9.5	2.4	4.1	2.6
stable—unstable										
Public	6.5	5.8	10.5	30.4	17.1	11.9	11.4	6.4	4.2	3.6
Bureaucrats	5.2	13.1	18.3	34.8	12.9	8.9	4.6	2.1	3.4	2.3

reference to each of the ten pairs of adjectives. The range of non-responses for the public was from 5.1 per cent ('pleasant—unpleasant') to 7.6 per cent ('brave—cowardly') and that of the bureaucrats was from 1.7 per cent ('pleasant—unpleasant') to 3.7 per cent ('brave—cowardly'). Thus, the range of non-response was considerably lower for the bureaucrats, which indicates, as might be expected, that they are better able to relate to the concept of 'public bureaucrat' and are consequently more likely to hold an elaborate image of it. Overall, these findings indicate that 'public bureaucrat' does, indeed, loom large in the life of the political community.

Israeli bureaucrats are not only better able to relate to the concept of 'public bureaucrats' than are members of the general population, their image of it is also likely to be more homogeneous. This is to be expected, of course, in view of their greater familiarity and experience with public bureaucrats. Moreover, it suggests that, despite the import- ance of different styles and outlooks within the Israeli civil service, com- mon patterns of socialisation may exist. Thus, whereas the range of variances for the bureaucrats is from 1.9 ('good—bad') to 2.9 ('active— passive'), that of general public is from 2.7 ('honest—dishonest') to 4.2 ('fast—slow'). Within each of the groups, relative homogeneity is especial- ly noticeable on the 'good—bad' and 'honest—dishonest' scales. Relative heterogeneity, on the other hand, is most pronounced with regard to the adjectives 'active—passive' and 'fast—slow'. In other words, Israeli bureaucrats have a more coherent and uniform image of 'public bureau- crat' than does the general public, and within both groups the greatest consistency in images exists with regard to the evaluative elements con- cerning honesty and 'goodness'. The greatest disagreement concerns the activity elements of 'active—passive' and 'fast—slow'.

The public's and civil servants' images of 'public bureaucrat' are con- veniently summarised and compared in Figure 5.1, which displays the mean profiles for the two groups. It is evident that neither the public nor the bureaucrats hold an extremely positive or negative image. How- ever, the public's image of 'public bureaucrat' is substantially less favourable, especially on the evaluative dimension. Thus, to the average Israeli citizen, public bureaucrats are more dishonest, unpleasant, and inefficient than they are to the average Israeli bureaucrat. It is also interesting to compare the high peaks of the two profiles. In so doing, it can be noted that the Israeli citizen's most extreme images of 'public bureaucrat' are with regard to slowness, inefficiency, and passiveness. Those of the bureaucrats, on the other hand, are most extreme in terms of honesty, stability, and deepness. These cleavages indicate that public

Figure 5.1: Mean Profiles for Public and Bureaucrats

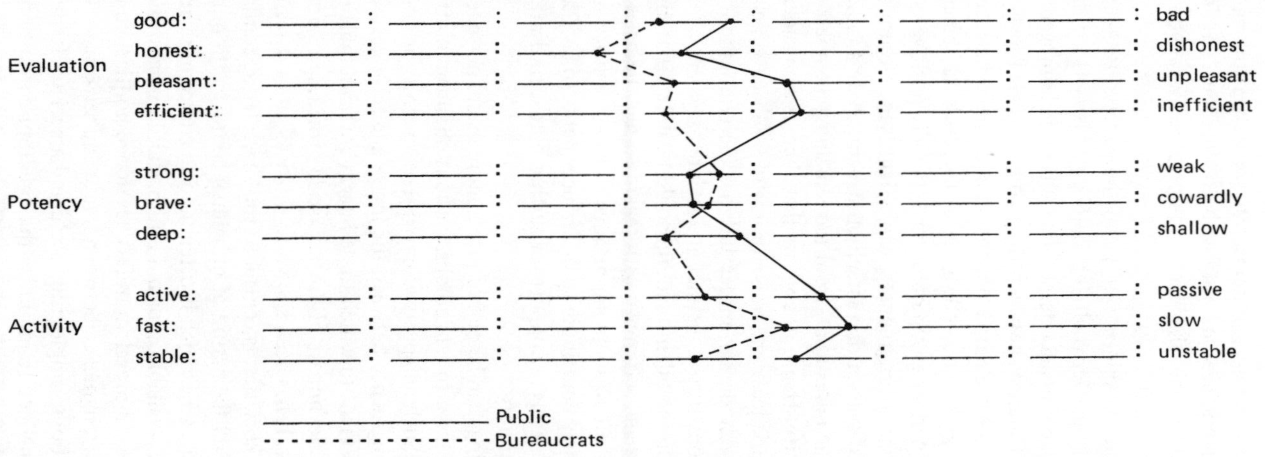

good: : bad
Evaluation honest: : dishonest
pleasant: : unpleasant
efficient: : inefficient

strong: : weak
Potency brave: : cowardly
deep: : shallow

active: : passive
Activity fast: : slow
stable: : unstable

——— Public
-------- Bureaucrats

bureaucrats do not perceive themselves precisely as they are perceived. Nevertheless, the images are not highly incongruous, and hence are unlikely to present a major barrier to co-operation between citizens and bureaucrats.

In sum, then, the concept of 'public bureaucrat' is salient and familiar enough to the overwhelming majority of Israelis for them to hold images of it. The bureaucrats' self-image is more homogeneous and favourable. Differences between the two groups are most pronounced with regard to the evaluative dimension and smallest concerning the 'strong—weak' and 'brave—cowardly' scales. It should be emphasised, however, that neither group holds an extremely positive or negative image. Moreover, incongruences, while significant, do not appear to be large enough to suggest that Israeli bureaucrats have a radically different image of 'public bureaucrat' from the remaining members of the political community. Hence, it appears that there is a considerable amount of shared experience, communication, and feedback which tends to produce relatively similar images and that therefore, the Israeli bureaucrats do not constitute a distinct and isolated segment of the political community. On the other hand, it should be noted that differences between image and self-image with regard to such items as efficiency and 'goodness' are of some importance to Israeli politics and administration and may contribute to differences between civil servants' and other citizens' levels of support for further bureaucratisation of the political community.

These findings can be placed into a more useful perspective, perhaps, by comparing them to related observations obtained in different political communities. Such an approach provides standards for assessing the degree of incongruence between the image and self-image of bureaucrats and the extent to which these images are favourable or unfavourable. Perhaps the 'honest—dishonest' scale provides the best indicator in this context. It has been shown to evoke significant responses in highly diverse societies, is central to the character of administrative performance and the nature of individual contact with bureaucrats, and, in fact, is an element which is often used to characterise entire national bureaucracies. Available data and interpretation suggest that bureaucratic corruption is most prevalent in less developed political communities[6] and that the incongruence between image and self-image is greatest in such polities. For example, Eldersveld and associates found that in India, 'officials are inclined to minimize the extent of corruption, while a majority of the public is ready to charge officials with corruption. About 60 per cent of our sample is convinced that half or more than half of the officials are corrupt; but only 20 to 30 per cent, roughly, of the officials in our sample have the pessimistic view'.[7] In the United States, on the other hand, Kilpatrick and associates found more positive images and a far narrower gap between the public's image of the federal employee and the latter's self-image. Thus, on a ten-point, 'high–low' scale concerning honesty, the general public gave federal employees a rating of 7.6, whereas the civil servants rated the honesty of their colleagues at 8.3.[8] These findings suggest that the image and self-image of Israeli bureaucrats occupies an intermediate position, as might be expected in view of the political community's pattern of development. At least with regard to honesty, the incongruence between image and self-image, while not insignificant, is dwarfed by comparison with the Indian example. To the extent that a high degree of incongruence limits the possibilities for changing the nature of the bureaucracy, then, Israel does not appear to face anywhere nearly as serious a problem as India in this regard. At the same time, however, the relatively low rating on honesty given to Israeli bureaucrats by both groups suggests that there is not a great deal of support for them or their activities and that, therefore, the bureaucratisation of public life in Israel has serious drawbacks from the point of view of building and maintaining a democratic political community. The images of those who largely control the major political input and output channels are not favourable with regard to several aspects of their performance and character, including the very basic element of honesty.

Variations in Image and Self-Image

The incongruences between the public's image of bureaucrats and the latter's self-image are indicative of some between-group disparity. However, there are also significant differences within groups and these, too, are of importance to bureaucratic culture. As argued in chapter 1, there is reason to believe that bureaucracy and the bureaucratisation of public life affects individuals in a differential manner. Some are better able to relate to and deal with bureaucracy than others. In view of the discussion and findings in the previous two chapters, a second level of argument is now apparent. Those who are least cognisant of the impact of bureaucracy are also least efficacious and competent with regard to it, and consequently they are least able to fulfil the roles of citizenship in a democratically-oriented, bureaucratised political community. At this juncture, it is necessary to determine whether such citizens also hold the least favourable images of bureaucrats. Bureaucrats, while not an elite in the Israeli context, nevertheless are a group of great political importance. If a significant segment of the population feels relatively unable to influence their activities and also believes that bureaucrats are inefficient, dishonest, and so forth, it vitiates the possibility that the civil service could be legitimately considered to play the role of enlightened, non-partisan keepers of the public interest. The latter, it will be recalled, is sometimes predicated as the most appropriate role for civil servants in democratic political communities.

Analysis of bureaucrats' patterns of evaluation of their colleagues is no less important. As this study of bureaucratic culture proceeds, it becomes increasingly clear that separate types of bureaucrats have distinct reactions to bureaucracy and bureaucratisation. Moreover, not only can variation be expected, but as Kilpatrick and associates suggest, it may be either functional or dysfunctional in terms of the specific needs of the bureaucracy and the political system. They found, for example, that in the United States, 'federal employees themselves are more favorable than the comparable nonfederal groups in their comments on the civil servant; but except for the federal executives, the upper-level federal groups yield fewer favourable replies than do those lower in the federal hierarchy'.[9] This was interpreted as one of several indicators that the federal service's appeal as an employer was most limited where its needs were greatest. Clearly, the images held by different types of bureaucrats concerning such characteristics as honesty and efficiency could indicate which were most and which were least objective and critical with regard to civil servants' performance. This, in turn, would suggest which types were most functional, at least in terms of these elements. For example, where there is overwhelming evidence that a bureaucracy is corrupt, such as in India, officials who either sincerely believe it to be honest or tend to look the other way are clearly dysfunctional if change is desired. Those who are personally honest, but view many of their colleagues as corrupt, on the other hand, would be the most functional. However, even where overriding evidence of dishonesty or inefficiency is absent, it may be possible to assess the functionality of different types of bureaucrats. For instance, in terms of the dimensions employed here and the Israeli context, higher ratings concerning evaluation, potency, and activity would generally be indicative of greater support for the bureaucracy and its personnel. Given the somewhat transitional, disorganised, and incoherent nature of the Israeli bureaucracy (as discussed in chapter 2), bureaucrats whose image of their colleagues involved a positive evaluation, and the attribution of a high degree of potency and activity, would tend to be the most functional for the administrative system at the present time. This is all the more so to the extent that one's view of one's colleagues' behaviour influences one's own behaviour and conditions individual and organisational expectations. Finally, it is important to investigate the images of the 'public bureaucrat' held by different types of civil servant in order to further our knowledge concerning the patterns through which individuals adapt to membership in public bureaucratic organisations.

The different images and self-images of 'public bureaucrat' which exist among the various types of citizens and civil servants can be conveniently summarised with reference to each of the dimensions of the semantic differential. Table 5.2 presents the images held by bureauphiles, bureautolerants, and bureautics with regard to the evaluative dimension. It will be recalled that this consists of scales pertaining to honesty, 'goodness', pleasantness, and efficiency. It is evident, as was noted in connection with Table 5.1, that overall, the Israeli public is somewhat negative in its image of public bureaucrats with respect to the evaluative dimension. Indeed, 44 per cent provide a negative rating concerning these characteristics, as compared to only 15 per cent who hold a positive image of bureaucrats on this dimension. However, it is also apparent that there is considerable variation among the different types. This is most readily observed with reference to negative ratings. Bureauphiles are far less negative in their evaluative images of public bureaucrats than are the other types, and bureautics are especially negative. In fact, 58 per cent of the latter hold negative images of public bureaucrats with respect to the evaluative dimension.

Table 5.2: The Evaluative Dimension by Types among the Citizenry

	Positive	Neutral	Negative	Total	
All respondents	15%	41%	44%	100%	(1,305)
Bureauphiles	22	53	25	100%	(312)
Bureautolerants	16	41	43	100%	(501)
Bureautics	9	33	58	100%	(492)

Gamma = .36 (p ⟨.01)

The activity dimension of the public's image of bureaucrats is also strongly related to type, as is demonstrated in Table 5.3. With reference to the scales of 'fast–slow', 'active–passive', and 'stable–unstable', it is clear that Israelis, in general, view public bureaucrats as largely inactive. Moreover, only a small segment of the population holds an image of public bureaucrats that characterises them as highly active. Indeed, even among bureauphiles, who are consistently more favourably predisposed to the Israeli bureaucracy than the other types, 47 per cent view public bureaucrats as inactive. Bureautics, as is to be expected, are even more likely to perceive them as inactive, with 69 per cent falling into this category.

Potency, the third dimension of the semantic differential, is also related to type, but to a lesser extent as is indicated in Table 5.4. This dimension consists of adjectives relating to strength, depth and courage. It is readily evident that relative to their images with regard to the eval-

Table 5.3: The Activity Dimension by Type among the Citizenry

	Highly Active	Neutral	Inactive	Total	
All respondents	7%	32%	61%	100%	(1,313)
Bureauphiles	12	41	47	100%	(312)
Bureautolerants	8	32	60	100%	(505)
Bureautics	4	27	69	100%	(496)
		Gamma = .27 (p <.05)			

Table 5.4: The Potency Dimension by Types among the Citizenry

	High Potency	Neutral	Low Potency	Total	
All respondents	22%	43%	35%	100%	(1,284)
Bureauphiles	23	52	25	100%	(309)
Bureautolerants	23	41	36	100%	(488)
Bureautics	19	40	41	100%	(487)
		Gamma = .15 (p <.001)			

uative and activity dimensions, Israelis display a greater tendency to view public bureaucrats as highly potent. Thus, 22 per cent of all Israelis view them in this manner, as compared to 15 per cent who hold positive images of them on the evaluative dimension, and 7 per cent who perceive them to be highly active. Moreover, this pattern is found among all types. The differences among bureauphiles, bureautolerants, and especially bureautics are also of interest. Bureauphiles are the least likely to view public bureaucrats as having low potency, whereas bureautics are the most likely to, with bureautolerants assuming their usual position between these two extremes. However, the image held by bureautics is especially worth noting in this context because whereas only 9 per cent of them hold a positive evaluative image, and only 4 per cent perceive public bureaucrats to be highly active, 19 per cent view them as highly potent. Bureautics, it will be recalled, are also the least cognisant of the bureaucracy's impact on daily life and national development, and they are the least efficacious and competent with regard to it. Together these findings suggest that to a considerable extent they constitute a categorical group which is unable to effectively fulfil the necessary citizenship roles with respect to bureaucratisation in a democratically oriented political community and that bureautics, more than any other type, tend to view the bureaucracy as a relatively unintelligible, uncontrollable, impotent force. At the same time, however, it should be stressed that this is only a relative condition, and that a greater percentage of all types hold an image of public bureaucrats which attributes low potency to them.

Turning to an analysis of variation in bureaucrats' self-images, it is evident that these are also related to type. Table 5.5 reports the responses of statesmen, service bureaucrats, job bureaucrats, and politicos on the evaluative dimension. All types of bureaucrats hold a more positive image of the 'public bureaucrat' than does the general public. Statesmen, as might be expected, given their orientations and other perceptions, are the most positive in their evaluative images, and politicos are the most negative. Job bureaucrats and service bureaucrats fall in between these extremes, with the latter being far more negative. It is significant that no type of bureaucrat is overwhelmingly positive in its evaluative image of its colleagues. This once again suggests that the Israeli civil service has yet to develop into a coherent institution with a relatively uniform self-image and sense of self-worth. This is especially true in view of the centrality of honesty and efficiency, two of the elements which compose the evaluative dimension.

Similar patterns exist with regard to the activity and potency dimensions. The former is presented in Table 5.6, which indicates that relative to the public, all types of bureaucrats view the 'public bureaucrat' in a more active fashion. However, no type characterised public bureaucrats as more highly active than inactive. Thus, although job bureaucrats and especially statesmen are the most likely of any of the types to hold an image of public bureaucrats as being active, even they are more inclined to view them as inactive. Table 5.7 shows that the self-image of all public bureaucrats is one which connotes greater potency than is attributed to them by the image held by the general population. Moreover, overall, the bureaucrats are equally likely to view 'public bureaucrat' as having high potency as low potency, although a large proportion (42 per cent) are neutral in their self-image on this

Table 5.5:   The Evaluative Dimension by Bureaucratic Types

	Positive	Neutral	Negative	Total
All respondents	35%	41%	24%	100% (540)
Statesmen	44	39	17	100% (140)
Service bureaucrats	29	42	29	100% (69)
Job bureaucrats	38	42	19	99% (203)
Politicos	22	43	35	100% (128)

Gamma = .20 (p $<$ 001)

Table 5.6:   The Activity Dimension by Bureaucratic Types

	Highly active	Neutral	Inactive	Total
All respondents	21%	38%	41%	100% (545)
Statesmen	29	34	36	99% (143)
Service bureaucrats	14	37	49	100% (70)
Job bureaucrats	19	41	40	100% (202)
Politicos	15	37	48	100% (130)

Gamma = .12 (p $<$ 01)

Table 5.7:   The Potency Dimension by Bureaucratic Types

	High potency	Neutral	Low potency	Total
All respondents	29%	42%	29%	100% (530)
Statesmen	34	38	28	100% (138)
Service bureaucrats	28	33	39	100% (67)
Job bureaucrats	26	48	26	100% (199)
Politicos	25	40	35	100% (126)

Gamma = .07 (p $<$ 05)

dimension. The bureaucrats are also more homogeneous on this dimension than on the other two. Nevertheless, a familiar tendency is evident in that statesmen and job bureaucrats are the least likely to view public bureaucrats as having low potency, and service bureaucrats and politicos are the most likely to perceive them in this fashion.

In terms of self-image, then, there is considerable variation among the bureaucratic types. Statesmen tend to have the most optimistic view of the Israeli civil service, whereas politicos tend to be highly critical. No type, however, is highly positive in its image of the 'public bureaucrat', and this does not bode well for the Israeli bureaucracy. Political communities which have not achieved self-sustained political and economic development need an effective public bureaucracy which can mobilise support, elicit a sense of mission and importance from its personnel, and play an active role in the life of the nation if such development is to be attained. None of the bureaucratic types found in Israel expresses a high level of confidence in the bureaucracy's ability to perform these functions. Nevertheless, within the range of differences among the bureaucrats with regard to self-image, it is the statesmen who tend to emerge as the most functional type and the politicos are clearly the least functional. Presumably, statesmen's image of public bureaucrats lends the most internal legitimacy to the bureaucracy's performance of developmental roles and generates the greatest support and impetus for its activity in this sphere. Although politicos could be in favour of change, their perceptions in this case do not appear to comport well with objective reality, in so far as it can be ascertained, and their image of public bureaucrats seems to be overly negative and more indicative of alienation than of a functional self-critical mood. Indeed, they appear to extend little support for the bureaucracy's functions in developmental areas (chapter 3) or to bureaucratic personnel. It would appear, therefore, that a bureaucracy employing politicos in positions of critical importance would not function well in a political community striving for rapid development. Among the other types, job bureaucrats, likewise, would tend to be more functional than service bureaucrats in this regard. It should be emphasised again, though, that as a whole, the bureaucrats' self-image strongly suggests that the Israeli civil service has several undesirable characteristics from the point of view of furthering political and economic development.

Taken together, the findings presented in this chapter provide considerable contributions to our understanding of bureaucratic culture. It is clear that the concept of 'public bureaucrat' is salient enough to most Israelis to evoke an image. Moreover, it is evident that different types among the public and the bureaucrats have different images of the Israeli bureaucrat. Nevertheless, overall, the variance among these images is limited and the image and self-image of Israeli bureaucrats is not favourable. The public's image does not attribute to them either high character, skill, efficiency, or strength. Although the bureaucrats' self-image is more favourable, it nevertheless displays a distinct lack of elan, uniformity, and sense of organisational worth. Statesmen and job bureaucrats, who believe that public personnel matters are achievement-oriented, hold the most favourable images of the 'public bureaucrat'. Politicos, on the other hand, tend to view the Israeli bureaucrat in a highly negative fashion. This suggests that to the extent that one's behaviour in an organisational setting is conditioned by one's view of one's colleagues, statesmen, and to a lesser extent job bureaucrats, would tend to be the most functional types in terms of the needs of creating an effective national bureaucracy in an effort to further the development of the political community. In general, though, the images of the Israeli bureaucrat held both within and outside the civil service are not supportive of bureaucratic personnel and are likely to present substantial barriers to the mobilisation of support for bureaucratic action and activity.

Variations in the images of 'public bureaucrat' held among the Israeli citizenry are suggestive of an additional problem. It is increasingly evident that bureautics, a large group, have not been incorporated fully or success-fully into democratic citizenship roles. They hold the least favourable image of public bureaucrats and the gap between them and the other types is narrowest on the potency dimension. Thus, the group most opposed to bureaucratisation and least able to deal with it, nevertheless is only slightly less likely than the rest of the population to attribute high potency to bureaucratic personnel. This suggests that for bureautics, public bureaucrats are anything but a relatively benign or incon-sequential force in the political community and that bureaucratic person-nel, as well as other characteristics of bureaucracy, present a barrier, at least in a subjective sense, to their full integration into the political system.

Finally, it should be noted that although there are incongruences between the citizenry's image of public bureaucrats and the latter's self-image, these do not appear to be substantial enough to present major obstacles to administrative change or to co-operation between citizens and civil servants. Indeed, relative to a less-developed polity such as India, it appears that these are quite limited. Hence, to a large extent, Israeli bureaucrats see themselves as others do, which may be a pre-requisite for the adoption of a self-corrective mood.

Notes

1. Samuel Eldersveld, V. Jagannadham, and A.P. Barnabas, *The Citizen and the Administrator in a Developing Democracy* (Glenview: Scott, Foresman, 1968), p. 91.
2. Franklin P. Kilpatrick, Milton C. Cummings, Jr., and M. Kent Jennings, *The*

Image of the Federal Service (Washington: Brookings Institution, 1964). Indeed, in ch. 7 *infra*, it is indicated that the Israeli population views the bureaucracy as being more politicised than do the bureaucrats, and that perceived politicisation limits its recruitment potential.

3. For a comprehensive exposition of the method and its various applications, see James G. Snider and Charles E. Osgood (eds.), *Semantic Differential Technique* (Chicago: Aldine, 1969).

4. Only scales with a response rate of 80 per cent or higher were retained in the final questionnaire.

5. See for example, Charles E. Osgood, 'Semantic Differential Technique in the Comparative Study of Cultures', *American Anthropologist*, 66 (1964), 171-200; and Hideya Kumata and Wilbur Schram, 'A Pilot Study of Cross-Cultural Meaning', *Public Opinion Quarterly*, 20 (1956), 229-38.

6. See Arnold J. Heidenheimer (ed.), *Political Corruption* (New York: Holt, Rinehart & Winston, 1970), part 2 and part 4.

7. Eldersveld *et al.*, *Citizen and Administrator*, p. 93.

8. Kilpatrick *et al.*, *Image of the Federal Service*, table 10-3, p. 219.

9. Ibid., p. 240.

6 BUREAUCRATIC CULTURE AND SOCIAL CLEAVAGES

In chapter 1 it was argued that several features of public bureaucracy could be expected to engender differential reactions among the members of a political community. In the past three chapters, we have seen that this is indeed the case. Bureauphiles, bureautolerants, bureautics, and the types among the public servants, all manifest distinct patterns of cognitive, affective, and evaluative orientations towards bureaucratic objects. As noted in chapter 1, however, our typologies are only loosely associated with social group, despite the fact that there are important social cleavages in Israel. Therefore it is both necessary and desirable to continue our discussion of bureaucratic culture by addressing its relationship to these divisions within the polity. This can be accomplished conveniently within the broad framework of theories of representative bureaucracy.

Social Representation

Political and administrative analysts have long been concerned with the extent to which the social composition of public bureaucracies is representative of the membership of the political communities of which they are a part.[1] This has been especially true with regard to political systems having a moderate or high degree of structural differentiation in which governmental bureaucracies play an instrumental role in the formulation and implementation of wide-ranging public policies. Such concern stems from several sources. At the simplest level, it has been argued that the social representativeness of a public bureaucracy can have independent effects of considerable consequence on a polity. For instance, it has been maintained that 'bureaucracies . . . symbolize values and power realities'[2] and, therefore, that their composition provides clues and generates expectations regarding social and political behaviour. Hence, it has been asserted that 'social conduct and future behavior in a society may be channelized and encouraged through the mere constitution of the bureaucracy'.[3] Somewhat more specifically, it has been argued that social representation is of great importance because

A major task of governance is to gain support for policies. No matter

how brilliantly conceived, no matter how artfully contrived, government action usually requires societal support. And one of the oldest
methods of securing such support is to draw a wide segment
of society into the government to convey and to merchandise a
policy.[4]

Moreover, 'bureaucracy is . . . at least potentially more representative
than other arms of government'.[5]

In democratically-oriented political systems, social representation in
public bureaucracies is of additional importance in so far as there exists
'the simple representational notion that all social groups have a right to
political participation and to influence'.[6] Overt efforts to exclude members of some groups from employment in a public bureaucracy may be
viewed as discriminatory and affect their status in the society at large.
Krislov, for instance, argues that public employment has a 'multiplier
effect' in that small changes in the nature of public personnel administration can have widespread ramifications throughout the polity. Discrimination against some groups and/or their 'under-representation' in
a bureaucracy may influence their orientations towards it, the regime,
and the political community as a whole. As Krislov expresses it:

> Finally we must note the 'ratchet effect' involved in governmental
> recognition or withdrawal of power for a group. There is a significant
> social 'multiplier effect' in what is politically done both because
> such actions tend to be highly visible and because they tend to be
> enveloped in the invisible rays of legitimacy. What government does
> is what fixes social policy. The treatment of its constituent individuals
> and constituent groups in political form is a tip-off and a harbinger of
> social action in other guises.[7]

These theoretical perspectives on the importance of social representation in a public bureaucracy lead to the conclusion that the nature of its
composition is likely to be of considerable visibility throughout a society
and of high salience to the members of certain groups. It may also reflect
and reinforce social cleavages and tend to bind groups to, or alienate
them from, governmental policy and the political community in general.
There is reason, therefore, to believe that social representation can be of
great importance to groups' patterns of orientations towards public bureaucracy. While the independent effects of such representation on bureaucratic culture are virtually impossible to trace, something can nevertheless
be learned about their relationship to one another by comparing levels of

representation with social groups' patterns of cognition, affect, and evaluation regarding public bureaucracy. For example, if Krislov is correct, all other things being equal, we would expect the least well represented groups to feel the least affinity for their public bureaucracy and to evaluate it in the most negative terms. It is to an exploration of these elements within the context of the Israeli polity that we now turn.

An assessment of social representation in a bureaucracy involves an investigation into the 'source of origin of individuals and the degree to which, collectively, they mirror the total society'.[8] Taken literally, a representative bureaucracy in this sense would be one 'in which *every* economic class, caste, region or religion in a country is represented in exact proportion to its numbers in the population'.[9] In practice, however, research has concentrated on the most significant social cleavages found in a society. In Israel, this would involve either a study of the differentiations between Arabs and Jews or an analysis of the divisions within the latter population alone. Although the former might prove interesting and enlightening, it is effectively foreclosed by the fact that the Israeli Civil Service Commission maintains data on personnel by the categories of Jews and non-Jews, and by place of birth within these groups. Consequently, while one can determine the number of non-Jews in the bureaucracy, one cannot ascertain the number of Arabs since the two groups are not identical. In any event, because about 98 per cent of all civil servants are Jews, such a study would be almost entirely fruitless. A more theoretically relevant reason for concentrating on the Jewish population is that, as noted in chapter 2, the cleavages within it are in many ways the most important ones found in the political community. Overall, Israel's inability to integrate fully its Arab *citizens* is far less threatening to the polity than its continued difficulty in fully absorbing those Jews who emigrated from North African and Asian nations.

Perhaps the nature of the cleavages within the Jewish population is best summed up in the following terms:

(1) Relations between European and non-European Jews are asymmetrical; European Jews serve as a positive reference group for non-Europeans. While there is considerable prejudice against non-European Jews, the attitude of non-European Jews towards Europeans is usually favorable.

(2) Ethnic hostilities between Jewish communities are tempered by a sense of interdependence in the face of the conflict between

Israel and its neighbors.[10]

Furthermore, in the words of S.N. Eisenstadt:

> The development by the Oriental immigrants of specific subcultures
> within the Israeli system of stratification is indicated by several dif-
> ferent reinforcing trends and is closely related to the continuous
> coalescence—especially within oriental groups—of low occupational,
> educational, and economic status.
>
> . . .
>
> The crystallization of the specific ethnic element as distinct and
> divisive also becomes apparent in the data on intermarriage between
> groups of different origin. These show that in 86 per cent of all
> marriages performed in 1959, partners were of similar ethnic origin,
> whereas in only 14 per cent were their origins 'mixed.'[11]

Moreover, the overall pattern was one of hypergamy. Although there is
evidence that these divisions are becoming less pronounced, they continue to retain great importance for Israeli society.

The nature of these cleavages is such that one would expect members
of the Oriental group to be under-represented, in a proportional sense,
in the Israeli bureaucracy. National bureaucracies can never be fully
representative of the social composition of a political community. Of
necessity, they tend to over-represent professional and clerical occupational categories and to under-represent others. With few, if any important
exceptions, however, these over-represented skills are not distributed
equally among all social groups in societies, and therefore some groups
fare better than others with regard to civil service employment. In general, it is the least economically advanced and the least socially integrated
groups which tend to be most under-represented in public bureaucracies.
However, there is sometimes a complicating factor in that public personnel regulations may be aimed specifically at the inclusion or exclusion of
certain groups from the civil service. For example, in the United States,
throughout much of the nineteenth century, blacks were formally barred from employment in some federal positions, whereas today, conversely, special procedures exist to facilitate their entrance into the bureaucracy.[12] Similarly, the Indian central government has developed a
system of reserving civil service positions for members of scheduled
castes and tribes.[13] Needless to add, perhaps, in many cases differential
treatment is not formalised. For the most part, such practices are absent
from the Israeli scene. Although discrimination against Orientals in

personnel actions is sometimes alleged, it has not been pinpointed in a
systematic fashion.[14] Nor is there substantial evidence that they receive
preferential treatment.[15]

It is convenient to begin our analysis of the social representation of
Jewish groups within the Israeli bureaucracy by presenting the information contained in Table 6.1, which displays their distribution in the
civil service for selected years between 1953 and 1967, the latest year
for which such data are available. Although the table does not assess
the proportional representation of these groups, it nevertheless shows
some interesting trends. It is evident that the size of the Israeli-born and
Asian—African born components increased over the fourteen-year period,
whereas that of the European—American born group declined sharply.
The considerable expansion of the Asian—African group is particularly
impressive because, coupled with the overall growth of the bureaucracy,
it indicates that they received a very large share of the new positions
which were created. This in turn suggests that, at least in terms of its
personnel policies, the bureaucracy has been an avenue for their social
and political integration. If the group believes this to be the case, it
might affect their perceptions and attitudes towards it in a favourable
way. In a somewhat different vein, these data also provide evidence of
Israel's commonality with other political systems, such as the United
States, which have made widespread use of the distribution of public
service positions in connection with the process of absorbing large
immigrant populations. Finally, the table is suggestive of the difficulties
Israel has faced in establishing integrated and uniform traditions or styles
within its civil service.

Table 6.1:   The Ethnicity of Jewish Civil Servants in Israel, 1953-67

Place of Birth	1953	1955	1960	1967
Israel	18%	17%	20%	22%
Asia Africa	14	16	20	27
Europe America	67	66	58	50
Total	24,157	24,829	31,437	40,282

Source: *Twenty Years of Service* (Jerusalem: Civil Service Commission, 1968), p.
79.

Tables 6.2 and 6.3 deal with the proportional representation of these
social groups. They employ a commonly used method for determining

the degree of social representation found within a bureaucracy (or other government unit). It is generally referred to as the 'index of representation', and compares the proportion of all members of a political community who fall into a specific social category, such as a racial, ethnic, or religious group, to the proportion of all civil servants who likewise belong to the same social unit. This comparison is expressed in the form of the following ratio:

$$\text{Index of Representation} = \frac{\% \text{ of all civil servants with characteristic 'x'}}{\begin{array}{c}\% \text{ of all members of the political community} \\ \text{with characteristic 'x'}\end{array}}$$

A value of 1.0, therefore, symbolises perfect proportional representation, more than 1.0 designates a degree of 'over-representation', in a proportional sense, of the group under consideration. Because the available data define the groups under consideration in terms of place of birth, and due to the fact that Israel is a nation with a large immigrant population thereby making the median age of native-born citizens considerably lower than that of others, it is desirable to consider the index of representation with reference to the working-age population as well as the overall population.

In so doing, it can be seen that in terms of the general Jewish population and the entire bureaucracy (Table 6.2), native-born Israelis are considerably under-represented, the Asian–African born are perfectly represented, and the European–American group is significantly over-represented. However, when representation with reference to the working-age population is considered a very different picture emerges. Here the Israeli-born are the most over-represented group, European–Americans are only slightly over-represented, and the Asian–Africans are moderately under-represented. Although there are some differences, the general pattern is the same with regard to social representation in the Uniform Schedule (Table 6.3). Sometimes, however, such overall assessments can be misleading and it is often desirable to examine social representation with reference to hierarchical position as well. This was done in Table 6.4, which reports the ratio of the proportion of a social group's employees within selected grades in the Uniform Schedule to the proportion of all civil servants in those grades. The results make it evident that Israeli and European–American born Jewish civil servants tend to be over-represented in the higher grades and under-represented in the lowest ten grades, whereas the opposite is true for Jews of Asian—African birth. The disparities are particularly acute in the highest levels, where European—Americans are very much over-represented and the Asian—African born component of the civil service is extremely under-represented.

Table 6.2: Social Representation in the Israeli Civil Service, 1967

Group	% of pop.	% of civil service	Index of rep.	% of pop. 20-69 yrs.*	Index of rep.
Israeli	42.8	22.3	0.52	16.5	1.36
Asian— African	27.5	27.6	1.00	37.8	0.73
European— American	29.7	50.1	1.69	45.7	1.10

*Not more than 1.5 per cent of the civil service was not in this age group.
Sources: *Comparative Research on the Composition of the State Workforce* (Jerusalem: Civil Service Commission of Israel, 1968); *Statistical Yearbook of Israel* (Jerusalem: 1968), 'Population and Settlements'.

Table 6.3: Social Representation in the Uniform Schedule of the Israeli Civil Service, 1967

Group	% of pop.	% of civil service	Index of rep.	% of pop. 20-69 yrs.	Index of rep.
Israeli	42.8	21.8	0.51	16.5	1.33
Asian— African	27.5	31.9	1.16	37.8	0.84
European— American	29.7	46.3	1.56	45.7	1.01

Sources: *Comparative Research on the Composition of the State Workforce* (Jerusalem: Civil Service Commission of Israel, 1968); *Statistical Yearbook of Israel* (Jerusalem: 1968), 'Population and Settlements'.

Table 6.4: Index of Social Distribution,* 1967

| Group | Index of distribution of grades | | |
	16-20	11-15	1-10
Israeli	1.00	1.10	0.90
Asian— African	0.23	0.75	1.45
European— American	1.40	1.09	0.79

*The index of social distribution is the proportion of a group within selected grades in the Uniform Schedule/the proportion of all civil servants in those grades.

These patterns of social representation are comparable to those existing in some other nations having heterogeneous populations. Although disadvantaged social groups often have moderately high representation in an entire bureaucracy, they nevertheless tend to be highly concentrated in the lower levels. In the United States, for example, disadvantaged groups such as blacks and native Americans are well represented and even over-represented in the federal bureaucracy as a whole, but are nevertheless very much under-represented, and in some cases virtually non-existent, in its upper levels.[16] Yet, because the most consequential bureaucratic policy-making takes place in the upper levels, it is here that social representation is potentially of greatest importance. This being the case, it is desirable to enquire further into the composition of the top five grades of the Israeli career service.

Table 6.5 presents the ethnic origins and education of higher civil servants in 1969. It re-emphasises the paucity of those of Asian—African birth in the upper grades and leads to the conclusion that, indeed, they have only token social representation at best. At the same time, however, the table serves to dispel any notion that there might be a homogeneous bureaucratic elite. Although the European—American born dominate these positions, the educational background of higher civil servants varies widely. Perhaps it is most noteworthy here that a plurality of them have only secondary or lesser education. As mentioned in chapter 2, this can be attributed in part to earlier Zionist ideologies de-emphasising the importance of formal education and technical training.

Table 6.5: Social Characteristics of Higher Civil Servants, 1969

Ethnicity	
Israeli	24% (118)
Asian—African	5% (23)
European—American	71% (355)
Total	100% (496)
Education	
Secondary or less	42% (208)
High with no degree	32% (59)
University degree	26% (129)
Total	100% (496)

Source: Civil Service Researches and Surveys, *Senior Civil Servants in the General Grading Scale* (Jerusalem: CSC, 1971), pp. 44, 48.

In sum, social representation in the Israeli bureaucracy follows a familiar pattern. Although the most disadvantaged Jewish group is well represented in terms of the overall population, it is under-represented as a proportion of the working-age population. Civil servants of Asian—African birth also hold disproportionately fewer of the positions in the upper half of the Uniform Schedule and they are almost entirely excluded from its top five grades. If several aspects of theories of representative bureaucracy are correct, then the Asian—African group's lack of proportionally equal social representation should have a marked impact on their perceptions and attitudes towards the bureaucracy. It is to an investigation of this matter that we now turn.

Social Group Orientations Towards the Bureaucracy

It is possible to learn more about the general relationship of social cleavage and social representation to bureaucratic culture by comparing the Asian—African's patterns of cognitive, affective, and evaluative orientations towards the Israeli bureaucracy with those of the remaining members of the political community. In terms of theories of representative bureaucracy, it could be expected that the most disadvantaged group would not only be the least well socially represented in a public bureaucracy, but would also have the least favourable reactions towards it and perceive the greatest difficulty in interacting with it. Furthermore, its members would probably feel less bound to policies emanating from it and be less cognisant of its impact on their daily lives. It could also be anticipated that such a group would have low expectations of equal treatment from an institution in which they are poorly represented, and that, in general, they would have less overall confidence in it than would groups which are better socially represented. Unfortunately, the causal links here must remain speculative. However, it could be assumed that those with proportionally fewest members of the community in a political or administrative structure would have the fewest functional contacts in it, and would have the greatest difficulty in understanding its operations. It would also be more difficult for them to empathise with those in its major roles. These factors, in turn, would probably increase the group's suspicions and lack of efficacy with regard to the institution and, perhaps, consequently tend to generate the belief that it fails to understand their special problems and treats them unfairly. Several of these propositions are suggested, for example, by those aspects of theories of representative bureaucracy which hold that 'the wider the range of talents, types, and regional and family contacts found in a bureaucracy, the more likely it is to be able to fulfill its functions, with respect to both internal efficiency and social setting'.[17] It should also be noted in this context that political communities with politicised social cleavages often attach considerable importance to even token social representation in their major political structures.[18]

Several aspects of the Asian–African group's orientations towards the Israeli bureaucracy are compared with those of the rest of the population in Table 6.6. It is evident that the findings revealed there are broadly congruent with theories of representative bureaucracy. The table indicates that the Asian–Africans are, indeed, substantially more likely to perceive the bureaucracy as being too complicated to be readily understood and they also feel considerably less efficacious towards it. Thus, whereas 71 per cent of the Asian–African group feel that the bureaucracy is complex, only 52 per cent of the remaining members of the political community share this outlook. Similarly, with regard to efficacy, 49 per cent of the Asian–Africans, as compared to 34 per cent of their fellow citizens, believe that there is nothing they could do to prevent the implementation of unjust bureaucratic regulations. As might be anticipated in view of the nature of social cleavages in Israel, there is also a sizable gap concerning expectations of equal treatment from the bureaucracy. Here, 61 per cent of the Asian–Africans actually expect *unequal* treatment, whereas less than half of the remaining group share this expectation. This finding is particularly important in view of the fact that leaders of the Asian–African community often charge that Israel's European and *Sabra* (native-born) establishment engages in official discrimination against members of their group. At the same time, however, perhaps as a function of the role the bureaucracy and civil service employment has played in their absorption by the political community, there is a somewhat greater tendency for Asian–African citizens to believe that the bureaucracy has promoted social integration. Finally, they are somewhat less likely than others to attribute to the bureaucracy an impact on their daily lives, and, as might be expected from these findings, they are slightly more negative in their overall evaluation of it.

The differences between the perspectives of Asian–Africans and other Israelis indicate that social cleavages can have a very important bearing on bureaucratic culture. Moreover, they suggest that social representation is an element of considerable consequence in the development of a group's patterns of orientations towards bureaucracy. This being the case, it is imperative to investigate further the nature of social representation by examining whether its importance is limited to its symbolic qualities or whether it leads to a more active kind of representation as well.

Table 6.6:   Selected Issues of Bureaucratic Culture by Ethnic Groups

Issues	Non-Asian—African citizens	Asian—African citizens	Yule's Q
Impact of bureaucracy on daily life			
Great and some Impact	78%	63%	.35 (p<.001)
No impact	22	37	
Total	100% (1,078)	100% (365)	
Perceived complexity			
Complicated	52	71	-.38 (p<.001)
Not complicated	48	29	
Total	100% (1,058)	100% (385)	
Promoting social integration			
Yes	48	55	-.14 (p<.05)
No	52	45	
Total	100% (925)	100% (325)	
Bureaucratic efficacy			
High efficacy	66	51	.32 (p<.001)
Low efficacy	34	49	
Total	100% (1,075)	100% (382)	
Expectations of equal treatment			
Equal	58	39	.37 (p<.001)
Unequal	42	61	
Total	100% (1,071)	100% (384)	
Evaluation of bureaucrats			
Positive	62	54	.16 (p<.01)
Negative	38	46	
Total	100% (1,091)	100% (390)	

Bureaucrats and Social Cleavages

It has been found that in a political community with politicised social cleavages, different groups have different patterns of cognition, affect, and evaluation towards their public bureaucracy. Members of these groups, however, are not confined to the ranks of the ordinary citizenry, they are also found in the bureaucracy. Consequently, some of them have an opportunity to participate directly in the formulation and implementation of policies which can have a major impact on the social and political life of the nation. A central question which emerges, therefore, is whether certain features of bureaucracy, including impersonality, formalisation, functional specialisation, and hierarchy, militate against the potential impact of social background characteristics and thereby serve to standardise perceptions and attitudes across social groups; or whether, on the other hand, predispositions associated with social group continue to have a significant impact on bureaucrats' orientations even after the latter 'cannot squirm out of the apparatus in which [they are] harnessed'.[19] This, of course, is also a question of great relevance to democracy and the development of 'balanced' administration. As was noted in chapter 1, there is an overall incompatibility between the requirements of democracy and those of bureaucratic organisation which creates a tendency for the latter to be unresponsive to the demands of political authorities and the membership of the political community in general. The crux of the matter has been well put by Frederick Mosher:

> The accretion of specialization and of technological and social complexity seems to be an irreversible trend, one that leads to increasing dependence upon the protected, appointive public service, thrice removed from direct democracy. Herein lies [a] central and underlying problem . . . how can a public service so constituted be made to operate in a manner compatible with democracy? How can we be assured that a highly differentiated body of public employees will act in the interests of all the people, will be an instrument of all the people?[20]

One partial answer that has frequently been suggested is 'by ensuring that such a civil service is also socially representative of the body politic'.

This aspect of the theories of representative bureaucracy is also of considerable relevance to bureaucratic culture. Although the precise linkage between the social background characteristics of bureaucrats and the behaviour of a bureaucracy has yet to be explored fully, many have argued that there is a strong overall relationship between the two. If this line of reasoning is accurate, and if we are correct in our assumption that a bureaucracy's performance has a significant impact on the development of individuals' patterns of orientation towards it, then bureaucrats' social origins may be an important explanatory factor affecting the nature of bureaucratic culture. Discussions along these lines are abundant in the literature on bureaucracy. For example, Weber argued that, 'The question is always who controls the existing bureaucratic machinery. And such control is possible only in a very limited degree to persons who are not technical specialists. Generally speaking, the trained permanent official is more likely to get his way in the long run than his nominal superior, the Cabinet Minister, who is not a specialist.'[21] Relatedly, after studying how a politically conservative bureaucracy stifled political authorities seeking radical political change, Lipset concluded that

> the behavior of government bureaucrats varies with the nongovernmental social background and interest of those controlling the bureaucratic structure. Members of a civil service are also members of other nongovernmental social groups and classes. Social pressures from many different group affiliations and loyalties determine individual behavior in most situations. The behavior of an individual or group in a given situation cannot be considered as if the individual or group members had no other life outside the given situation one is analyzing.[22]

Finally, Krislov summed up these concerns in the following fashion:

> The effect of an administrative directive can be as far reaching as a statute.
>
> Who writes the directive—his or her style, values, concept of role— is as significant as who gets to be president, congressman, senator, member of parliament, or cabinet minister . . . The issue of the composition of a country's civil service is a basic one for political analysts and students as well as for citizens anxious to understand and activists interested in reform.[23]

Although some, including Mosher, have cautioned that 'the fact is that we know too little about a man's background and pre-employment socialization on the one hand, and his orientation and behavior in office on the other', and that 'undoubtedly, there are a good many other intervening variables'[24] affecting this relationship, there are some significant historical examples of the social composition of a public bureaucracy having had a pronounced effect on its political and administrative behaviour. For instance, in the United States, the 'Jacksonian Revolution' thoroughly altered the social composition and behaviour of the federal service. Although there is some dispute as to whether the two Jackson administrations effectively deposed elites from the top levels of the federal service,[25] there is widespread agreement that he set in motion forces which eventually made the bulk of the bureaucracy more socially representative of the nation as a whole. Leonard D. White, for example, concluded that 'certain it is that the year 1829 marked the end of an era, politically and administratively. The gentlemen who since 1789 had taken the responsibility of government were driven from the scene, to be replaced by a new type of public servant and by other ideals of official action'.[26] Three decades after Jackson's first inauguration, a major historian observed that as a result of the spoils system,

> the government formerly served by the elite of the nation, is now served to a very considerable extent by its refuse . . . In the year . . . 1859, the fact of a man's holding office under the government is presumptive evidence that he is one of three characters, namely, an adventurer, an incompetent person, or a scoundrel. From this remark must be excepted those who hold offices that have never been subjected to the spoils system, or offices which have been 'taken out of politics.'[27]

Another instance in which the social composition of a public bureaucracy affected its behaviour was studied by Lipset. He was able to identify the processes through which the politically conservative and upper social class dominated civil service of the Canadian Province of Saskatchewan undermined the goals of the radical and lower class supported Co-operative Commonwealth Federation after it took over the reins of government. He found that:

> Civil-service modification of C.C.F. goals took three major forms: (1) the continuation of traditional and, from the C.C.F. point of view, reactionary procedure in government departments; (2) changes in the intent of new laws and regulations through administrative practices; (3) influence on cabinet ministers to adopt policies advocated by top-level civil servants.[28]

Lipset also argues that these obstructionist tendencies were partially due to the fact that

> the opinion of government officials on the feasibility of any proposal is necessarily colored by their political outlook and by the climate of opinion in their social group. Many top-ranking civil servants in Saskatchewan are members of the upper social class of Regina. Most

of their social contacts are with people who believe that they will be adversely affected by many C.C.F. policies. Government officials who belong to professional or economic groups whose position or privileges are threatened by government policies tend to accept the opinion of their own group that reforms which adversely affect the group are wrong and will not work. Cabinet ministers who desire to make social reforms may therefore be dependent for advice on permanent civil servants who, in part, are members of the special-interest group which the ministers oppose. In Saskatchewan, as in other places, civil servants have been known to reduce the significance of reforms directed against their own group.[29]

It should be noted, however, that arguing from such historical examples is not altogether satisfying. One could dispute the interpretations and cite counter examples. The best known of the latter, of course, is the British civil service after the Labour Party gained control of the government for the first time. Although much difficulty was anticipated in some quarters and the social class bases of the party and the bureaucracy were considerably divergent, in fact, the bureaucrats adhered to the principle of administrative neutrality and serious conflict was avoided.[30] Yet, in general, it nevertheless does appear that elite bureaucracies do behave differently from more representative ones. Thus Van Riper argues that it is precisely the representative qualities of the United States Federal Service which account for its overall harmony and integration with other central features of the political system,[31] whereas Chapman suggests that the unrepresentative nature of some Western European bureaucracies places them in tension with political authorities seeking social and political reform.[32] More importantly for the study of bureaucratic culture, elite and representative bureaucracies tend to engender different patterns of deference, prestige, and other orientations. For instance, those who staff elite-based bureaucracies are likely to be considered 'officials', while their counterparts in more representative structures may be thought of as 'servants'. This distinction, of course, is not inconsequential with regard to citizens' and bureaucrats' perceptions of bureaucracy. Similarly, in a broad sense, there appears to be some relationship between the historical social composition of a public bureaucracy and the legal position of civil servants with regard to political participation, job protection, and even formal efforts to ensure their prestige, such as laws against insulting state employees.[33]

From the perspectives of bureaucratic culture, however, it is not only important to understand the impact of a bureaucracy's social

composition at the aggregate level, it is also necessary to comprehend
the relationship between the background characteristics of individual
bureaucrats and their patterns of orientations towards aspects of bureaucracy. Such knowledge, in turn, might lead to a further understanding
of their behaviour and the nature of bureaucratic policy-making. Despite
its desirability, though, information along these lines has remained
elusive. Perhaps, as Mosher argues, there are too many variables and too
little data. He suggests, for example, that the following factors could be
of importance:

> length of time in the organization, or the time-distance from his
> background; the nature and strength of the socialization process
> within the organization; the nature of the position . . . the length
> and content of preparatory education; the strength of associations
> beyond the job and beyond the agency; etc.[34]

In order to learn more about the perceptions of bureaucrats and their
relationship to social characteristics, we compared the orientations of
Israeli bureaucrats of Asian—African background with those of all
other civil servants.

Table 6.7 presents Israeli bureaucrats' perceptions, beliefs, and
attitudes concerning several aspects of bureaucratic culture by social
group and by rank. It provides insights into the way in which bureaucratic employment impacts upon orientations associated with social
group background. At the simplest level, the table compares low ranking
Asian—African bureaucrats to all other civil servants in the same grades.
Here, it can be seen that there are several important differences which
suggest that social cleavages are indeed carried over into the bureaucratic
arena. Hence, there are important differences between the two groups
in that:

(1) The Asian—Africans are less likely to believe that the bureaucracy has a great impact on the average citizen's daily life.

(2) They are *more* likely to feel highly efficacious.

(3) They are less likely to believe that all are treated equally by
the bureaucracy.

(4) Asian—Africans are more likely to believe that the bureaucracy
promotes social integration.

(5) They tend to evaluate it more positively than do other low-
ranking bureaucrats.

Table 6.7: Selected Issues of Bureaucratic Culture by Ethnic Group and Rank

Issue	Non-Asian–African bureaucrats			Asian–African bureaucrats		
	Low rank	Middle and high rank	Yule's Q	Low rank	Middle and high rank	Yule's Q
Impact of bureaucracy on daily life						
Great impact	79%	88%	-.32 (p<.05)	73%	89%	-.53 (p<.05)
No impact	21	12		27	11	
Total	100%	100%		100%	100%	
	(265)	(206)		(70)	(59)	
Complexity						
Complicated	56	49	.14 (p>.05)	51	69	-.39 (p>.05)
Not complicated	44	51		49	31	
Total	100%	100%		100%	100%	
	(255)	(194)		(67)	(50)	
Promote social integration						
Yes	55	64	-.19 (p<.05)	60	80	-.45 (p<.05)
No	45	36		40	20	
Total	100%	100%		100%	100%	
	(247)	(179)		(68)	(25)	
Bureaucratic efficacy						
High efficacy	53	63	-.20 (p<.05)	85	61	.55 (p<.05)
Low efficacy	47	37		15	39	
Total	100%	100%		100%	100%	
	(200)	(142)		(52)	(44)	
Expected treatment						
Equal	61	69	-.18 (p>.05)	55	59	-.08 (p>.05)
Unequal	39	31		45	41	
Total	100%	100%		100%	100%	
	(263)	(202)		(68)	(55)	
Evaluation						
Positive	65	84	-.54 (p<.001)	73	89	-.51 (p<.05)
Negative	35	16		27	11	
Total	100%	100%		100%	100%	
	(267)	(203)		(70)	(55)	

It is evident, therefore, that the mere acts of seeking and obtaining bureaucratic employment do not displace particularistic perspectives by the creation of a uniform 'bureaucratic outlook'. Moreover, in terms of the overall directions of these relationships, the Asian–African lower-level civil servants bear a striking resemblance to members of their group in the general population. It will be recalled from Table 6.6, for example, that Asian–African citizens also tend to be less cognisant of the bureaucracy's impact on daily life, less expectant of equal treatment, and more likely to view it as an important contributor to the processes of social integration. On the other hand, Asian–Africans in the general population differ from their counterparts in the lower levels of the bureaucracy with regard to sense of efficacy and evaluation. These divergencies can be explained, perhaps, by the likelihood that Asian–African civil servants' self-images are positively reinforced by their sense of accomplishment at having overcome social barriers in obtaining employment in the bureaucracy. Overall, these findings suggest that scepticism regarding the translation of social representation into some more active form of representation may be unjustified. Clearly, as Lipset argues, becoming and being a bureaucrat do not fully remove the effect of one's social roots. At the same time, however, these activities are not inconsequential and there are obvious differences between the perceptions, beliefs, and attitudes of Asian–Africans in the general population and those in the bureaucracy, despite important similarities in their tendencies *vis-à-vis* members of their community.

It is possible to learn more about the impact of bureaucratic employment on orientations towards bureaucracy associated with social group by controlling for rank. Hierarchy is perhaps the hallmark of bureaucratic organisation. Its centrality is such that it could be expected to have a greater impact on bureaucrats' orientations than most—perhaps all—other organisational features. For example, several analysts have suggested that one's position in a bureaucratic hierarchy alters one's perceptions and self-image. Thus, Thompson writes: 'Prolonged enactment of a role reacts upon the personality. People become what they do. The deference accorded a person who performs a hierarchical role gradually modifies his self-characterization'.[35] To the extent that this is the case, therefore, it could be anticipated that hierarchy, more than impersonality, seniority, and similar organisational variables, would militate against the effects of membership in a disadvantaged social group. As Kenneth Clark has pointed out, a group's collective image is partly created by the internalisation of the external world's view of it.[36] For high-ranking bureaucrats, however, as Thompson argues, there is a built-in shield against the internalisation of negative views which, although by no means impermeable, is likely to encourage the development of perspectives that are different from those of the larger groups to which one belongs.

In its comparison of higher-ranking Asian–African bureaucrats with all other civil servants in the same hierarchical levels, Table 6.7 indicates that rank does indeed tend to reduce the impact of social background on bureaucrats' perceptions and attitudes, although there is a major qualifying factor. Thus, whereas among low-ranking civil servants, Asian–Africans are less aware of the bureaucracy's impact on the daily life of the citizenry, there is no difference between the groups in the middle and highest ranks. Asian–African bureaucrats' patterns of efficacy and evaluation are also far more congruent with those of their bureaucratic peers at the higher rather than lower levels. These findings therefore strongly suggest that rank serves to erase the effects of particularistic perspectives associated with social group background. However, it is also evident that this is not the case with regard to the two items of greatest salience to the Asian–African's peculiar situation in the Israeli political community. Thus, in terms of expectations of equal treatment, the gap between high-ranking Asian–Africans and those of their group in the lower levels is small in comparison to the difference between the former and other high-ranking bureaucrats. Moreover, there is a consistent pattern. Throughout the society and the civil service Asian–Africans are less expectant of equal treatment from the bureaucracy than are their counterparts belonging to other social groups. The same pattern is found with regard to perceptions concerning the bureaucracy's role in fostering social integration. Here, however, higher rank reinforces the tendency of Asian–Africans to believe that the bureaucracy has had an important impact in this area. Thus, not only are both higher and lower Asian–African civil servants as well as members of their group in the general population all more likely than their peers of different background to view the bureaucracy as a significant promoter of social integration, entering the bureaucracy and obtaining high rank actually reinforces this perception. Indeed, this is exactly what might be expected, given that Asian–African bureaucrats, and especially those of higher rank, are to some extent living proof that the 'system' can work for members of their group. But as Lipset and others argue, that is precisely the point—particularistic perspectives associated with social background do carry over into the ranks of bureaucratic organisation and may even be reinforced by it.

These findings have considerable implications for bureaucratic culture and democratically 'balanced' administration. Social representation is more than simply a symbolic matter. It involves social groups' patterns of orientations towards public bureaucracy and it may also concern the actual representation of these groups in bureaucratic policy-making. It is apparent from this analysis that although obtaining bureaucratic employment and advancing through its ranks does affect the relationship between social background and bureaucratic culture, it does not necessarily erase the importance of this factor, and indeed, may even reinforce it where matters of high salience to the nature of social cleavages and a group's peculiar position in the political community are involved. This, in turn, suggests that it may be possible to alleviate the tension between bureaucracy and democracy by making bureaucracy highly representative in a social sense. It is useful to return to Janowitz's formulations in this context. Theoretical perspectives concerning representative bureaucracy suggest that the relationship between social representation and bureaucratic culture contribute to the achievement of at least two of his four criteria for 'democratically balanced' public administration. Thus, it appears that the more faithfully social representation in a public bureaucracy replicates the composition of the political community: (1) the more likely all segments of the population are to have 'knowledge about the operations of the public bureaucracy', and (2) the more likely they are to believe that 'the public bureaucracy is guided in its actions by a set of principles guaranteeing equal and impersonal treatment'.[37] Finally, although our findings with regard to Janowitz's remaining criteria are somewhat ambiguous, there is reason to believe that greater social representation of groups would increase the extent to which the public would 'consider that its self-interest is being served by the public bureaucracy' and it might enhance the prestige of civil service employment.[38] As argued above, Asian–Africans probably view the Israeli bureaucracy as having contributed more to social integration than other groups do partly because of the role civil service employment played in their absorption by the political community.

It is also apparent that social representation can foster democracy in another way as well. It can contribute to the establishment of a representative bureaucracy in an active sense.[39] Given that public bureaucracies may be more representative socially than legislatures,[40] and in view of the fact that they may have more important policy-making functions, they are potentially more representative in an active sense as well. This is not to imply that there are not important constraints on bureaucratic policy-makers; certainly several factors, including the nature of the position one holds, are of great relevance to one's ability to actively represent a constituency. Yet, as Lipset indicates, such representation does take place. Its potential intensity and salience is better indicated by Krislov:

> The failure of a white, middle-class administered poverty program to stir up much except controversy is related to its social bearing. In New York City an educational crisis is best understood as a conflict of values between a rabidly suspicious Black community and a bureaucracy—largely Jewish—which finds departures from its own sense of academic priorities personally threatening. In Nigeria a civil war emerged from the fantastic success of the Ibos in securing bureaucratic power over other tribes through personal efficiency—an efficiency which could only be dealt with by a massacre of the Ibos. Fear of similar conflict reluctantly led the Tunku Abdul Rahmin, premier of Malaysian states, to suggest dismemberment of the Union so that the energetically successful Chinese concentrated in Singapore would not arouse the animosity of his compatriots. In short, throughout the world, bureaucracy is the blood, bone, and sinews of political power. Its composition dictates and reflects policy.[41]

However, there is nothing inevitable about bureaucratic domination by a single group. Bureaucracies, as Norton Long argues, can be broadly representative of a nation as a whole and may even serve as a counterweight to the unrepresentativeness of other political institutions.[42] This being the case, the nature of recruitment takes on paramount importance, and it is the focus of the next chapter.

Notes

1. On representative bureaucracy see Samuel Krislov, *Representative Bureaucracy* (Englewood Cliffs: Prentice-Hall, 1974); Samuel Krislov, *The Negro in Federal Employment* (Minneapolis: University of Minnesota Press, 1967), chs. 3 and 4; V. Subramaniam, 'Representative Bureaucracy: A Reassessment', *American Political Science Review*, 61 (December 1967), 1010-19; Dennis L. Dresang, 'Ethnic Politics, Representative Bureaucracy and Development Administration: The Zambian Case', ibid., 68 (December 1974), 1605-17; Kenneth J. Meier, 'Representative Bureaucracy: An Empirical Analysis', ibid., 69 (June 1975), 526-42; and Frederick C. Mosher, *Democracy and the Public Service* (New York: Oxford University Press, 1968), pp. 10-14.
2. Krislov, *The Negro*, p. 64.
3. Ibid.
4. Krislov, *Representative Bureaucracy*, pp. 4-5.

5. Ibid., p. 63.

6. Krislov, *The Negro*, p. 64.

7. Krislov, *Representative Bureaucracy*, p. 129.

8. Mosher, *Democracy and the Public Service*, p. 12.

9. Subramaniam, *American Political Science Review*, 61, 1010.

10. Yochanan Peres, 'Ethnic Relations in Israel', *American Journal of Sociology*, 76 (May 1971), 1021.

11. S.N. Eisenstadt, *Israeli Society* (New York: Basic Books, 1967), p. 217.

12. See David H. Rosenbloom, 'The Civil Service Commission's Decision to Authorize the Use of Goals and Timetables in the Federal Equal Employment Opportunity Program', *Western Political Quarterly*, 26 (June 1973), 236-51; and David H. Rosenbloom, 'Implementing Equal Employment Opportunity Goals and Timetables in the Federal Service', *Midwest Review of Public Administration*, 9 (April/July 1975), 107-20.

13. See Marc Galanter, 'Compensatory Discrimination in Recruitment to the Indian Public Service', unpublished paper delivered at the Meeting of the American Society for Public Administration, Denver, Colorado, 19 April 1971.

14. David Rosenbloom and David Nachmias, 'Bureaucratic Representation in Israel', *Public Personnel Management*, 3 (July-August 1974), 302-13.

15. Donna Robinson, 'Patrons and Saints: A Study of the Career Patterns of Higher Civil Servants in Israel', unpublished Ph.D dissertation, Department of Political Science, Columbia University, 1970, suggests that there may be informal mechanisms for attempting to increase the number of Asian-Africans in the upper levels of the Israeli civil service. See pp. 142-3.

16. See US, Civil Service Commission, *Study of Minority Group Employment in the Federal Government*, 1974 (Washington: CSC, 1975); and David H. Rosenbloom, *Federal Equal Employment Opportunity* (New York: Praeger, 1977), ch. 1.

17. Krislov, *The Negro*, p. 64.

18. For instance, Israel's northern neighbour, Lebanon, excelled in this regard. See Krislov, *Representative Bureaucracy*, pp. 97-101. In Krislov's words, 'Since 1943 there has been no census for fear the changing population proportions will wreck the fragile settlement and agreement on new ratios would not be possible' with regard to representation in political institutions (p. 98).

19. Max Weber, *From Max Weber: Essays in Sociology*, trans. and ed. H.H. Gerth and C.W. Mills (New York: Oxford University Press, 1958), p. 228.

20. Mosher, *Democracy and the Public Service*, pp. 3-4.

21. Max Weber, *The Theory of Social and Economic Organization*, trans. Talcott Parsons and A.M. Henderson (New York: Oxford University Press, 1947), p. 338.

22. Seymour Martin Lipset, 'Bureaucracy and Social Change', in Robert K. Merton *et al.* (eds.), *Reader in Bureaucracy* (New York: Free Press, 1952), p. 230.

23. Krislov, *Representative Bureaucracy*, pp. 7-8.

24. Mosher, *Democracy and the Public Service*, p. 13.

25. Sidney Aronson, *Status and Kinship in the Higher Civil Service* (Cambridge: Harvard University Press, 1964) and David H. Rosenbloom, 'A Note on the Social Class Composition of the Civil Service, 1789-1837', *Polity*, 5 (Fall 1972), 136-8.

26. Leonard D. White, *The Jeffersonians* (New York: Free Press, 1965), p. viii.

27. James Parton, *The Life of Andrew Jackson* (Boston: Houghton, Mifflin, 1887), vol. III, p. 220.

28. Lipset, 'Bureaucracy and Social Change', in Merton *et al.* (eds.), *Bureaucracy*, p. 225.

29. Ibid., pp. 227-8.

30. See Krislov, *Representative Bureaucracy*, pp. 13-15. In a somewhat related vein, Dresang, *American Political Science Review*, 68, pp. 1605-17, found that the ethnicity of bureaucrats did not affect the distribution of funds for development

administration in Zambia.

31. Paul P. Van Riper, *History of the United States Civil Service* (Evanston: Row, Peterson, 1958). Meier, *American Political Science Review*, 69, pp. 526-42, employing a somewhat different concept of representative bureaucracy, concluded, on the other hand, that the United States federal bureaucracy is not as representative as was once thought.

32. Brian Chapman, *The Profession of Government* (London: Unwin University Books, 1959), chs. 14 and 16. See also John A. Armstrong, *The European Administrative Elite* (Princeton: Princeton University Press, 1973); Geraint Parry, *Political Elites* (New York: Praeger, 1969), pp. 80-3; and Ezra Suleiman, *Politics, Power, and Bureaucracy in France* (Princeton: Princeton University Press, 1974), esp. part 2.

33. See Chapman, *Profession of Government*, pp. 315-20, 287-95; see also Roger Grégoire, *The French Civil Service* (Brussels: International Institute of Administrative Sciences, 1952), esp. pp. 360-1.

34. Mosher, *Democracy and the Public Service*, p. 13. Meier, *American Political Science Review*, 69, p. 529, argues that 'the assumption . . . that socioeconomic characteristics determine values for upwardly mobile, adult bureaucrats is in need of revision . . .'.

35. Victor Thompson, *Modern Organization* (New York: Knopf, 1961), p. 73.

36. Kenneth Clark, *Dark Ghetto* (New York: Harper & Row, 1965), p. 64.

37. See Samuel J. Eldersveld *et al., The Citizen and the Administrator in a Developing Democracy* (Glenview: Scott, Foresman, 1968), p. 5.

38. See ch. 7 *infra*.

39. Mosher, *Democracy and the Public Service*, pp. 11-12, defines active representation as a situation '. . . wherein an individual (or administrator) is expected to press for the interests and desires of those whom he is presumed to represent, whether they be the whole people or some segment of the people'.

40. See Krislov, *Representative Bureaucracy*, ch. 4; Roger H. Davidson, 'Congress and the Executive: The Race for Representation', in A. DeGrazia (ed.), *Congress: The First Branch of Government* (New York: Anchor, 1967); and Norton Long, *The Polity* (Chicago: Rand McNally, 1962), pp. 68-73.

41. Krislov, *Representative Bureaucracy*, p. 40.

42. Long, *The Polity*, esp. p. 70.

7 RECRUITMENT: ENTRANCE, EXIT, AND BUREAUCRATIC CULTURE

The nature of patterns of recruitment to public bureaucracies is an additional area of importance to the study of bureaucratic culture and one which provides a capstone to our entire discussion thus far. Recruitment, in a broad sense including both patterns of entrance to and exit from public bureaucracies, is intertwined with virtually every aspect of the distribution of cognitive, affective, and evaluative orientations towards public bureaucracy among the members of a political community. At the most general level, recruitment is related to the political and administrative performance of public bureaucracies. In reality, bureaucratic organisations are much more than the tightly structured, formalistic hierarchies of value-free automatons portrayed by the ideal type model. Despite their behavioural regularities and the pressures they place on their employees to conform to organisational norms, demands, and processes,[1] they also have a more 'human side'[2] in that bureaucracies are collections of individuals who bring talents, values, and idiosyncrasies to them. Indeed, a good part of this study has been spent demonstrating and elaborating this point. Thus, it has been found that statesmen, job bureaucrats, service bureaucrats, and politicos defy the uniformity implied in the ideal type characterisation. Put simply, they perceive bureaucracy differently and the ways in which they view it are related to the nature of their aspirations and their experiences in it. Similarly, in the previous chapter, it was observed that bureaucratic organisation does not necessarily quash the importance of influences on its employees which stem from their social backgrounds, and therefore, as was noted, recruitment is of great importance in this context as well. In short, despite the dehumanising tendencies of bureaucracy, the consequences of which should not be minimised, there is nevertheless a human element in such organisations. Informal organisations[3] may emerge and contribute to the functionality or dysfunctionality of the formal 'bureaucratic machine'. Indeed, in some political communities employee dissatisfaction with being little more than an appendage to such formal, impersonal, ritualistic, and 'mechanised' economic organisations has encouraged some of these to adopt more pluralistic and democratic styles which allow for greater individualism and self-actualisation.[4] It follows therefore that the characteristics of those who enter a bureaucracy will affect the nature of its operations and outputs. As a member of the Planning Commission of India summarised these thoughts:

> Social scientists and students of administrative sciences have increasingly realized that organizations are more and more led by the dynamic and behavioural components than by the formalized systems; that organizational effectiveness depends heavily upon the behaviour of its personnel. The essential ingredients of the bureaucratic behaviour are the various personnel values reflected in day-to-day operations. These would include attitudes to work, degree of professionalization, attitudes towards superiors, towards subordinates, attitudes to delegation of authority and acceptance of responsibility, and several others which have a direct impact on the operational aspects of an organization. These behavioural inputs of the bureaucracy play a vital part in shaping the character and the effectiveness of the entire organization.[5]

However, if the premises of this investigation are correct, the nature of bureaucratic processes and outputs affects the ways in which people perceive and react to such organisations. Thus, bureautics find them complex and unfair; bureauphiles do not share these perceptions; and bureautolerants concur in part and dissent in part. Moreover, these basic outlooks are associated with almost all aspects of individuals' orientations towards public bureaucracy. Recruitment, though, is not only related to bureaucratic processes and outputs and therefore to these patterns of orientations; the latter, in turn, are also associated with patterns of recruitment. The processes at work here are well described by Kilpatrick and associates:

> People usually perceive occupations and employing organizations, not precisely and realistically, but in terms of vaguely generalized cultural pre-judgments, which not only are undiscriminating in application, uncertain as to origin, and resistant to modification, but also tend to be self-perpetuating and self-enhancing by virtue of their selecting and modifying effect on current experience and perception. This is the pattern of stereotypes which . . . add up to the *images* the individual has of kinds of employment and employing organizations. Thus, one of the keys to 'attractiveness' is not what *is*, but *how it is perceived.*[6]

Hence, recruitment bears a circular relationship to bureaucratic culture.

Each reinforces the other in a consistent direction. Recruitment affects bureaucratic performance and bureaucratic performance affects recruitment. The more favourably performance is perceived by the members of a political community, the easier it will be to recruit the talents and types desired. Conversely, the worse the perceived performance, the more difficult it will be to obtain the latter. Politically and administratively, this means that any polity that wants to upgrade its bureaucratic apparatus faces a significant difficulty. Upgrading requires the infusion of new types of personnel, which, however, is dependent upon upgrading.

This is a problem which is faced by almost all political communities in one way or another, but it is most acute where the processes of self-sustained political and economic change have not been attained. Indeed, the complexity of administrative requirements in less developed nations is intimidating:

> In modern, developed societies today we are more than ever inclined to emphasize the importance and complexity of the roles of administrators. In developing societies these roles are preeminent, particularly in societies dedicated to massive programs of social innovation. In such developing societies the communication of welfare-state goals, the education of the populace, the mobilization of citizen support, and the translation of this support into new patterns of action make administrative structures and personnel centrally important. The roles of others, such as the politician, the intellectual, the entrepreneur, are important, but the administrator is a vital cog in the achievement of social planning.[7]

It is obvious, perhaps, as Heady notes, that the resource base upon which such societies may draw is relatively limited and there may be intense competition for those individuals with the skills desired.[8] Indeed, to some extent, as the term 'brain drain' suggests, this competition is international. The problem, it should be emphasised, is rarely one of finding enough individuals to fill bureaucratic posts, it is rather one of attracting those citizens the administrative apparatus needs most to fulfil its functions in the most effective fashion. Moreover, it appears that even in highly developed nations, public bureaucracies have difficulties in this regard. For example, Kilpatrick and associates found that in the United States:

> the image of the federal service harmonizes closely with the

occupational values and attitudes of those groups in society from whom its personnel needs in relation to available resources are least; it is dangerously out of phase with the occupational values and attitudes of those groups in society for whom its present and projected personnel needs are greatest, and for whom competition from the private sphere and other levels of government will be most severe.[9]

It is useful, therefore, to keep the following perspectives in mind while analysing patterns of recruitment:

The distribution of human effort, skills, and talent among the various enterprises in a society is a significant clue to both the nature and the probable lines of development of that society. It is a matter for grave public concern when any major enterprise essential to social welfare and progress fails to receive its necessary share of these resources.[10]

Politics and Recruitment

Recruitment to positions in public bureaucracies is necessarily a political affair. Personnel 'needs' and the desired 'skills', 'talents', and 'types' are seldom, if ever, determined without reference to political values. In Krislov's words, 'A public office makes for public fuss. The process of prefering one or another set of criteria is one of policy making, of agenda setting, of preference ordering, of cue giving for the other sectors as well.'[11] Moreover, despite the tendency of authors of public personnel textbooks to write in terms of techniques designed 'to assure that the government service attracts its proper share of the *best qualified* persons',[12] in reality 'qualification is a relative conception',[13] and 'there is no natural dividing line between intrinsic and extrinsic criteria'.[14] Politics impinges upon recruitment in at least two ways. First, it is instrumental in 'selecting-out' members of certain groups. Second, the extent to which politics is believed to influence the nature and performance of a public bureaucracy is associated with its attractiveness, as an employer, to members of the political community.

The political nature of recruitment patterns is most visible in spoils or patronage-oriented public bureaucracies. Even here, however, attention has largely focused on the relationship between spoils and the development of viable political parties and there has been a tendency to underestimate the extent to which these practices have been associated with the deliberate inclusion of some groups in and the exclusion of others from public bureaucratic positions. In Western nations such as England and France prior to the development of mass political parties, administrative patronage was used to bolster the upper social class nature of regimes against emerging pressures from the bourgeoisie. On the other hand, after the advent of modern political parties in a country such as the United States, patronage was associated with the displacement of upper social strata from positions of political authority. Thus, President Jackson ushered in the spoils system with a view to changing the social class basis of national politics in the United States,[15] and to a considerable extent, given that subsequent administrations also made heavy use of patronage practices, his 'reform' was successful. Historically, merit systems were also often introduced at least as much in connection with demands for a redistribution of political and administrative authority as to secure better economy, efficiency, and technical competence. Civil service reform in the United States, Great Britain, and sixth—tenth century China present just three such examples.

In the United States, the civil service reformers of the post Civil War era thought that, in the words of one of their leading advocates, 'The question whether the Departments at Washington are managed well or badly, is, in proportion to the whole problem, an insignificant question.'[16] What they sought, as they clearly stated, was 'to restore ability, high character, and true public spirit once more to their legitimate spheres in our public life, and to make active politics once more attractive to men of self-respect and high patriotic aspirations'.[17] In short, nothing less than a fundamental change in political leadership. In Great Britain, as J.D. Kingsley observed, 'the debate occasioned by the Northcote-Trevelyan recommendations ran clearly along class lines',[18] and the overall issue was the distribution of political power, rather than more efficient administration. In China, 'after several centuries of division, the Sui (589-618) dynasties saw in the training and recruitment of a centralized civil service the best means of overcoming the powers of regionalism and of the hereditary aristocracy'.[19] Although there is some doubt as to whether 'the rise of this aristocracy of merit . . . definitely freed the dynasty from its dependency on an older, hereditary aristocracy',[20] there is widespread agreement that changes in the recruitment process were introduced with this prospect in mind. In the United States and Great Britain, on the other hand, there is considerable evidence that reform was, in fact, associated with many of the political changes for which its supporters had hoped.[21] Finally, it is worth noting that in the United States today, equal opportunity and social representation have become the major political concerns associated with public personnel administration and many have charged that the 'merit system' inherently discriminates against members of minority groups. Moreover, as a consequence, race, ethnicity, and sex have become legitimate criteria to be taken into account in recruitment and promotion procedures.[22]

There is evidence that the complexity of the relationship between politics and recruitment is compounded by the impact that perceived 'politicisation' has on the attractiveness of public bureaucracies as employing institutions. For example, even in the United States where over 90 per cent of all federal service positions are filled almost entirely without regard to political affiliation or partisan views and where norms and regulations pertaining to political neutrality are strong, it was discovered that a significant number of top-level business employees found the prospect of working in the bureaucracy unappealing because 'there would be too many political pressures involved in the job'.[23] Moreover, the extent to which the perceived politicisation of public bureaucracies enhances or reduces their recruitment potential may vary considerably among the members of a political community. Thus, in the United States, the above group was the only one studied having this reaction. Others either did not perceive the bureaucracy as politicised or did not consider politicisation to be unattractive. In Israel, on the other hand, where many believe that there is a wide gap between the depoliticisation of the bureaucracy in form and its politicisation in reality, it could be expected that perceived politicisation would be an even stronger factor bearing on the civil service's recruitment potential. For example, it has been found that among Israeli bureaucrats, some (politicos and service bureaucrats) tend to view the recruitment process as one which involves factors of a political nature, whereas others believe it is more achievement oriented. At the same time, however, these perspectives are associated with different views on a broad number of items concerning the attractiveness of the bureaucratic work environment. It stands to reason, therefore, that some members of the political community might be drawn to bureaucratic employment because of its perceived politicisation, whereas others would be repelled by the same perception. The patterns through which this occurs and their overall impact on recruitment processes, of course, are also major elements in the nature of a polity's bureaucratic culture.

These matters can be investigated in several stages. At the broadest level, the Israeli bureaucracy appears to be largely unattractive, as a place in which to work, to members of the political community. When asked, 'Would you prefer to be employed in the public bureaucracy?' slightly less than two-thirds of our respondents answered in the negative.

At the same time most Israelis indicated a preference for further depoliticisation of the civil service. Thus about 80 per cent of the members of
the political community want politics to be further separated from
administration. The extent to which the perceived existence of partisan
political pressures within the bureaucracy is associated with individuals'
preferences for entering its ranks or remaining outside is indicated in
Table 7.1. It is clear that the overwhelming majority of Israelis believe
that public bureaucrats are subjected to at least moderately strong
partisan pressures. Equally important, however, there is an association
between the perception of a high degree of such pressure and a propensity not to prefer employment in the bureaucracy. Thus, whereas only
28 per cent of those who indicate a preference for joining the ranks of
the civil service believe bureaucrats are subjected to a great deal of
partisan pressure, 39 per cent of those who would prefer not to enter

Table 7.1: Citizens' Propensity to Enter the Israeli Bureaucracy by its
Perceived Politicisation*

Propensity to enter	Politicisation			
	Low	Medium	High	Total
Would enter	20%	52%	28%	100% (485)
Would not enter	3	58	39	100% (912)
Total	9	56	35	100% (1,397)
		Gamma = .36 (p<.001)		

*Actual text of question: 'To what extent are civil servants influenced by political
parties?'

share this perception. This suggests that the Israeli bureaucracy's inability
to convey the image of having successfully divorced partisan politics
from administration, not to mention the lack of such a separation in
reality, has reduced its recruitment potential. However, the question of
'To whom is bureaucratic employment most attractive?' remains to be
investigated.

Given their wide divergencies on a number of aspects of bureaucratic
culture, it is to be expected that bureauphiles, bureautolerants, and bureautics would react differently to the prospect of accepting employment in the Israeli bureaucracy. Interestingly, however, it is true only
to a limited extent. Thus, taking the polar extremes, 37 per cent of the
bureauphiles and 24 per cent of the bureautics express a desire to join
the workforce of the bureaucracy. The latter figure is somewhat surpris-

ing, but apparently the job security and other employment benefits offered by the bureaucracy are sufficient enough to induce a considerable proportion of bureautics to overcome their basic distaste for its structural and procedural characteristics.

A more highly refined picture of how perceptions concerning politicisation of the bureaucracy affect its recruitment potential can be obtained by focusing on the extent to which members of the political community consider the *public personnel system* itself to be politicised, or at least non-achievement-oriented. Although the *general* image of an institution may be of considerable importance to its overall attractiveness, it may also be the case that among those who would seriously consider working in a public bureaucracy, the nature of its personnel procedures would be of greatest salience. Indeed, it should be remembered in this connection that one of the elements upon which our typology of bureaucrats rests is the nature of their perceptions concerning the personnel processes employed in the Israeli civil service. In addition, in Israel, the United States, and other countries, many believe that job security is one of the most attractive features of public employment. In any event, the ways in which members of a political community perceive and react to public personnel procedures, in the context of whether they would prefer to join the ranks of a public bureaucracy, are of considerable importance to patterns of bureaucratic culture because they provide information concerning the distribution of norms of relevance to bureaucratic employment. Analysis of this question makes it evident that perceptions regarding politicisation of public personnel administration do affect the bureaucracy's recruitment potential in a marked fashion.

Figure 7.1 presents a 'breakdown analysis' of potential recruitees by their perceptions of the personnel process and by the nature of individuals' personal orientations, that is, whether they are inner-oriented or community-oriented. Although it is not reported in the figure, the overwhelming number of those who would *not* prefer to be employed in the public bureaucracy believe that its personnel procedures reward civil servants on the basis of non-achievement-oriented criteria. The converse of this relationship can be seen by examining those who would prefer to join the ranks of the bureaucracy. Of the individuals in this group, 69 per cent believe that promotions in the civil service are based on achievement factors, whereas only 31 per cent view other elements as being central. In other words, employment in the bureaucracy is far more attractive to those who view its promotional procedures as being depoliticised.

Taken together, these findings concerning politicisation and recruitment potential are extremely important to the nature of bureaucratic
culture in Israel, and presumably, in other political systems as well. It is
clear that the Israeli bureaucracy has limited recruitment potential in
part because of its politicised image. Thus, there is a greater tendency

Figure 7.1. Citizens' Propensity to Enter the Bureaucracy, by Orientation and Perception of the Personnel System

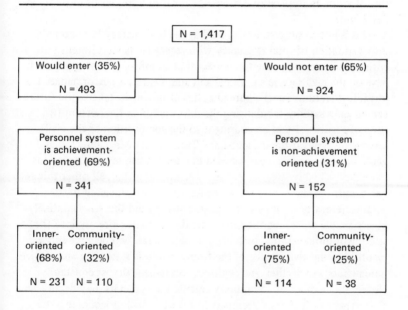

among those who would prefer *not* to join its ranks to believe that bureaucrats are subjected to very substantial partisan political pressures.
Moreover, there is even a stronger tendency among this group to perceive its personnel procedures as being politicised, or at least non-
achievement-oriented. This suggests, therefore, that the bureaucracy is
least attractive to those who favour partisanly neutral, achievement-
oriented public administration, but find it absent from the Israeli civil
service. However, as LaPalombara argues, the extent to which an
achievement-orientation applies to political recruitment and role differentiation is an important indicator of a political community's tendency

towards political change. It may be, therefore, that in so far as the Israeli polity is seeking further political development, the bureaucracy's image as an employer is dysfunctional. Furthermore, to the extent that the political community favours the establishment of goal-oriented public administration in connection with national development and social integration, it is evident that its efforts have been hampered by the bureaucracy's inability to compete effectively for large segments of the working population. Moreover, there is little reason to suspect that this situation is atypical of nations at similar or lesser levels of political development.

This is not to suggest, however, that the bureaucracy has entered into a situation of total stagnancy with regard to its recruitment potential or to underestimate the impact that an influx of new types might have on the civil service's political and administrative performance. The possible directions Israel's bureaucratic culture might take in the future can be addressed by tabularising the information in the bottom two rows of Figure 7.1 and comparing it to the composition of the civil service, by type, at the present time. This was done in Table 7.2, and while such an approach can be used in a speculative fashion only, it is nevertheless highly suggestive. The table indicates that, all other things being equal, in the future the bureaucracy will be appealing to somewhat different types than in the past. Thus, *if* (and this seems unlikely in any simple sense) recruitment potential translates directly into the staffing of bureaucratic positions, job bureaucrats will become more plentiful in the civil service of the future, whereas statesmen and service bureaucrats will decline, and politicos will remain almost constant. Hence, the number of community-oriented bureaucrats may decline and the extent to which bureaucrats perceive personnel procedures to be achievement-oriented, and therefore, perhaps, the degree to which they are in fact achievement-oriented, appears likely to increase. At the same time, however, the politico element may remain strong and stable. Given the different patterns of cognitive, affective, and evaluative orientations of these types towards the bureaucracy, it is likely that such changes, if they were to occur, would have a substantial impact on bureaucratic performance and bureaucratic culture. It must be reiterated, though, that these tendencies are propensities at best. Moreover, it must be borne in mind that the bureaucracy is attractive as an employer only to a minority of the members of the political community.

Social Background and Recruitment

In view of our findings in the previous chapter, no analysis of the relation-

Table 7.2. Actual Versus Potential Employees in the Israeli Bureaucracy

Types	Actual	Potential
Statesmen	26%	22%
Service bureaucrats	13	8
Job bureaucrats	37	47
Politicos	24	23
Total	100%	100%
	(557)	(493)

ship between patterns of entrance, or more precisely, potential entrance, and bureaucratic culture would be complete without an examination of the impact of social background characteristics on the bureaucracy's recruitment potential. It will be recalled that social representation in the Israeli bureaucracy was found to be of relevance to some aspects of groups' patterns of orientations towards it and their active represent-ation by it. Education is a second background factor of considerable importance to the relationship between recruitment and bureaucratic culture. Although earlier Israeli ideologies and recruitment practices de-emphasised the importance of formal education and professional training, the complexity of public administrative tasks in virtually all political communities places a premium on technically trained civil servants. Moreover, a substantial increase in the formal educational level of middle- and higher-ranking civil servants would almost certainly have a consider-able impact on the bureaucracy's performance, image, and self-image. A third social background characteristic which should be considered is sex. This division has not become politicised in Israel to a significant extent, but it is nevertheless worth exploring in the context of recruitment because studies elsewhere, notably in the United States, have found a tendency for women to be more favourably predisposed towards public employment.[24] The relationship of these three factors to the recruit-ment potential of the Israeli civil service is portrayed in Figure 7.2.

First, with regard to the cleavages among social groups within Israel's Jewish population, it can be seen that among those who would prefer to be employed in the public bureaucracy most are of European-American heritage and least are of Israeli (*Sabra*) background, with Asian-Africans occupying an intermediate position. To the extent that these divisions are indicative of the future social composition of the Israeli civil service, it is interesting to note that the proportion of European—Americans would decline somewhat, that of Asian—Africans would remain about the same, and the social representation of Israelis would increase. It

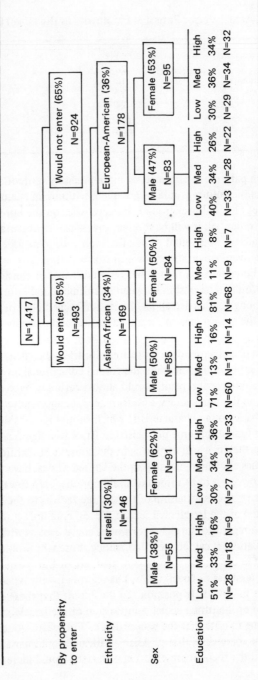

Figure 7.2. Citizens' Propensity to Enter the Bureaucracy, by Ethnicity, Sex, and Education

should also be noted that among the respondents in our sample, Asian—Africans were the group having the highest proportion (44 per cent) indicating preference for employment in the bureaucracy and Israelis were the group having the least (30 per cent). This follows a pattern which has been observed elsewhere as well, especially in the United States with reference to federal and municipal employment, whereby the most disadvantaged social groups in the political community tend to prefer jobs in the public sector, perhaps because of the security they offer.[25] The figure also indicates that overall, women constitute a majority among those who would prefer employment in the civil service and that this tendency is particularly strong among those of Israeli background. Again, similar findings have been obtained in the United States, and job security and equal pay for equal work, regardless of sex, which is not a principle consistently applied throughout most sectors in Israel,[26] are probably the major factors explaining this relationship.

Finally, it is evident that the recruitment potential of the bureaucracy is strongest among those with the *least* formal education, except among women of Israeli and European—American background. The tendency of those among the members of the political community who would prefer employment in the bureaucracy to be less well educated is particularly strong in the case of Asian—Africans, who as a group lack a high degree of formal education, and in that of male Israelis. Again, studies elsewhere suggest such a relationship can be largely explained by a desire for job security. To the extent that these preferences signify a propensity actually to enter the civil service and in so far as education is associated with entrance and advancement through the ranks, these data suggest that Israeli (*Sabra*) women and European—Americans of both sexes will be among the bureaucracy's leading members in the future.

These patterns of preference and recruitment potential reinforce the earlier interpretation that the Israeli bureaucracy faces a difficult situation with regard to its attractiveness as an employer. In terms of education, its appeal is clearly strongest where its needs are currently least. Moreover, this is especially true within the Asian—African group, which is already largely concentrated in the lower levels and severely under-represented, in a social sense, in the upper ranks. Concerning social representation itself, it does not appear from the social composition of the group which would prefer employment in the bureaucracy, that the most serious overall imbalance will be redressed. Furthermore, it appears that the bureaucracy's major strength as an employing institution is the security and equality of treatment it affords its employees, rather than the nature of the opportunities and careers it offers. Thus approximately 35 per cent of our respondents who expressed a desire to enter the civil service, cited 'job security' as its most important personnel feature. This has been found to be the case elsewhere as well, and perhaps it is endemic to the nature of public bureaucratic employment, but, at least in the Israeli context, these patterns of recruitment potential are somewhat dysfunctional and pose a serious dilemma for its bureaucratic culture.

Patterns of Exit

Patterns of exit are also related to the human composition of public bureaucracies and therefore may be as politically and administratively important as those of entrance. The departure of public employees for non-governmental work can create significant costs. Despite the popular image of the immovable and irremovable public bureaucrat, voluntary separations are often of a very considerable magnitude. When upper-level bureaucrats believe that they would be better off in private employment, the prestige, image, and morale of a public service is likely to suffer. This, in turn, has the effect of deterring other qualified personnel from seeking public bureaucratic positions and thereby makes it difficult for a bureaucracy to obtain and maintain the talent it often desperately needs. High turnover rates in the upper levels may also create discontinuities in the formulation and implementation of public policies. At all levels, exit creates additional training, socialisation, and recruitment costs. It also involves costs in terms of aborted careers. Although patterns of exit can be administratively beneficial, it appears that, in general, those who are most needed often have the greatest propensity to leave voluntarily. For example, Kilpatrick and associates found that in the United States Federal Service,

> The vast majority of federal employees presently intend to continue with the federal government. However, those who are thinking of leaving and/or least sure of staying are most often the specialized, high-ranking personnel (except for veteran executives), and younger and newer employees. Thus the retention problems occur in the groups for whom the needs are likely to be most critical now and in the future. Similarly, past thoughts of leaving the federal establishment occurred much more frequently among the higher-placed and better-educated employees.[27]

To a very large extent, actual exit is a function of opportunities for employment outside public bureaucracies. However, it can be anticipated that the *desire* or *propensity* to exit is conditioned by bureaucrats' patterns of cognitive, affective, and evaluative orientations towards the organisations in which they work.

Unfortunately, political scientists and students of public administration have tended to concentrate their research on the entrance side of public employment, and not much is known about the political and administrative correlates of patterns of exit. Thus, it has been argued that 'forty-five years of collecting and analyzing turnover data have not materially enhanced our knowledge about the process of loss of membership from groups and organizations'.[28] In large part, this is due to the tendency of traditional studies to fail to relate exit 'to the determinants of human behavior—needs, attitudes, frustrations, and so on'.[29] More can be learned about the relationship between bureaucratic culture and the propensity to exit, therefore, by analysing these tendencies by bureaucratic types. This is achieved in Table 7.3, which provides strong evidence that the two are associated. It is apparent that statesmen are the most likely to express a desire to remain in the bureaucracy, and that politicos have the greatest propensity to leave. Indeed, almost half of the latter express a desire to exit, whereas only about a quarter of the former do. The propensities of job bureaucrats and service bureaucrats to exit fall between these extremes, with job bureaucrats being closer to politicos, and service bureaucrats closer to statesmen. These finding are surprising in several ways. Perhaps most interesting is that the propensities of all types of Israeli bureaucrats to exit appears to be extremely high. For example, Kilpatrick found that in the United States less than 7 per cent of all general employees and less than 3 per cent of all executives in the federal service planned to leave the bureaucracy.[30] Thus, relative to the views of bureaucrats elsewhere, Israeli civil servants are unenthusiastic about remaining in the bureaucracy. This is especially true of those who are inner-oriented (politicos, job bureaucrats) rather than community-oriented, perhaps because of the bureaucracy's relative incoherence and low prestige. It should be noted however, that perhaps because of their community orientation, service bureaucrats, who, it will be recalled, are the least efficacious and the least sanguine of the types with regard to the bureaucracy's role in political and economic development, nevertheless express a relatively strong preference for remaining in its employ. Finally, the job bureaucrats merit attention. It has been found that among those in the *general population* who would prefer to enter employment in the bureaucracy, the largest single group possess the orientations towards work

Table 7.3:   Bureaucrats' Propensity to Exit the Bureaucracy by Types[*]

Type	Exit	Ambivalent	Remain	Total
Statesmen	24%	8%	68%	100% (195)
Service bureaucrats	35	7	58	100% (72)
Job bureaucrats	42	10	48	100% (206)
Politicos	45	9	45	99% (128)

Gamma = -.26 (p<.001)

[*]Actual text of question: 'Would you prefer to be employed outside the public bureaucracy?'

and the bureaucracy's personnel practices that are associated with job bureaucrats. Yet, once in the bureaucracy, the latter express a very considerable desire to seek employment elsewhere. It may be, therefore, that this inner- and achievement-oriented group is highly mobile, at least subjectively, in employment. It is necessary to analyse further the propensities of Israeli bureaucrats to exit before the ramifications of these patterns can be fully assessed.

One of the complexities of the bureaucratisation of public life, and an element of broad importance to the study of bureaucratic culture, is the relationship between the power position of public bureaucracies and bureaucrats as a collective group, and the powerlessness of individual bureaucrats *vis-à-vis* the organisations of which they are a part. Indeed, individual powerlessness and collective power has been a theme running throughout discussions of bureaucracy at least since Balzac referred to such organisations as 'giant power wielded by pygmies'.[31] Several studies of organisation and alienation have addressed the issue of individual powerlessness and it is generally seen as a central and highly salient aspect of bureaucratic employment.[32] From the perspectives of public administration, and especially with regard to political and economic development, dynamic, persuasive, and aggressive bureaucrats tend to be deemed desirable, at least in so far as they are adequately checked by other political institutions. Indeed, as noted in chapter 1, there are some who argue that it is such bureaucrats that make polyarchial political systems function well. It stands to reason, therefore, that individual bureaucrats' sense of power or powerlessness could be associated with their propensities to exit, and that this association could have major repercussions for political communities. Table 7.4 shows the propensity of Israeli bureaucrats to exit by their sense of powerlessness. It leaves no doubt that those who feel the greatest sense of powerlessness desire to exit most strongly. Thus, whereas 56 per cent of those with a high sense of powerlessness show a propensity to exit, only 26 per cent of those with a low sense of powerlessness share this tendency. These findings strongly suggest, therefore, that many Israeli civil servants do feel a

Table 7.4. Bureaucrats' Propensity to Exit by Powerlessness*

Powerlessness		Propensity to exit			Total
		Exit	Ambivalent	Remain	
High sense of powerlessness	1	56%	11%	33%	100% (85)
	2	40	8	52	100% (305)
	3	29	12	59	100% (170)
Low sense of powerlessness	4	26	14	60	100% (14)
			Gamma = .24 (p $<$.001)		

*Actual text of question: 'To what extent can people in positions like yours influence decisions made by higher-ups?'

considerable sense of powerlessness and to the extent that propensities to exit are transformed into actual exit, those bureaucrats remaining in the civil service will probably be more in keeping with the needs of the political community in connection with its efforts to develop a dynamic and forceful public administrative apparatus.

Thus far, it has been argued that bureaucratic type and bureaucrats' sense of powerlessness are two elements of interest to bureaucratic culture which are associated with propensities to exit the public bureaucracy. Politicisation is an additional factor which needs to be considered. Although there has been no definitive study on the subject, it is plausible that highly politicised bureaucracies have substantial turnover rates. This, of course, is almost necessarily the case where spoils systems prevail, and if the United States during the nineteenth century can serve as an example, the rate of exit can be very rapid indeed.[33] Yet, very little empirical knowledge exists about the relationship of politicisation to patterns of *voluntary* exit. It has been suggested, however, that there is a tendency for professionals and some categories of upper-level bureaucrats to resent political encroachment upon their work and to reject political interference in personnel matters.[34] Nevertheless, at the same time, it has been observed that politicisation may increase the power of high-ranking generalists and increase their ability to achieve political and administrative goals.[35] These matters are addressed, in part, in Table 7.5, which shows the association between the perceived influence of political parties on bureaucrats and their propensities to exit, by rank. The table indicates that there is a significant difference between the exit-propensities of low-ranking bureaucrats who perceive the bureaucracy to be politicised and those who view it as non-politicised, whereas in the highest ranks the difference, while not negligible, is very much smaller. This suggests that politicisation is less offensive to high-ranking bureaucrats, perhaps because they must interact with politicians and rely on partisan support to accomplish some aspects of their jobs.

Table 7.5:   Bureaucrats' Propensity to Exit by Politicisation* Controlling for Rank

Politicisation	Rank	Propensity to Exit			Total
		Exit	Ambivalent	Remain	
	Low	47%	9%	44%	100% (167)
Highly	Middle	48	12	40	100% (122)
politicised	High	27	15	58	100% (26)
		Gamma = .07 (p>.05)			
	Low	27	7	66	100% (136)
Non-	Middle	31	11	58	100% (74)
politicised	High	21	8	71	100% (24)
		Gamma = .04 (p>.05)			

*Actual text of question: 'To what extent are civil servants influenced by political parties?'

This interpretation is strengthened considerably by the information contained in Table 7.6. It indicates that, in general, the greater the amount of actual interference with a bureaucrat's work by politicians, the more likely the bureaucrat is to express a desire to exit. This tendency, however, declines with increasing rank, and high-ranking bureaucrats who report the most frequent interference appear to have the least propensity to prefer employment outside the bureaucracy. The propensity to exit of middle- and lower-ranking bureaucrats, whose work is frequently subject to political interference, though, is overwhelming. The table further suggests that to a very considerable extent individual public bureaucrats in Israel do not experience interference with their own work by politicians, despite a general tendency on the part of both civil servants and citizens to view the bureaucracy as at least moderately politicised.

Finally, in view of the importance of social cleavages to bureaucratic culture and their effect on patterns of recruitment, it is desirable to exam-

Table 7.6. Bureaucrats' Propensity to Exit by the Frequency of Political Interference,* Controlling for Rank

Frequency of interference	Rank	Propensity to exit			Total	
		Exit	Ambivalent	Remain		
Frequent interference	Low	57%	13%	30%	100%	(62)
	Middle	54	10	36	100%	(48)
	High	7	28	65	100%	(14)
		Gamma = .29 (p<.05)				
No interference	Low	32	9	59	100%	(267)
	Middle	38	9	52	99%	(163)
	High	27	8	65	100%	(38)
		Gamma = -.05 (p>.05)				

*Actual text of question: 'How frequently do politicians interfere with your work?'

ine the relationship between social background and propensity to exit the public bureaucracy. Table 7.7 indicates that bureaucrats of different social groups have considerably divergent preferences for employment outside the bureaucracy. Throughout all ranks, European—Americans are the least likely to express a desire to exit. In the lower ranks, those

Table 7.7: Bureaucrats' Propensity to Exit by Ethnicity, Controlling for Rank

Rank	Ethnicity	Propensity to exit			Total	
		Exit	Ambivalent	Remain		
Low	Israeli	42%	9%	49%	100%	(188)
	Asian-African	37	6	57	100%	(67)
	European-American	24	12	64	100%	(84)
Total		37	9	54	100%	(339)
		Gamma = .23 (p<.05)				
Middle and high	Israeli	41	14	45	100%	(92)
	Asian-African	47	8	45	100%	(59)
	European-American	28	12	60	100%	(120)
Total		37	11	52	100%	(271)
		Gamma = .21 (p<.01)				

of Israeli (*Sabra*) background have the greatest propensity to exit, and in the higher ranks, it is the Asian—Africans who most frequently express a preference for other employment. The latter finding is especially important because Asian—Africans are very under-represented, in a social sense, at these levels. To the extent that these propensities result in actual exit, then, the higher ranks of the Israeli bureaucracy are likely to become less representative of the major social groups in the Jewish population. This, in turn, as was argued in chapter 6, will tend to decrease the active representation of the Asian–African group by the civil service and is likely to affect adversely the orientations of citizens of Asian–African background towards the bureaucracy.

Analysis of citizens' propensities to enter employment in a public bureaucracy and civil servants' preferences for exiting it yields several findings of importance to an understanding of bureaucratic culture. At the broadest level, these patterns add a dynamic element to bureaucratic culture because the human composition of bureaucracies is inevitably intertwined with their images and performance. The latter elements, in turn, are associated with orientations towards public bureaucracies, which bear upon their recruitment potential and turnover rates. Hence, there is a circular process involved: individual orientations towards the bureaucracy influence its recruitment potential; recruitment potential influences the bureaucracy's image and performance; performance influences bureaucrats' self-images and propensities to exit; and, finally, exit and performance influence individual orientations. To the extent that a political community seeks to change the patterns of orientations towards its public bureaucracy found among its members, then, it faces a serious dilemma. Change is somewhat dependent upon the human composition of a public bureaucracy, but the latter may also be dependent upon change. The nature of this dilemma is well illustrated by the Israeli case.

To a considerable extent, Israelis both inside and outside the bureaucracy find it a relatively unattractive place in which to work. Clearly, it has been unable to compete effectively for the scarce human resources it needs. It tends to be most attractive to those citizens with lesser education and to members of disadvantaged groups (Asian–Africans, and in the employment context, women, as well). At the same time, high-ranking bureaucrats of Asian–African background express the greatest desire to exit. Politically, in view of the nature of social cleavages in Israel, this is potentially of great consequence. Taken together, and coupled with the lack of support among members of the political community for the bureaucracy, these findings are not encouraging. It will obviously be difficult for the bureaucracy to upgrade its operations, in so far as these are dependent upon its human composition. Among the barriers to a stronger recruitment and retention potential are perceived and actual politicisation, the image of the personnel system, and a sense of powerlessness among public bureaucrats. While one is tempted to reason that the negative impact of some of these features could be overcome by offering better salaries and employment conditions, such an approach does not contain the full answer. For what differentiates those who would join and remain from those who would not are not simply job features of this sort, but rather ingrained political and administrative practices and images.

Nevertheless, there is reason to believe that bureaucratic culture contains some dynamic elements and is unlikely to remain stagnant. Thus, in Israel it is apparent that there will be some tendency for the bureaucracy to draw substantially upon different types in the future than it currently employs, and that the impending changes in this regard may well be functional. Relatedly, patterns of propensity to exit indicate a degree of dynamism. Among the bureaucrats, it is those who are inner-oriented and feel most powerless who are most likely to desire to exit. The fact that Israel has been able to establish a bureaucracy which is most attractive as an employer to civil servants who are community-oriented and are able to resist organisational pressures which generate a high sense of powerlessness in others, is in itself encouraging. To the extent that such bureaucrats become more prevalent in the future, it would appear that the bureaucracy will play a more satisfactory role in the further development of the political community.

Finally, it is necessary to return to the theme of incongruence between the perceptions of citizens and bureaucrats. Here, as elsewhere in this study, the gap between the two groups is of importance. Bureaucrats tend to view the civil service as less politicised than does the average citizen. As individuals, they also report far less actual political interference with their work than either they, as a group, or the citizenry imagines. Yet the image of politicisation is a limitation on the bureaucracy's recruitment potential and militates against support for administrative action. This points, once again, therefore, to the necessity of establishing better communication between bureaucrats and the public, and even among the bureaucrats themselves. The possibilities of establishing such communication, and its functionality, are the subject of the concluding chapter.

Notes

1. See Robert K. Merton, 'Bureaucratic Structure and Personality', *Social Forces*, 18 (1940), 560-8, for an analysis.

2. Douglas McGregor, *The Human Side of Enterprise* (New York: McGraw-Hill, 1960). See also the 'human relations' approach which is conveniently outlined in Amital Etzioni, *Modern Organizations* (Englewood Cliffs: Prentice-Hall, 1964), ch. 4.

3. See among others, Melville Dalton, *Men Who Manage* (New York: Wiley, 1959), pp. 222-32, for a general discussion.

4. See George Berkley, *The Administrative Revolution* (Englewood Cliffs: Prentice Hall, 1971).

5. V.A. Pai Panandiker, 'Developmental Administration: An Approach', in Nimrod Raphaeli (ed.), *Readings in Comparative Public Administration* (Boston: Allyn & Bacon, 1967), p. 209.

6. Franklin P. Kilpatrick, Milton C. Cummings, Jr., M. Kent Jennings, *The Image of the Federal Service* (Washington: Brookings Institution, 1964), p. 7.

7. Samuel J. Eldersveld, V. Jagannadham, A.P. Barnabas, *The Citizen and the Administrator in a Developing Democracy* (Glenview: Scott, Foresman, 1968), pp. 1-2.

8. Ferrel Heady, *Public Administration: A Comparative Perspective* (Englewood Cliffs: Prentice-Hall, 1966), p. 70.

9. Kilpatrick *et al., Image of the Federal Service*, p. 244.

10. Ibid., p. 1.

11. Samuel Krislov, *Representative Bureaucracy* (Englewood Cliffs: Prentice-Hall, 1974), p. 4.

12. Felix Nigro, *Public Personnel Administration* (New York: Henry Holt, 1959), p. 155.

13. E. Pendleton Herring, *Federal Commissioners* (Cambridge: Harvard University Press, 1936), p. 5.

14. Krislov, *Representative Bureaucracy*, p. 4.

15. See Andrew Jackson, *The Correspondence of Andrew Jackson*, ed. J.S. Bassett (Washington: Carnegie Institution, 1926), vol. IV, p. 32, for a statement. See David H. Rosenbloom, *Federal Service and the Constitution* (Ithaca: Cornell University Press, 1971), ch. 2 for an analysis.

16. Carl Schurz, *Speeches, Correspondence, and Political Papers of Carl Schurz*, ed. F. Bancroft (New York: Putnam, 1913), vol. II, p. 123.

17. Editorial in *Harper's Weekly*, XXXVII, p. 614.

18. J. Donald Kingsley, *Representative Bureaucracy* (Yellow Springs: Antioch Press, 1944), p. 63.

19. See *The Chinese Civil Service*, ed. Johanna Menzel (Boston: D.C. Heath, 1963), p. vii.

20. Ibid.

21. Reform in the United States contributed to a change in the overall nature of national politics and a decline in the importance of political machines. However, it does not seem to have enabled social leaders such as the reformers to obtain high-level elective position. With regard to Great Britain, J.D. Kingsley wrote, 'I have been at some pains to show that the achievement of such a basic unity was a principal object of middle class reform of the Civil Service and that the reforms of 1855 and 1870 were eminently successful in this respect', *Representative Bureaucracy* (Yellow Springs: Antioch Press, 1944), p. 278.

22. See David H. Rosenbloom, 'The Civil Service Commission's Decision to Authorize the Use of Goals and Timetables in the Federal Equal Employment Opportunity Program', *Western Political Quarterly*, 26 (June 1973), 236-51.

23. Kilpatrick *et al., Image of the Federal Service*, p. 129.

24. See ibid., pp. 245-6, for a summary of the nature of women's more favourable dispositions towards the federal service.

25. For instance, blacks are more favourably disposed towards the federal

service than are whites. See ibid., pp. 88, 90, 96. See also L.D. White, *The Prestige Value of Public Employment In Chicago* (Chicago: University of Chicago Press, 1929) and *Further Contributions to the Prestige Value of Public Employment* (Chicago: University of Chicago Press, 1932).

26. See Y. Agassi, 'The Occupational Distribution of Women in Israel', *Labour and National Insurance*, 9 (September 1975), 283-8; and CSC, 'Women in the National Bureaucracy', ibid., 294-7 (in Hebrew).

27. Kilpatrick *et al., Image of the Federal Service*, p. 205.

28. Geoffrey Y. Cornog, 'The Personnel Turnover Concept: A Reappraisal', *Public Administration Review*, 17 (1957), p. 255.

29. Ibid.,

30. Kilpatrick *et al., Image of the Federal Service*, p. 188. It should be noted that these data are not fully comparable. There is a difference between preferences for exit and plans to exit. However, even when those in Kilpatrick's sample who were not sure if they planned to continue in the federal service, or responded in the 'don't know' category are added to those who planned to leave, Israeli bureaucrats, including statesmen, still express a much greater propensity to exit.

31. Honoré de Balzac, *Les Employés*, quoted in Martin Albrow, *Bureaucracy* (New York: Praeger, 1970), p. 18.

32. See among others, Charles M. Bonjean and Michael D. Grimes, 'Bureaucracy and Alienation: A Dimensional Approach', *Social Forces*, 48 (March 1970), 365-73.

33. See Rosenbloom, *Federal Service and the Constitution*, pp. 64-6; see also Fred W. Riggs, 'Bureaucrats and Political Development: A Paradoxical View', in Joseph LaPalombara (ed.), *Bureaucracy and Political Development* (Princeton: Princeton University Press, 1963), pp. 120-67.

34. Frederick C. Mosher, *Democracy and the Public Service* (New York: Oxford University Press, 1968), ch. 4, esp. p. 109.

35. See Marver Bernstein, *The Job of the Federal Executive* (Washington: Brookings Institution, 1958), p. 15.

8 CONCLUSION: BUREAUCRATIC CULTURE AND DEMOCRACY

The central question of this study has been 'with special reference to the nature of citizenship and the processes of nation-building, what are the political consequences of the bureaucratisation of public life in democratically-oriented political communities?' Having explored in some depth citizens' and bureaucrats' patterns of cognitive, affective, and evaluative orientations towards a national bureaucracy, and having compared these with findings obtained in a variety of political communities, we are now in a position to integrate two central themes running throughout this discussion and to provide some conclusions. One of these themes concerns the importance of incongruences between the orientations of citizens and civil servants, and the other involves the tensions between bureaucracy and democracy. They are related in that incongruence contributes to the difficulties of maintaining democracy in a bureaucratised political community.

Profiles among the Public

Our strategy for ascertaining the impact of bureaucratisation on the nature of citizenship has been to determine the ways in which citizens and civil servants relate to the bureaucratic form of organisation. This has been accomplished by constructing typologies which tap elements associated with bureaucracy that have been identified by organisational theorists as central to the nature of individual interaction with it. It is desirable now to bring these findings together by delineating profiles of the various types of citizens and bureaucrats. It should be borne in mind, as we do so, that these typologies are only loosely associated with such factors as socio-economic status, ethnicity, organisational rank and seniority, and even the frequency of contact with bureaucratic officials. Rather, they are the product of citizens' and bureaucrats' predispositions and perceptions towards highly salient features of bureaucratic organisation. Hence, although these typologies have not been constructed as an end in themselves, they nevertheless represent an important contribution to this study. Thus, it has been found that how an individual perceives a public bureaucracy with regard to its complexity and fairness is associated with almost all of his or her cognitive, affective, and evaluative orientations towards it. Similarly, among those who work in a national bureau-

cracy, the way in which the personnel system is viewed and the extent
to which individuals are community-oriented or inner-oriented are
associated with dispositions towards their organisation. This being the
case, there is little reason to believe that these typologies would not
have utility in other democratic political communities, although the
patterns of distribution among them might differ.

With reference to the general citizenry, the following profiles emerge:

1. Bureauphiles

These are the relatively well-adjusted clients of public bureaucracy and
the citizen-consumers of bureaucratic policy and action in a bureaucratised political community. They are more likely than other citizens to
attribute a considerable impact to the bureaucracy on the daily life of
the average citizen. They are also somewhat more likely to believe that
the bureaucracy has an important impact on the development of the
political community and the maintenance of democracy. Although somewhat negative in their evaluation of this impact, they are nevertheless
more positive in their characterisation of it than are other types of
citizens. Bureauphiles also feel considerably more efficacious with
regard to the bureaucracy and they are most inclined to use bureaucratic
channels in attempting to influence the course of its actions. In keeping
with these findings, they are also most positive in their overall evaluation
of public bureaucrats, and they have a somewhat greater propensity to
enter employment in the national bureaucracy. It is important to note
that bureauphiles are not characterised by an unthinking supportiveness
of the national bureaucracy; they are a long way from finding it totally
acceptable or desirable. However, relative to other citizens, their views
are indeed more sanguine. In short, perceiving the bureaucracy to be
intelligible and fair, bureauphiles feel better able to deal with it and
tend to see it in a more positive light.

2. Bureautics

These are the polar opposite of bureauphiles. In keeping with Thompson
and Gouldner's theories about them,[1] they are poorly adjusted to the
bureaucratisation of public life, and consequently are unable to play
effectively certain citizenship roles in the democratic political community.
They find bureaucracy to be complex and unfair, and in part this is due
to their difficulty in dealing with impersonal situations. Indeed, they
tend to view the bureaucracy as an unwelcome and threatening force in
polity and do not feel as able as other citizens to interact successfully
with it. Specifically, bureautics subjectively tend to reduce the impact

that the bureaucracy has on the life of the average citizen and on that of the nation. Their evaluation of its performance of nation-building roles is far more negative than that of other citizens. Thus, almost 60 per cent of them do not think that the bureaucracy and bureaucrats perform their functions well. Given their overall view of the bureaucracy, it is not surprising that, relative to other citizens, they feel a low sense of efficacy with regard to influencing its decisions and activities. Moreover, their aversion to bureaucracy is apparent in their rejection of bureaucratic channels as a means of influencing the national bureaucracy. Their overall image and evaluation of bureaucrats is also the most negative of any of the types and they are the least likely to express a preference for obtaining bureaucratic employment. In sum, then, bureautics constitute a categorical group of citizens who are poorly adjusted to the roles of public bureaucracy in a modernising polity. Consequently they have difficulty in coping with it and functioning as full citizens in a bureaucratised, democratic political system.

3. Bureautolerants

This type consistently falls in between the previous two. Sometimes their orientations are closer to those of bureauphiles and sometimes they are closer to bureautics. In general, however, it appears that bureautolerants, while sharing with other citizens a somewhat negative outlook concerning the national bureaucracy, are nevertheless receptive to bureaucracy and willing to accept it on its merits and reject it on its shortcomings. Unlike bureauphiles and bureautics, they are neither positively nor negatively predisposed towards bureaucracy, but rather believe it is either fair or at least something that is intelligible to them.

It should be pointed out that the between-types variance depends, to a certain extent, on the examined facet of bureaucracy. Nevertheless, it is rarely inconsequential. For example, variability is considerably greater with regard to feelings of bureaucratic efficacy than in relation to the overall image of the public bureaucrat. Furthermore, although other factors, such as education and ethnicity, may affect citizens' orientations towards public bureaucracy in some respects, these do not erase the impact of the central predispositions with which we are dealing. This suggests that although devices external to bureaucracy, such as education or non-bureaucratic channels for exercising influence over the bureaucracy, may exert a measurable impact on citizens' orientations, they are insufficient to generate vastly different perspectives, or to surmount major differences among the types. This observation is of considerable significance when addressing the tensions between bureaucracy and democracy. Before exploring its implications, however, we will briefly develop profiles of the public bureaucrats.

Profiles among the Bureaucrats

Although there have been several attempts to typologise public bureaucrats, none appears to be as comprehensive and empirically grounded as the one presented here. Ultimately, such typologies are desirable because they can serve to predict bureaucrats' attitudes and the nature of bureaucratic behaviour. Consequently, if they were related to on-the-job performance and if political, psychological, and social outlooks could be incorporated better into public personnel administration, it might eventually become possible to use such typologies not only as an analytical tool, but also for the selection of public administrators. Here, it has been found that four types of public bureaucrats are of importance to the concerns of bureaucratic culture. However, in contrast to the general citizenry, less consistency and more complexity is evidenced. We can profile our bureaucratic types in the following fashion:

1. Statesmen

This group is the most positive in its cognitive, affective, and evaluative orientations towards the Israeli bureaucracy. Statesmen are community-oriented and they believe that public personnel actions are based on merit and achievement. As such, they are in some respects the most desirable type of public bureaucrat. This is especially true from the perspectives of political and economic development, at least to the extent that their community orientation fosters effective bureaucratic participation in development roles, and in so far as their perception of the personnel system supports the kind of practices which they believe exist. Specifically, statesmen tend to believe more than any other type of bureaucrat that the bureaucracy has a great impact on the daily life of the average citizen, on national development, social integration, and on the maintenance of democratic government. Furthermore, they are the most likely to assess the character of these impacts in a positive fashion. Statesmen also feel the most efficacious with regard to influencing the course of bureaucratic activity and their overall evaluation and image of public bureaucrats is substantially more positive than those of the other groups. Finally, statesmen display a markedly lower propensity to leave their bureaucratic posts for positions elsewhere in society. Thus, they appear to be well adjusted to their organisational roles and the bureaucratic structure in which they are employed. As in the case of bureauphiles, they appear to be optimistic, but not over-sanguine concerning the bureaucracy.

2. Service Bureaucrats

This type is considerably more complex in its orientations and in some ways appears to be the least well adjusted to the bureaucracy as a work environment. Service bureaucrats are community-oriented. However, they believe that the personnel system is non-merit oriented and it appears that they consider bureaucratic structure, processes, and personnel to be obstacles to be overcome in their attempt to render effective public service. Hence, while relative to other types of bureaucrats they tend to believe that the bureaucracy has a great impact on the daily life of the average citizen, they also tend to view it as having less impact in the areas of nation-building and the maintenance of democracy. Moreover, their evaluation of the character of its impact is the most negative of any of the types. Their overall evaluation and image of the public bureaucrat also tends to be relatively negative, and they feel less efficacious with regard to the bureaucracy than any other type. On the other hand, with the exception of statesmen, they display the lowest propensity to exit the bureaucracy. Consequently, they appear to have a good deal in common with Presthus' 'ambivalents'.[2] They feel that, by and large, the bureaucracy is potentially an appropriate institution through which they can serve the public, but concurrently they believe that it does not enable them to do so adequately at the present time. They are at once tied to the organisation and highly critical of it—perhaps largely because of their perception of the personnel system.

3. Job Bureaucrats

This group is inner-oriented and perceives the personnel system to be merit-oriented. As in the case of service bureaucrats, their patterns of orientation are complex and less consistent than those of statesmen. Job bureaucrats tend to fall between statesmen and service bureaucrats in their overall orientations towards the bureaucracy. This is true with regard to the way in which they perceive and characterise its impact on nation-building and the maintenance of democracy and in connection with their overall evaluation and image of public bureaucrats. They are second only to statesmen in their feelings of bureaucratic efficacy. On the other hand, they display the second greatest propensity to seek employment outside the bureaucracy. Hence, they appear to be a categorical group which is oriented towards upward mobility and primarily concerned with its own advancement. From this perspective, job bureaucrats appear to be archtypical modern 'organisation men', who are loyal to and supportive of the organisation, but more interested in their own personal advancement than that of either their employer or the community at large.

4. Politicos

Although they are sometimes more positive in their orientations than are service bureaucrats, politicos tend to be the most negative type in their overall outlook on the national bureaucracy. They are the polar opposite of statesmen, being inner-oriented and viewing the personnel system as non-merit oriented. In their case there is every reason to believe that their perceptions of the personnel system influence their own behaviour, and it may be that politicos constitute a considerable proportion of the recipients of patronage who still staff some bureaucratic positions. With the possible exception of service bureaucrats, politicos appear to be least satisfied with their employment in the bureaucracy and they are the most likely to express a desire to leave it. Put simply, they do not consider the bureaucracy to be an effective instrument. They attribute to it the least impact on the daily life of the average citizen. They believe it has had little impact on nation-building and that its impact has been undesirable. Relatedly, their overall evaluation and image of bureaucratic personnel is the most negative of any of the groups. On the other hand, in comparison to service bureaucrats, they feel relatively efficacious in determining the bureaucracy's course. This may be a reflection of their perception of the personnel system and a tendency to act on the basis of political connections. Overall, politicos appear to be the least desirable of the types for a national bureaucracy upon which a political community is placing emphasis as a tool for fostering national development. Their negative orientations appear to be overly so; they are unsupportive of the bureaucracy, its personnel and activities; and their presence would almost certainly militate against a bureaucracy's effectiveness in contributing to modernisation.

It should be stressed that rank, which is perhaps the most salient aspect of one's position in a bureaucratic organisation, affects these types of bureaucrats in a differential manner. For example, in contrast to other higher-ranking civil servants, service bureaucrats in these ranks are markedly less likely to attribute to the bureaucracy a considerable impact on national development, social integration, and the maintenance of democracy. Similarly, unlike other high-ranking bureaucrats, politicos in the upper levels are somewhat less likely to feel highly efficacious than politicos in lower ranks. This emphasises the extent to which it is the type, rather than the rank, which is more strongly related to bureaucrats' patterns of orientation towards the Israeli bureaucracy.

Citizens and Bureaucrats

Having completed our profiles of types of citizens and bureaucrats, it is desirable to proceed one step further and to summarise the nature of the orientations of the average citizen and the average bureaucrat. Only then will it be possible to suggest ways in which some of the negative aspects of these orientations might be overcome.

It is evident that there is substantial incongruence between the orientations of Israeli citizens and Israeli civil servants towards their national bureaucracy. As a whole, Israeli citizens report that the bureaucracy has a considerable impact on their daily lives, that it is of high salience to them, and that they interact with it frequently. They also feel that it has a considerable impact on national development, social integration, and democracy, although less so with regard to the latter. Nevertheless, Israelis are overwhelmingly negative in their characterisation of the bureaucracy's impact in these areas. Moreover, they tend to dislike bureaucratic interaction, finding it characterised by 'red tape' and wasted time, and they are far more negative than positive in their characterisation of Israeli civil servants. At the same time, Israeli citizens tend to display a high sense of efficacy with regard to the bureaucracy and feel that there exist appropriate channels through which they can exercise influence over it. Although most feel that successfully influencing the course of the bureaucracy is unlikely, a sizable minority (30 per cent) believe that such success is at least moderately likely. These subjective characteristics of the Israeli general population are important from the perspectives of integrating bureaucracy with democracy. They suggest that Israelis feel a measure of control over their national bureaucracy. However, this interpretation is clouded by the fact that only a relatively small minority (17 per cent) have ever actually tried to influence the course of bureaucratic action. In view of their general evaluation of bureaucrats and the bureaucracy, the latter finding does not presage well for the achievement of such an integration. Finally, in contrast to some less developed nations, Israelis do not attach great prestige to civil service employment and about 35 per cent express a preference for joining the ranks of the bureaucracy. To some extent, the bureaucracy is unappealing as an employer because it is perceived to be politicised. In sum, then, Israelis find their national bureaucracy and its employees to be undesirable features of the political community, which have a considerable, yet largely unfavourable, impact on their lives.

The average Israeli bureaucrat, in contrast, is considerably more sanguine with respect to his or her orientations towards the national bureaucracy. On the whole, the civil servants tend to attribute to the bureaucracy a greater impact on the daily life of the nation. They also feel that it has had a greater impact on national development, the maintenance of democracy, and especially on the promotion of social integration. Moreover, the bureaucrats are far more positive in their characterisation of the bureaucracy's impact in these areas, and this is particularly the case in the higher ranks. In addition, although their overall evaluation and image of civil servants are more favourable than those of the general public, they are, nevertheless, somewhat more negative than positive. Relatedly, a large proportion of the bureaucrats express a desire to be employed outside the national bureaucracy, their propensity to exit is associated with a sense of powerlessness and, especially for those in the lower and middle ranks, perceived politicisation. At the same time, bureaucrats tend to feel more efficacious than the general population, tend to embrace more readily bureaucratic channels in attempting to exercise influence, tend to engage more often in actual attempts to affect the course of bureaucratic action, and tend to rate their chances of success at this as being greater. In general, then, Israeli civil servants are more supportive of bureaucratic personnel and action than is the general public, but nevertheless their characterisation of its activities, performance, and composition is largely unfavourable.

Bureaucracy and Democracy

These incongruences between and among the bureaucrats and the public are of importance to the establishment of a 'democratically balanced' national bureaucracy and to its integration with other elements of the political system. By and large, among the public the bureaucracy is seen as a salient, negative, and non-democratic force in the life of the political community. In terms of a 'democratically balanced' public administration it is clear that the orientations of the bureaucrats are closer to the ideal, although they too may fall considerably short. It will be recalled that such a balance consists of the following elements: (1) widespread knowledge about the bureaucracy; (2) a feeling that the public's self-interest is being served by the bureaucracy; (3) a feeling that the bureaucracy provides equal treatment, and (4) the bureaucracy must have an adequate prestige value. As will be discussed shortly, the theorising of many would suggest that more interaction between citizens and bureaucrats in a participatory sense might tend to diminish the extent to which the Israeli public does not

meet these criteria for democratic balance. Yet, while citizen participation has emerged as a potential and practical contribution to the
democratisation of bureaucracy and to the minimisation of such incongruences between policy-maker and policy-consumer, our analysis of
bureaucratic culture suggests that it is only one technique for reducing
the more general tension between the bureaucratisation of public life
and the maintenance of democratic political communities. Other
elements in such an endeavour would have to include: (1) a high level
of social representation; (2) participatory decision-making within a
bureaucracy, and (3) the participation of public bureaucrats in national
debate over public policy choices. Before expounding upon these
elements and indicating how the present study supports their utilisation,
other 'grand designs' for bureaucratic reform should be reviewed briefly
in order to place our call for 'participatory bureaucracy' into perspective.

A. The Spoils System

The nature of the tension between bureaucracy and democracy was
discussed in chapter 1. Essentially, the question is one of simultaneously
ensuring that a public bureaucracy will be reasonably efficient and responsive to the citizenry of a democratic political community. The former,
although often immeasurable, is a determinant of the effectiveness of
any modern government; and the latter is necessary for the maintenance
of democracy in a highly bureaucratised polity. To date, there have been
three major and a few minor attempts at achieving these goals. The first
major attempt to come to grips with this problem in a democratic polity
came under the presidency of Andrew Jackson in the United States.
Prior to his inauguration in 1829, public administration was effective
and efficient, but also dominated by elites and unrepresentative of the
general population. Jackson called for a rotation of office-holders, which
he considered to be 'a leading principle in the republican creed'[3] and
one which would provide 'healthful action to the system'.[4] He argued
that the entrenchment of bureaucrats led to their corruption, especially
in the sense of their irresponsibility to political authorities and the
citizenry. He concluded, therefore, that 'more is lost by the long con-
tinuance of men in office than is generally to be gained by their
experience'.[5] The spoils system contributed to the democratisation of
the bureaucracy and the political community. For example, it encouraged the growth of strong political parties by enabling them to reward
their faithful followers with public service jobs and to finance themselves indirectly through the public treasury by levying assessments on
the salaries of public employees. During this period of United States

history, the partisanship of the presidency changed more frequently than in any other, political participation was relatively high, and democratic attitudes and social practices took firmer hold in the society at large.

However, as democracy thrived in conjunction with Jacksonian administrative practices, administration itself faltered. To some extent administration did fit better the democratic character of the polity at the time. Selection and promotion were more democratic in the sense that they were determined by elected political authorities. Consequently, bureaucrats were more likely to reflect the political attitudes and values of a majority of the population. The bureaucracy also became more representative in a social sense.[6] Nevertheless, Jackson's reforms did not achieve his ostensible goal of increasing the efficiency of the public service. Spoils created a great deal of administrative instability and discontinuity. Instability, in turn, contributed to corruption and inefficiency. In addition, democracy was mitigated by coercion of federal employees to engage in political activity and to contribute to campaign funds. Eventually, however, as public policy in the United States became more regulatory and involved greater penetration of the society by the bureaucracy, the corruption and inefficiency associated with the spoils system became too much to bear and a second kind of reform was instituted.

B. Civil Service Reform

For the most part, civil service reform in the United States shared the characteristics of such reform movements in other democratic political communities and is illustrative of a second 'grand design' for simultaneously achieving bureaucratic responsiveness and efficiency, and thereby fostering the integration of bureaucracy and democracy. As elsewhere, the introduction of the merit system in the United States was aimed not only at the reform of the civil service, but rather at a transformation of the political system as a whole.[7] However, on the level of administration itself, the reformers argued that merit selection and merit tenure would ensure an efficient and effective public service. Yet in and of themselves, merit systems do nothing to ensure that such a civil service will be politically responsive. Indeed, so vulnerable were the civil service reformers in the United States on this point that they argued that political responsiveness was unnecessary because politics had no place in public administration. As Woodrow Wilson expressed it, 'administrative questions are not political questions'.[8] In the reformers' view, in so far as it was articulated, political direction could be achieved through the strict subordination of administrators to the federal Congress and the political executive. While their dichotomy between politics and administration may have made sense during certain periods of United States history, it does not provide a useful description of the nature of public administration in any developed or developing political community today. Politics inevitably enters administration; administrators make policy; and the *means* by which they choose to implement it and the policies established by others are themselves often intensely political. Consequently, while merit reforms can improve the efficiency of a public bureaucracy, and depending on the political and social circumstances may even make it more representative, they nevertheless do not provide a satisfactory guarantee of political responsiveness. In fact, spoils systems along the Jacksonian lines are far stronger in the latter regard.

C. Scientific Management

Another 'grand design', like that of merit reforms, tended to be international in character. The Scientific Management Movement[9] and its aftermath had much in common with merit reforms but went further in attempting to secure efficiency, perhaps because its proponents had fewer ulterior political motives. They sought smooth-running, efficient production and organisation. With regard to public bureaucracies, Scientific Management urged an institutionalisation of the dichotomy between politics and administration through proper organisation. Its advocates believed that politics and administration are two heterogeneous functions which cannot be combined without inefficiency.[10] In their view, politics interfered with the efficient organisation of public bureaucracy, and they became

> preoccupied with the anatomy of Government organization and concerned primarily with arrangements to assure that (1) each function is assigned to its appropriate niche within the Government structure; (2) component parts of the executive branch are properly related and articulated; and (3) authorities and responsibilities are clearly assigned.[11]

Such a mode of organisation would not only be more efficient, but it would contribute to the broad direction of administration by political executives. In the United States, this logic was expressed by the Brownlow Commission,[12] which advocated a consolidation of the executive branch and the establishment of organisational units which would enable the President to control, direct, and co-ordinate the bureaucracy.

The President would become the manager-in-chief and other political elements would be largely excluded from the organisation and operation of the federal bureaucracy.

Although the Scientific Management approach made contributions to the rational organisation of public administration and to its direction by political authorities, it nevertheless failed to come to grips with bureaucratic politics and the extent to which administrative agencies wield influence over their politically appointed heads. It has also led to the mistaken belief that it is possible to 'resolve deepseated and intractable issues of substance by reorganization'.[13] Moreover, its emphasis on structure, hierarchy, and the division of labour sometimes militated against efficiency. Hence, while the Scientific Management approach offered some help in the effort to resolve the tension between responsiveness and efficiency, its utility has been limited by an inadequate understanding of the extent to which administration is infused with political questions and of the divergence between formal organisational arrangements and informal realities.

D. Limited Approaches

None of the 'grand designs' addressed to the achievement of political responsiveness and efficiency in public bureaucracies in democratic political communities has been fully satisfactory. While merit reforms have contributed to efficiency and Scientific Management approaches have fostered rational organisation and better political direction, few if any democratic nations have totally escaped the overall dilemma. For example, in Western Europe the integration of public bureaucracies into political systems and political communities has produced mixed patterns, perhaps, as Chapman observes, because 'in every country the increase in public services has not been accompanied by sufficient serious thought as to the best way to absorb them into the structure of the modern state'.[14] Thus, in Italy and France problems of inefficiency and unresponsiveness are relatively acute. In Chapman's words, 'The Italian . . . considers his public services to be venal and sporadically corrupt. He believes they are sometimes manipulated for private advantage and used as arenas for political manoeuvering. The services are regarded as inefficient, dogmatic, and obscurantist.'[15] Although the French public service is better in this regard, nevertheless, 'At regular intervals publicists, journalists, and jurists devote themselves to bitter attacks on the plethora of public officials, their dilatoriness, their red tape, their brusqueness, their abuse of office'.[16] In terms of responsiveness, it has been observed that it 'would seem . . . that the French bureaucracy remains as impervious to control as it always was. This, however, is not entirely the case, because political control over the bureaucracy has changed under the Fifth Republic in one very important respect: when a minister has been determined to push through a reform opposed by his civil servants he has usually been able to win, though not without conflict and even crisis'.[17] With the exception of West Germany, elsewhere in Western Europe public officials are largely accepted in a somewhat contemptuous and distrusting fashion. In nations such as Denmark and Belgium, civil servants remain aloof and consider themselves the guardians of state and public interest, if not the state itself.[18] Elsewhere in the democratic world comparable patterns can be found.

In the United States, where the federal bureaucracy is often charged by political authorities and politicians with inefficiency and unresponsiveness, where the bureaucracy suffers from a lack of legitimacy as a fullfledged partner in the government, and where all of the 'grand designs' have run their course, a number of more limited practices and processes have somewhat reduced the tension between responsiveness and efficiency. To an extent, these are illustrative of related developments in other democratic political communities. Among these practices has been the use of 'in and outers', or high-level business executives and professionals who go back and forth between government and private employment, or who accept public assignments for relatively brief periods of time. It is generally thought that such people contribute expertise and special skills to government management and administration, and within the political context of the United States, they certainly tend to lend legitimacy to it. They also tend to infuse public bureaucracies with values representative of those dominant in the private sphere and make it more cognisant of the attitudes and ideas prevalent in the areas from which they come. Thus, 'in and outers' may increase efficiency and political responsiveness, at least to a particular segment of the population. However, one of the costs of this process is 'making conflict-of-interest a principle of government'.[19]

Another element contributing to efficiency and greater political responsiveness has been the politics of pluralism, both in its traditional and 'interest group liberal' version.[20] The assumption here has been that public bureaucracies can be structured to advance the politics of interest waged through competition. In the classical conception, interest groups would state their needs and preferences before government agencies, which acting as impartial and expert judges would adopt the policies best suited to the public interest. Presumably such a system maximises the amount of information available to administrators in making their decisions. In the interest group liberal conception, in contrast, government agencies are not considered impartial judges, but rather advocates of the causes of special interests. In this view, agencies are essentially captured by interest groups and become part of policy-interest complexes, such as a 'military-industrial complex'. Although both of these models are descriptive of some elements of bureaucratic politics in democratic nations such as the United States and Israel, and can increase efficiency and responsiveness through the participation of relevant groups in policy-making processes, neither is fully satisfactory. Not all segments of a citizenry have an equal opportunity or ability to organise or to be effectively represented by interest groups or complexes. A lack of competition often characterises the nature of the relationships among interest groups, which indeed is why they tend to blend into complexes. Moreover, as McConnell has effectively argued, groups and complexes tend to represent pertinent populations only on narrow levels of interest, and generally ignore wider elements in their political thinking.[21]

Towards a 'Participatory Bureaucracy'

This review of 'grand designs' and more limited approaches aimed at the simultaneous maximisation of political responsiveness and efficiency in the public bureaucracies of democratic polities suggests that both singularly and collectively they have been insufficient. Furthermore, our analysis of citizens' orientations towards a national bureaucracy throughout this study has indicated that changes external to a bureaucracy, such as increasing the average level of educational achievement in a society, are likely to have only a modest impact at best on individuals' patterns of reactions towards the bureaucratisation of public life. Consequently, it appears that reforms directed towards greater efficiency and responsiveness will have to be instituted in bureaucracies themselves, despite the inadequacies of past attempts along these lines. At the present time the most promising reforms of this nature are those which we have referred to under the label of 'participatory bureaucracy'. They have emerged to an extent in several democratic political communities, especially the United States and some Western European nations. The movement towards 'participatory bureaucracy' stresses social representation, more participatory decision-making within the bureaucracy, a more participatory role for public employees in the political life of the community, and greater participation by ordinary citizens in bureaucratic policy-formulation. Taking up these items in their respective order, it can be seen that there is an internal logic to them; that their utility is supported not only by our own findings, but by the theoretical

propositions and empirical observations of others as well; and that while
there is no fully participatory public bureaucracy in existence, some of
these elements have been incorporated into several national bureaucracies.

A. Representation

The arguments in favour of a socially representative bureaucracy have
already been dealt with at some length and require only brief reiteration
here. Basically, it is urged that the more socially representative a public
bureaucracy is the more in tune it will be with the norms, values, and
attitudes of the political community; the better able it will be to bind all
groups to the policies and procedures emanating from it; and therefore,
the more efficient and responsive it will be with regard to the implementation and formulation of policies for dealing with the most pressing
problems facing the political community. It has long been argued that
efficient public bureaucracies can only be effectively integrated with
modern democratic governments if they are 'at all points sensitive to
public opinion'.[22] Social representation is often viewed as one way of
institutionalising such a sensitivity. Our findings strongly support this
approach. Although, as discussed in chapter 6, there has been some
dispute over the existence of a connection between social representation
in public bureaucracies and their policy outputs, this study, as well as
others, indicates that becoming and being a bureaucrat do not necessarily erase the impact of ethnicity and other social characteristics on
one's political and social attitudes. Thus, it will be recalled that the
perspectives of Israelis of Asian-African background differ considerably
from those of other Israelis both within the general population and within the bureaucracy, and that there is substantial congruence between
the views of Asian—African citizens and those of their 'social representatives' in the civil service. Moreover, despite the fact that higher rank
tends to militate against this congruence, it does not eradicate it in
areas of high salience to the particularistic perspectives of the Asian—
African community. Indeed, because 'real-world' bureaucracies never
completely manifest the conditions of the ideal type bureaucracy, they
always include a human element (in contrast to total dehumanisation or
impersonality), and therefore it is to be expected that perspectives
associated with social group will not be obliterated by bureaucratic
structure and process. As a matter of fact, in some countries such as the
United States, a stress on social representativeness follows partly from a
realisation that although public bureaucracies may be partisanly neutral,
they can rarely be politically neutral in a wider sense. Once this is con-

ceded, and as the political role of public bureaucracy expands, an increasing emphasis is placed on making it a representative institution which will reflect the character of the community at large. In democracies, it seems the absence of neutrality requires representation. But will a socially representative public bureaucracy also be representative in an active sense? In large part this depends upon the extent to which an opportunity is provided for 'social representatives' to express their views and to participate in policy-making. This, then, leads to the second and third elements of 'participatory bureaucracy'.

B. *'Organisational Democracy'*

The next feature of 'participatory bureaucracy' entails (1) fully-fledged participation by middle-level civil servants in general bureaucratic policy-making, and (2) the participation of all employees in decisional processes involving the organisation of work and the nature of public personnel administration. Taking the latter element first, it has been argued increasingly that expanding the role of rank and file employees in the structuring of work-processes and the formulation of personnel procedures tends to produce greater efficiency. Moreover, there are now enough advocates, analyses, and successful examples of this approach to lead some to conclude that in the workplace, at least, 'democracy is inevitable'.[23] Although arguments in favour of this approach are diverse and too plentiful to review in their entirety, they may nevertheless be readily summarised. Basically, the impetus for democratisation of organised work can be traced back to the well-known Hawthorne experiments (Western Electric Researches).[24] It was demonstrated there and subsequently by those associated with the early Human Relations Approach,[25] that productivity could be increased by involving employees in decisions concerning the organisation of work processes, allowing them to develop self-leadership, encouraging the development of informal groups among employees, and by avoiding strict and punitive supervision. More recently, such an approach has been advocated by such organisational theorists as Douglas McGregor, George Berkley, and Warren Bennis,[26] to name but a few. In *The Human Side of Enterprise*, for example, McGregor argues that 'traditional' management practices of direction and control, whether of the 'hard', 'soft' or 'firm-but-fair' varieties, simply fail to generate adequate commitment to organisational objectives in a developed and affluent society. Drawing upon Maslow's concept of a hierarchy of needs, he concludes that traditional management fails because direction and control are unsatisfactory methods of motivating people whose physiological and safety needs are reasonably

satisfied and whose social, egoistic and self-fulfilment needs are pre-
dominant. McGregor called traditional and more authoritarian management practices, 'theory X', and contrasted them with 'theory Y'. In his
view, motivation, efficiency, and productivity are increased where
employees are participative and management is consultative, power
and responsibility are decentralised, despecialisation (job enlargement)
is emphasised, and employee evaluation is primarily self-evaluation.

In speculating about the nature of organisations of the future, Bennis
also concludes that they will be more participative. Hitting upon many
of the same points as McGregor, he argues that hierarchy and specialisation, as they now exist, will be replaced:

> People will be differentiated not vertically, according to rank and
> role, but flexibly and functionally according to skill and professional
> training.
>   Adaptive, problem-solving, temporary systems of diverse special-
> ists linked together by co-ordinating and task evaluating specialists in
> an organic flux—this is the organizational form that will gradually re-
> place bureaucracy as we know it.[27]

Berkley, who is in general agreement with the 'theory Y' and Bennis
approaches, is more empirical in his orientation. He cites several examples
of 'the new administration at work'.[28] These include several private
firms in the United States and elsewhere, but even more impressive are
the general patterns emerging in some European democracies. Berkley
writes,

> Both Sweden and West Germany, along with Norway and Holland,
> have enacted laws giving workers the right to elect representatives to
> the boards of directors of their companies. West Germany at the
> start of 1974 was preparing new legislation to enlarge this right. It
> would allow employees of the [country's] 650 largest firms to elect
> half of the directors of these companies.[29]

Presently, Sweden is considering legislation which 'would give workers
a share in virtually all the decisions private industry has traditionally
reserved for management—from the appointment of directors to pricing
policies and mergers'.[30] Nor are such examples confined to the private
sector.

In the United States and France, two countries which have been somewhat resistant to the 'theory Y' and related participative approaches, sig-

nificant steps have been taken to afford public employees a greater input into the organisation of work processes and personnel administration. In Berkley's words, 'Even France, a country not known for having highly developed democratic institutions, has what are called round table commissions in most government departments. Consisting half of employee representatives, these commissions make decisions on promotions and dismissals within their own administrative units.'[31] In the United States, the 1960s saw the development of a whole new era with regard to labour relations in the federal service. Prior to that time, there was little support for and much opposition to the development of effective labour organisations and participatory labour relations in the government. In 1962, however, President Kennedy issued an executive order which provided for labour organisations which would have the right to '. . . be represented at discussions between management and employees or employee representatives concerning grievances, personnel policies and practices, or other matters affecting general working conditions . . . [and to] meet at reasonable times [with agency representatives] and confer with respect to personnel policy and practices'.[32] In addition, federal employees were given greater protection in adverse actions and a larger opportunity to participate in grievance proceedings.[33] Although the specific procedures governing the new relationship between rank and file federal employees and agency management have undergone almost continuous modifications, it is clear that unions currently play a greater role than ever before in determining the nature of working conditions and personnel practices in the federal service. Moreover, they have provided a base upon which advocates of greater participation have attempted to '. . . organize employees around their work grievances, and, from the institutional base of a strong organization of workers, to seek changes in their agencies' working conditions, personnel practices, and substantive policies'.[34] Significant examples of a more participatory approach have also taken place in the actual organisation of work in some bureaus, particularly those of the Social Security Administration.[35]

Other examples could be cited as well and the trend in Western democratic political communities is clear. Greater worker participation in such matters is virtually inevitable, and while part of its inevitability stems from democratic values and the influence of organised labour in industrialised democratic nations, its inroads have also been largely due to its contributions to efficiency and productivity in a technological age. Our analysis of bureaucratic culture supports the rationality of this trend. Although participation in personnel matters is prevalent in Israel, it is not as developed as elsewhere, and there is little effective participation in the organisation of public service work, at least in the civilian sector. By and large, labour relations in the Israeli bureaucracy tend to centre around bargaining between the Civil Service Commission and the civil service unions, and there is little interaction between employees and their individual supervisors concerning the structuring of work or the nature of personnel matters. The findings presented here suggest that the Israeli bureaucracy pays a considerable price for this.

Israeli bureaucrats do not agree on the specific characteristics of the bureaucracy as a work environment, but they are largely dissatisfied with it. At the most general level, a very sizable proportion express a desire to leave the bureaucracy for employment elsewhere. Their overall image of the 'public bureaucrat' is largely negative. These aspects of bureaucrats' orientations towards the institution in which they are employed are symptomatic of serious personnel and organisational problems. Inevitably they are costly in terms of low morale, inadequate efficiency, and turnover. While we have not explored fully the roots of the bureaucrats' dissatisfaction, but rather concentrated our efforts on those elements which are of political relevance, it is evident that at least two of the major factors which contribute to employee dissatisfaction could be largely overcome by more participatory management and personnel relations. Among the important antecedents of the propensity to exit the Israeli bureaucracy are a feeling of powerlessness and a rejection of politicisation, in several senses. It has often been observed that a sense of powerlessness on the part of those who are 'harnessed' to the bureaucratic 'machine' can grow out of the clash between bureaucratic norms and Western values. For example, as noted in chapter 1, there are pressures on bureaucrats to be passive, subordinate, conformist, and dependent, both psychologically and otherwise, on superordinates. These pressures run contrary to Western individualism and concepts of freedom, and within the context of Western culture, at least, they militate against the development of a healthy adult personality.[36] Greater participation by rank and file bureaucrats in the structuring of work and in personnel matters, however, as Berkley and others observe, tends to counteract these pressures and feelings of powerlessness. In fact, participatory management has been found to reduce personnel turnover and other organisational pathologies associated with personality adaptation.[37]

The relationship between politicisation and propensity to exit is somewhat more complex because it is strongly affected by rank. Politicisation is less repulsive to bureaucrats in the higher ranks, and it is only in the middle and lower levels that it is markedly associated with a desire to obtain employment outside the bureaucracy. This is true whether politicisation is viewed as interference by politicians in the work of civil servants or is defined in terms of the role that non-achievement-oriented factors play in promotions. In either case, it is apparent that more participatory management would tend to overcome the repercussions of perceived politicisation. Employees would have a greater role in the structuring of work and this would make political interference more difficult, or at least more palatable. Affording rank and file civil servants greater input to personnel administration would inevitably place further limitations on politicisation and would tend towards the diminution of the gap between the depoliticised form and the more politicised reality. Moreover, in the Israeli context, greater participation in these matters would generate better communication among employees and would thereby tend to make the image of political interference more congruent with the reality. It will be recalled in this connection that although many Israeli bureaucrats believe that politicians interfere with their colleagues' work, a considerably lesser proportion have actually experienced such intrusions.

Greater employee participation in policy-making is another aspect of this feature of 'participatory bureaucracy', but one which has been less advanced. Although theoretical propositions and empirical analyses are less prevalent in this area, it is nevertheless possible to construct an argument for greater internal participation in policy-making and to cite some examples of its application. At the heart of this approach is the belief that public bureaucracies make and implement public policy and that policy made democratically, as opposed to hierarchically, will be more satisfactory. This is because it will be more pluralistic in its representation of perspectives and values. This is especially true where a bureaucracy is highly representative in a social sense as it would allow 'social representatives' a greater opportunity to become active representatives. Moreover, where democratic values are strong, policy that is democratically developed will also be considered more legitimate.[38] In a sense though, the converse of this argument is even stronger. Democracy may not always yield effective policy, but hierarchical policy-making has even more serious disadvantages. Hierarchy tends towards elitism and offers no guarantee that the elite will be responsive to either the public at large or to political authorities. Hierarchy also contradicts such basic democratic values as egalitarianism and respect for the dignity of the individual. It places greater value on the opinions of some on the basis of status rather than content, whereas democracy assumes that all citizens are competent to develop and articulate political ideas. Furthermore, hierarchy militates against a free and open exchange of ideas and information, and given that middle-level employees often have a great deal of expertise and knowledge concerning the policy arenas in which they work, it may thereby critically weaken the quality of input to decisional processes. Finally, in some political systems, such as the United States, hierarchy stands contrary to dominant political practices because it concentrates power rather than fragments it. In short, only by opening up policy-making processes to participation by middle-level employees can information, the diversity of ideas and values, including those stemming from social background, adherence to democratic values, and legitimacy be maximised and elitist, non-democratic tendencies minimised.

Some participation along these lines exists in Western Europe and there is a movement in its direction in the United States. With regard to the former, Berkley writes, 'As for the public sector, worker participation in many areas of policy formulation and decision-making has also gone forward. In Great Britain, West Germany and Scandinavia, rank-and-file representatives sit on a variety of policy boards and commissions throughout their respective bureaucracies.'[39] In the United States Federal Service, both management and employee organisations support such an approach, although there are important differences between them. Thus, a one-time executive director of the US Civil Service Commission, the government's central personnel agency, wrote: 'The more complex the system, the larger is the proportion (not just the absolute number) of its members who make professional contributions and participate in policy formulation and decision-making. Participative management, in this relative sense, is coming less from behavioral science theory than from the intrinsic requirements of business and complexity.'[40] In addition, during the late 1960s, a protest movement arose within the ranks of the federal service. At its core was the proposition that middle-level employees should have more influence in the determination of public policy. One organisation advocating such a state of affairs, Federal Employees for a Democratic Society, provided a vision of how the federal bureaucracy might operate under its programme. Among its major characteristics were:

1. Employees would have a voice in the basic policy formulation of their agency and in decisions affecting the programs they administer and conditions under which they work . . .

2. Privileges of class and status should be eliminated wherever they create barriers among workers . . .

    3. The hierarchy within the Federal Bureaucracy must be reduced to a minimum . . .

    4. Workers should be allowed to refuse to perform work which is contrary to their consciences or their sense of justice . . . [41]

Moreover, in at least one instance, the participatory ideal was nearly approached in an institutionalised fashion. In 1970, the Secretary of Health, Education, and Welfare, Robert Finch, agreed to discuss his personal leadership, department priorities, and national policies with 600 HEW employees. The discussion was to be carried by closed-circuit television to the cafeterias in HEW buildings in the Washington metropolitan area. It never came about, however, because Finch was taken ill and subsequently resigned his post in favour of one in the Executive Office of the President.[42]

Our findings suggest that several aspects of participation in the sense being described would be beneficial. We have seen that there are distinct types of bureaucrats with different predispositions and orientations towards the Israeli bureaucracy, its roles, performance, and personnel. It has also been observed that members of different social groups have divergent patterns of perceptions, beliefs, and attitudes towards bureaucracy. In some instances, it has been found that rank affects all bureaucrats in a uniform direction, whereas in others it affects them differentially. It stands to reason, therefore, that much is to be gained by including different types of bureaucrats, members of different social groups, and those holding diverse positions in the bureaucratic hierarchy in policy-making processes. Such participation would increase the diversity of perspectives brought to bear upon decisions, it would enhance the ability of 'social representatives' to represent actively the groups from which they come, and would add an element of 'built-in pluralism' to policy-making. In addition, with specific reference to the Israeli case, participation along these lines would help overcome some of the incoherence of the bureaucracy as an institution by increasing communication and the information available to middle- and upper-level bureaucrats. While it might be dysfunctional for bureaucrats to have uniform outlooks on all subjects of political importance, it would nevertheless improve the performance of the Israeli bureaucracy if its members were able to develop a greater degree of agreement and clarity on its proper place in the process of nation-building. As it stands now, some bureaucrats are advocates of further bureaucratic action, whereas others, and especially those in the middle and lower ranks, express minimal support for the bureaucracy's performance in this area. Inevitably, such diversity must contribute to important differences in the content of policy as well as the pace and tone of its implementation by different bureaus and agencies. This, in turn, contributes to the uneven character of political and economic development found in the political community, and means that the development of some sectors is restrained by the relative lack of development in others. Greater participation in policy-making by middle-level employees would at once tend to bind them to the policies adopted, enhance the pace of their implementation, and also provide higher-ranking bureaucrats with a better understanding of what is technically and organisationally feasible. As a result, it could be expected that eventually bureaucrats would develop a more coherent and uniform level of support for bureaucratic action, and this, consequently, would lead to more even administration.

C. Participation in Public Debate

The next feature of 'participatory bureaucracy' is that bureaucrats be allowed and even encouraged to contribute freely to public debate on matters of public policy. From the perspectives of bureaucratic culture this would have several beneficial effects. It would provide citizens with better knowledge about the operation, character, and perspectives of the national bureaucracy and its personnel. This would tend to reduce the degree of incongruence between the orientations of citizens and civil servants towards the bureaucracy. As such, it would be especially important where radically different orientations tend towards the perceptual isolation of bureaucrats and engender markedly different understandings of the bureaucracy's roles and character. In addition, it would enable the 'social representatives' of all groups, but especially those which are disadvantaged, to communicate better with their 'constituencies', and this would often tend to bind the latter more fully to the bureaucracy and to policies emanating from it.

In terms of democracy and the establishment of a 'democratically balanced' public administration, participation along these lines is potentially of great importance. At the broadest level, civil servants can play a substantial role in the political and administrative 'enlightenment' of the political community. The latter, of course, is generally considered a prerequisite to effective democracy. Thus, as noted earlier, it has been argued that 'the special kind of practical wisdom that characterizes the civil servant points to a more fundamental political function of the bureaucracy, namely to bring to bear on public policy its distinctive view of the common good or its way of looking at questions about the common good'.[43] More specifically, middle- and higher-level public employees tend to have a good deal of technical knowledge about what is feasible and how it may be obtained, they are more politically neutral in a partisan sense than most public officials, and they often know more than anyone else about the programmes and policies they implement. They may also be knowledgeable about the formulation of these policies and have an extensive understanding of their intent. As a result, they are in a unique position to contribute to public debate and to encourage a more informed public opinion to develop. They have the expertise, the facts, and often the detached outlook which can enable them to become a significant counterforce to inaccurate, misleading or meaningless political rhetoric and news management techniques. Their participation in public debate would offer a counterweight to that tendency towards the devitalisation and degeneration of democratic political systems which stems from a belief that the electorate cannot really judge policy options or the actions of politicians because they do not have enough information about them. The latter view encourages uninformed citizen participation through voting based upon the candidates' apparent personalities and upon vague statements about the political good and how it can be attained. In a very real sense, only civil servants and national statesmen are in a position to mitigate these tendencies.

It is interesting to note that some have urged such a role for bureaucrats upon their departure from the public service. Indeed, it has been argued that the executive branch of the United States would be strengthened by

the planting and rooting of a tradition of getting out [of the bureaucracy] and speaking out in a society and political system that have heretofore discouraged such behavior. Only through the development of such a tradition can the individual conscience be freed to act as a brake against the tyranny inherent in the American Presidential state and its ideology, the national security ethic.[44]

Yet this logic applies equally well to those civil servants who are intent upon continuing in their positions, and, in the United States at least, there have been a good number of examples of this phenomenon. For example, federal employees have taken open stands concerning civil rights policies and the United States military involvement in South-east Asia.[45] Although it might be argued that participation of this nature would impair the implementation of disputed policy and damage relationships among public employees, this does not seem to have been the case, even where employees were critical of their own agency's role in policy formulation. However, even if participation of this nature did have dysfunctional consequences along these lines, it could be viewed from the more optimistic perspective of breaking down the notion that a national bureaucracy is monolithic and thereby enhancing citizen control over it by providing information about the divisions within it.

D. Citizen Participation

Finally, 'participatory bureaucracy' requires citizen participation in bureaucratic policy-making. This is especially true of those citizens who are affected most by bureaucratic decisions in any given policy area, but in principle it applies in other cases as well. In recent years, the Western world has seen a resurgence of interest in participatory democracy. Much of this concern has centred on public bureaucracies, which have taken on more and more policy-making functions in recent decades as legislatures have atrophied. The arguments in favour of participatory democracy can be found in the writings of several political philosophers. Rousseau, for example, cites three benefits of citizen participation in government.[46] First, it plays an educative role which makes the citizen community-regarding and more aware of the needs and feelings of others. Second, it increases the value that a citizen attaches to political freedom because it provides citizens with a greater sense of their own freedom and more awareness of its utility. Third, participation plays an integrative function and gives the citizen a sense of belonging with regard to the political community. Another advantage was identified by Aristotle. Citizens are consumers of government policy, and it is sometimes the wearer rather than the creator who knows best where the 'policy shoe' pinches.[47] Overall then, it has been forcefully argued that participation makes both citizens and government officials more sensitive human beings, with a greater degree of civic maturity, toleration of others, and commitment to policy and community.

Citizen participation in bureaucratic policy-making also has distinct advantages from the perspectives of bureaucratic culture. As noted earlier, it would contribute to a 'democratically balanced' public administration by increasing knowledge about the bureaucracy, generating an impression that, collectively, the public's interest is being served by the bureaucracy, and by providing the feeling that, as individuals, citizens are treated equally. In addition, it would tend towards the reduction of incongruence between the orientations of civil servants and citizens towards a national bureaucracy. This, in turn, would diminish the tensions, misunderstandings, absence of support, and bureaucratic isolation which almost inevitably would follow from marked incongruence. Bureaucrats would learn to see themselves more as others view them, and citizens would view the bureaucrat in a more educated and realistic fashion. Impersonality in the sense of equal treatment of those in equivalent categories would not be replaced, but impersonality in the sense of bureaucratic organisation which does not express concern for the plight of its individual clients and consumers would be modified. Moreover, as citizens learned more about bureaucratic procedures, personnel, approaches, and perspectives, they would become better able to accept and play the kind of citizenship roles demanded of them by bureaucratised democratic political communities. Thus, participation would enable bureautics, the categorical group least able to deal with the bureaucracy, to overcome some of their lack of understanding of that form of organisation and to relate better to impersonality. In short, citizens and bureaucrats would become more knowledgeable about each other, and more responsive to each other's needs.

In this area as in the others, there have been several examples of the kind of participation under discussion. In the United States, for example, such participation has taken three major forms, only one of which does not have a long history. First, there are citizens' committees which act as advisory groups. These generally involve occupational groups, such as farmers, or areas of production, such as mining and metals. In some instances government agencies are required by law to consult with such bodies.[48] In the view of some, this form of participation tends to work to the advantage of the wealthier, more powerful units or segments of an economic sphere.[49] At the same time, however, few would deny that these practices have in fact made the government more responsive to external influences.

A second type of participatory structure is a citizen committee which acts as a governing group in a specific policy area. This has been used more on the local level in the United States than in the federal government. Such committees are especially prevalent as overseers of police and public school administration. Again, there is a tendency for 'elite' elements to play a more substantial role, although this may be a function of interest to an extent.[50] In any event, such approaches do afford citizens greater control over administrators.

The third type of citizen participation is more recent in origin, wider in scope, and far more controversial. It involves a concept of neighbourhood government in which individual citizens are afforded an opportunity to participate directly in the formulation of policy by the federal bureaucracy. The best known attempts at establishing participation of this type involved the Community Action Programs of the 'war on poverty' and the Model Cities Program of the Department of Housing and Urban Development. Despite a considerable literature on the subject, in some ways it is too early to pass judgement on participation of this type. Many programmes and efforts were abortive, others have been more participatory in name than in reality. Nevertheless, several observers have concluded that the benefits of citizen participation have outweighed its costs. For instance, participation of this nature has created a means of mobilising under-utilised resources, provided a source of knowledge, both corrective and creative, and become something of an affirmation of democracy itself.[51] In the view of one analyst who is far from oblivious to its limitations:

> Participation by providing a sense of community and participatory relationships is the key to improving the quality of life.
>
> . . .
>
> The simple conclusion of a comparison of the costs and benefits of participation of the poor in the Community Action and Model Cities Programs is that democracy would not and will not survive without such participation; that a basic reallocation and decentralization of power is required; and that the necessities as well as the benefits outweigh the costs.[52]

In sum, 'participatory bureaucracy' consists of four major elements: (1) a high level of social representativeness in a national bureaucracy; (2) participation by bureaucratic employees in decisions concerning the structuring of work, personnel matters, and the nature of public policy; (3) participation by bureaucrats in public political debate, and (4) citizen participation in the formulation of public policy by a national bureaucracy. It is important to emphasise that these elements can be readily integrated into a coherent approach for contributing to a resolution of the tensions between democracy and bureaucracy by at once making a national bureaucracy more politically responsive to the citizenry and more efficient in its operations. In fact, there is a strong internal logic to 'participatory bureaucracy'. The inability to render national bureaucracies completely apolitical strongly suggests that if democracy is to be safeguarded they must be socially representative. It appears that only in this fashion can it be assured that a bureaucracy will reflect, or at least be sensitive to the norms, values, and attitudes of the general population. However, once social representation becomes a goal, it is clear that the 'social representatives' must be given an oppor-

tunity to represent in an active fashion, if responsiveness is to be maximised. This requires less hierarchical and more participatory decision-
making, both with regard to matters of public policy and matters of
internal importance to the bureaucracy. Such participation ensures
that a wider range of perspectives will be brought to bear on decisional
choices, and increases the probability that these will be representative
of the major viewpoints found within the society at large. At the same
time, such participation is likely to increase the efficiency of a bureaucracy's operations. Given that policy formulation in such a bureaucracy
would be largely pluralistic and given that bureaucrats would be viewed
as 'representatives' to some extent, it follows that they should be able
to communicate more fully with their 'constituencies', to attempt to
mobilise public support for their positions, and to play a greater
educational role in the process. Internal bureaucratic disputes often
come to the attention of political authorities in democratic political
communities, and there appears to be little rationale for keeping them
from the electorate. Finally, communication between bureaucrats and
the public can only be complete if the public has a direct opportunity
to speak back. This could be effectively and democratically instituted
through popular participation in the formulation of public policy by
bureaucratic agencies. Such participation would strengthen democracy
overall, as well as the ability of bureaucrats to be responsive to and
reflect the popular will. At the same time, it would serve further to
educate the population with regard to matters of administrative and
political interest. None of this is to suggest, of course, that 'participatory bureaucracy' can be established rapidly or made to engulf all
bureaucratic operations and concerns, but rather only to say that it is
a promising strategy which is emerging in several democratic political
communities, and one which can have important application in a broad
range of policy areas.

To recapitulate the argument of this chapter and in large part the central
concern of the entire study, our analysis of bureaucratic culture indicates that not only is bureaucracy somewhat incompatible with democracy from a theoretical perspective, it engenders differential reactions
in citizens and bureaucrats which may enhance this tension in reality.
Bureaucrats may differ considerably among themselves, and this may
make unified policy approaches and their implementation difficult. As
a whole, however, they may also differ from citizens, thereby militating
against their responsiveness to the membership of the political community in general and contributing to their misperception of how they

are viewed by the citizenry at large. Citizens may also display different understandings of bureaucratic operations and some of them may be largely unable to relate to and deal with public bureaucracy in a satisfactory manner. Consequently, some citizens may not be able to play full citizenship roles in bureaucratised democratic political communities. Bureaucracy may be seen by these citizens as a powerful, relatively uncontrollable and threatening force in their lives and in that of the political community as a whole. This represents a failing of democracy to come to grips with the creation of suitable administrative structures. Although it has been argued that all governments must have a strong structural likeness, whether democratic or not, our analysis strongly suggests that such arguments avoid a central issue. The nature of an administrative system bears upon the nature of citizenship, and the nature of the latter is critical to the possibility of creating and maintaining a democratic political system. Traditional approaches for making bureaucracies more compatible with such systems have all fallen short, largely because they have failed to maximise efficiency or disregarded the full politicality of public bureaucracies. Indeed once it is recognised that public bureaucracies do make public policy and that therefore they cannot be politically neutral in a broad sense, it appears that there is but one choice left. If democracy is to deal successfully with the bureaucratisation of public life, it must modify that organisational form in such a fashion so as to make it at once efficient and politically responsive. Current developments in Western political communities and our findings in this study strongly suggest that this can be accomplished by replacing the ideal of neutrality with representativeness; by reducing hierarchy in favour of collegiality and equality; by affording bureaucrats the freedom to play an educational and wider political role in the polity and, thereby, also the opportunity to contribute to a revitalisation of political debate and perhaps even electoral processes; and finally, by increasing the role that citizens can play in the processes of policy formulation by bureaucratic agencies. It would be naive to suggest that 'participatory bureaucracy' would not have important costs and limitations of its own, for at best a resolution of the tension between bureaucracy and democracy is likely to be tenuous. Nevertheless, to the extent that the individual aspects of 'participatory bureaucracy' have been instituted in diverse settings, they have yielded considerable advantages and their overall integration promises to be even more beneficial. There is every reason to hope that in a political community with such a bureaucracy, bureauphiles and statesmen would abound and central administrative systems would at least have the potential of fulfilling the roles and functions demanded of them in modern and modernising democratic political communities.

Notes

1. See Victor Thompson, *Modern Organization* (New York: Knopf, 1961), pp. 170-7; and Alvin Gouldner, 'Red Tape as a Social Problem', in Robert K. Merton *et al.* (eds.), *Reader in Bureaucracy* (Glencoe: Free Press, 1952), pp. 410-18. See also the discussion in ch. 1 *supra*.

2. See Robert Presthus, *The Organizational Society* (New York: Random House, 1962), ch. 8; and the discussion in ch. 1 *supra*.

3. Quoted in James D. Richardson (ed.), *A Compilation of the Messages and Papers of the Presidents of the United States, 1789-1897* (Washington: US Government Printing Office, 1896), II, 449.

4. Ibid.

5. Ibid., p. 449. For a discussion of Jackson and the spoils system, see David H. Rosenbloom, *Federal Service and the Constitution* (Ithaca: Cornell University Press, 1971), ch. 2.

6. See ibid. for a summary of the evidence to this effect and the discussion in ch. 6 *supra*.

7. See Rosenbloom, *Federal Service*, ch. 3 for a discussion.

8. Woodrow Wilson, 'The Study of Administration', *Political Science Quarterly*, 56 (December 1941), p. 494.

9. For a convenient discussion of the Scientific Management Movement, see Amitai Etzioni, *Modern Organizations* (Englewood Cliffs: Prentice-Hall, 1964), ch. 3.

10. Luther Gulick, 'Science, Values and Public Administration', in *Papers on the Science of Administration*, ed. Gulick and L. Urwick (New York: Institute of Public Administration, Columbia University, 1937), p. 10.

11. Harold Seidman, *Politics, Position, and Power* (New York: Oxford University Press, 1970), p. 5.

12. President's Committee on Administrative Management, *Administrative Management in the Government of the United States* (Washington: January 1937).

13. Seidman, *Politics, Position, and Power*, pp. 3-4.

14. Brian Chapman, *The Profession of Government* (London: Unwin University Books, 1959), p. 320.

15. Ibid., p. 313.

16. Ibid., p. 312.

17. Ezra Suleiman, *Politics, Power, and Bureaucracy in France* (Princeton: Princeton University Press, 1974), p. 170.

18. Chapman, *Profession of Government*, pp. 310, 315, 296.

19. Theodore Lowi, *The End of Liberalism* (New York: W.W. Norton, 1969), p. 86.

20. See ibid., ch. 3.

21. Grant McConnell, *Private Power and American Democracy* (New York: Knopf, 1966), ch. 4 and pp. 342-5.

22. Wilson, *Political Science Quarterly*, 56, p. 500.

23. Warren Bennis and Philip Slater, 'Democracy is Inevitable', *Harvard Business Review*, 42 (March-April 1964), 51-9.

24. For a convenient discussion, see George C. Homans, 'The Western Electric Researches', in *Readings on Modern Organizations*, ed. Amitai Etzioni (Englewood

Cliffs: Prentice-Hall, 1969), pp. 99-114.

25. See Amitai Etzioni, *Modern Organizations*, ch. 4 for a convenient discussion.

26. Douglas McGregor, *The Human Side of Enterprise* (New York: McGraw-Hill, 1960); Douglas McGregor, *Leadership and Motivation* (Cambridge: MIT Press, 1966); Douglas McGregor, *The Professional Manager* (New York: McGraw-Hill, 1967); Bennis and Slater, *Harvard Business Review*, 42 (1965); and Bennis, 'Beyond Bureaucracy', *Transaction*, 2, No. 5 (1965), 31-5; George E. Berkley, *The Administrative Revolution* (Englewood Cliffs: Prentice-Hall, 1971); and George E. Berkley, *The Craft of Public Administration* (Boston: Allyn & Bacon, 1975).

27. Bennis, *Transaction*, 2 (July-August 1965), 35.

28. Berkley, *Craft of Public Administration*, pp. 478-86.

29. Ibid., p. 479.

30. *The New York Times*, 26 October 1975, sect. 4, p. 7.

31. Berkley, *Craft of Public Administration*, p. 480.

32. Executive Order 10988, U.S. *Federal Register*, 27: 551 (17 January 1962).

33. Executive Order 10987, ibid., p. 550 (17 January 1962).

34. Cary Hershey, *Protest in the Public Service* (Lexington: Lexington Books, 1973), p. 50.

35. Berkley, *Craft of Public Administration*, pp. 482-3.

36. See Chris Argyris, 'The Individual and Organization: Some Problems of Mutual Adjustment', *Administrative Science Quarterly*, II (June 1957), pp. 1-24; and Robert Merton, 'Bureaucratic Structure and Personality', *Social Forces*, 18 (May 1940), 560-8. See also the discussion in ch. 1 *supra*.

37. See Berkley, *Craft of Public Administration*, pp. 479, 481, 483.

38. The importance of this general approach can be observed in the United States. In November 1975, when President Ford fired Secretary of Defence Schlesinger, several members of Congress expressed concern that it would decrease the diversity of opinion within the Cabinet and that this would have undesirable effects on policy-formulation within the Presidential 'establishment'.

39. Berkley, *Craft of Public Administration*, p. 480.

40. Bernard Rosen, 'The Developing Role of Career Managers', *Civil Service Journal*, January-March, 1973. Quoted ibid., p. 489.

41. Hershey, *Protest*, p. 51, note a.

42. *New York Times*, 18 May 1970, p. 20.

43. Herbert J. Storing, 'Political Parties and the Bureaucracy', in *Political Parties, USA*, ed. Robert A. Goldwin (Chicago: Rand McNally, 1961), p. 154.

44. James C. Thomson, Jr., 'Getting Out and Speaking Out', *Foreign Policy*, 13 (Winter 1973-4); included in Peter Woll (ed.), *American Government*, 5th edn. (Boston: Little, Brown, 1975); pp. 549-62. The quoted passage appears on p. 562.

45. See David H. Rosenbloom, 'Some Political Implications of the Drift Toward a Liberation of Federal Employees', *Public Administration Review*, 31 (July-August 1971), pp. 420-6, for these and other examples. See also Hershey, *Protest*. Indeed, in 1970 a task force of the American Society for Public Administration strongly endorsed such behaviour: 'It isn't enough for us, as public executives, to take positions the way everyone else does. ASPA should have something special to say . . . In many instances, professional policy executors can make a contribution to the public debate on major issues that would be unique and listened to. Public executives should not just pirate what the influence-peddling organizations are saying, but should realize they have the ability of saying something unique to their role in society.' *New and Views*, American Society for Public Administration, October 1970, p. 7.

46. For a convenient discussion and analysis, see Carole Pateman, *Participation and Democratic Theory* (Cambridge: Cambridge University Press, 1970), esp. pp. 24-7.

47. See William L. Morrow, *Public Administration* (New York: Random House, 1975), p. 190.

48. See Seidman, *Politics, Position, and Power*, ch. 8; and McConnell, *Private Power*, pp. 259-80.

49. Morrow, *Public Administration*, p. 191.

50. This is the general conclusion reached in Robert Dahl, *Who Governs?* (New Haven: Yale University Press, 1961).

51. See Robert A. Aleshire, 'Power to the People: An Assessment of the Community Action and Model Cities Experience', *Public Administration Review*, Special Issue, September 1972, p. 442.

52. Ibid. On participation of this nature in general, see ibid.; Morrow, *Public Administration*, ch. 8; 'Symposium on Neighborhoods and Citizen Involvement', *Public Administration Review*, 32 (May-June 1972), pp. 189-223.

SELECT BIBLIOGRAPHY

Adedeji, A., ed. *Nigerian Administration and its Political Setting.* London: Hutchinson Educational, 1968.

Albrow, Martin. *Bureaucracy.* New York: Praeger, 1970.

Alford, Robert. *Party and Society.* Chicago: Rand McNally, 1963.

Almond, Gabriel A., and Verba, Sidney. *The Civic Culture.* Boston: Little, Brown, 1965.

Anderson, Charles W. *Politics and Economic Change in Latin America.* Princeton: D. Van Nostrand, 1967.

Armstrong, John A. *The European Administrative Elite.* Princeton: Princeton University Press, 1973.

Aronson, Sidney. *Status and Kinship in the Higher Civil Service.* Cambridge: Harvard University Press, 1964.

Balzac, Honore de. *Les Employes.* Eds. M. Bouteron and H. Longnon. Paris, 1910. In English *Bureaucracy; or a Civil Service Reformer.* Tr. Katherine Prescott Wormely. Boston, 1899.

Barker, Ernest. *The Development of Public Services in Western Europe, 1660-1930.* Hamden, Conn.: Archon Books, 1966.

Bendix, Reinhard. *Nation-Building and Citizenship.* New York: Wiley, 1964.

Berkley, George E. *The Administrative Revolution.* Englewood Cliffs: Prentice-Hall, 1971.

Berkley, George E. *The Craft of Public Administration.* Boston: Allyn & Bacon, 1975.

Bernstein, Marver H. *The Job of the Federal Executive.* Washington: Brookings Institution, 1958.

Bernstein, Marver H. *The Politics of Israel.* Princeton: Princeton University Press, 1957.

Birkhead, Guthrie S., ed. *Administrative Problems in Pakistan.* Syracuse: Syracuse University Press, 1966.

Blau, Peter, and Meyer, Marshall. *Bureaucracy in Modern Society.* New York: Random House, 1971.

Caiden, Gerald. *Israel's Administrative Culture.* Berkeley: Institute of Government Studies. University of California, 1970.

Chapman, Brian. *The Profession of Government.* London: Unwin University Books, 1959.

Chapot De Saintogne, R.A.A. *Public Administration in Germany.* London:

Weidenfeld and Nicolson, 1961.

Clark, Kenneth. *Dark Ghetto.* New York: Harper & Row, 1965.

Dahl, Robert. *Who Governs?* New Haven: Yale University Press, 1961.

Dalton, Melville. *Men Who Manage.* New York: Wiley, 1959.

Dang, N. *Viet-Nam.* Honolulu: East-West Center Press, 1966.

Djilas, Milovan. *The New Class.* New York: Praeger, 1957.

Downs, Anthony. *Inside Bureaucracy.* Boston: Little, Brown, 1967.

Eisenstadt, S.N. *Essays on Comparative Institutions.* New York: Wiley, 1965.

Eisenstadt, S.N. *Israeli Society.* New York: Basic Books, 1967.

Eldersveld, Samuel J., Jagannadham, J., and Barnabas, A.P. *The Citizen and the Administrator in a Developing Democracy.* Glenview: Scott, Foresman, 1968.

Elizur, Yuval, and Salpeter, Eliahu. *Who Rules Israel?* New York: Harper & Row, 1973.

Etzioni, Amitai. *Modern Organizations.* Englewood Cliffs: Prentice-Hall, 1964.

Etzioni, Amitai (ed.). *Readings on Modern Organizations.* Englewood Cliffs: Prentice-Hall, 1969.

Fein, Leonard. *Politics in Israel.* Boston: Little, Brown, 1967.

Gregorie, Roger. *The French Civil Service.* Brussels: International Institute of Administrative Sciences, 1964.

Hall, Richard. *Organizations: Structure and Process.* Englewood Cliffs: Prentice-Hall, 1972.

Heady, Ferrel. *Public Administration: A Comparative Perspective.* Englewood Cliffs: Prentice-Hall, 1966.

Heady, Ferrel, and Stokes, Sybil. *Comparative Public Administration: A Selective Annotated Bibliography.* Ann Arbor: Institute of Public Administration, University of Michigan, 1960.

Hershey, Cary. *Protest in the Public Service.* Lexington, Mass.: Lexington Books, 1973.

Hyneman, Charles S. *Bureaucracy in a Democracy.* New York: Harper Brothers, 1950.

Inkeles, Alex, and Smith, David H. *Becoming Modern.* Cambridge: Harvard University Press, 1974.

Jackson, Andrew. *Correspondence of Andrew Jackson.* Ed. J.S. Bassett. Washington: Carnegie Institution, 1926.

Jacoby, Henry. *The Bureaucratization of the World.* Berkeley: University of California Press, 1973.

Kernaghan, W.D.K., ed. *Bureaucracy in Canadian Government.* Toronto: Methuen, 1969.

Kilpatrick, Franklin P., Cummings, Milton, C., Jr., Jennings, M. Kent. *The Image of the Federal Service.* Washington: Brookings Institution, 1964.

Kingsley, J. Donald. *Representative Bureaucracy.* Yellow Springs: Antioch Press, 1944.

Krislov, Samuel. *The Negro in Federal Employment.* Minneapolis: University of Minnesota Press, 1967.

Krislov, Samuel. *Representative Bureaucracy.* Englewood Cliffs: Prentice-Hall, 1974.

Long, Norton. *The Polity.* Chicago: Rand McNally, 1962.

Lowi, Theodore. *The End of Liberalism.* New York: W.W. Norton, 1969.

McConnell, Grant. *Private Power and American Democracy.* New York: Knopf, 1966.

McGregor, Douglas. *The Human Side of Enterprise.* New York: McGraw-Hill, 1960.

McGregor, Douglas. *Leadership and Motivation.* Cambridge: MIT Press, 1966.

McGregor, Douglas. *The Professional Manager.* New York: McGraw-Hill, 1967.

MacKenzie, W.J.M., and Grove, J.W. *Central Administration in Britain.* London: Longman, 1957.

Menzel, Johanna, ed. *The Chinese Civil Service.* Boston: D.C. Heath, 1963.

Meyer, Alfred. *The Soviet Political System.* New York: Random House, 1965.

Morrow, William. *Public Administration.* New York: Random House, 1975.

Mosher, F. *Democracy and the Public Service.* New York: Oxford University Press, 1968.

Neustadt, R. *Presidential Power.* New York: Wiley, 1960.

Nigro, Felix. *Public Personnel Administration.* New York: Henry Holt, 1959.

Parry, Geraint. *Political Elites.* New York: Praeger, 1969.

Parton, James. *The Life of Andrew Jackson.* Boston: Houghton, Mifflin, 1887.

Pateman, Carole. *Participation and Democratic Theory.* Cambridge: Cambridge University Press, 1970.

Polanyi, Karl. *The Great Transformation.* Boston: Beacon Press, 1957.

Presthus, Robert. *The Organizational Society.* New York: Random House, 1962.

Riggs, Fred W. *Administration in Developing Countries—The Theory of Prismatic Society.* Boston: Houghton, Mifflin, 1964.

Riggs, Fred W. *Thailand.* Honolulu: East-West Center Press, 1966.

Rosenberg, Hans. *Bureaucracy, Aristocracy, and Autocracy.* Boston: Beacon Press, 1958.

Rosenbloom, David H. *Federal Equal Employment Opportunity.* New York: Praeger, 1977.

Rosenbloom, David H. *Federal Service and the Constitution.* Ithaca: Cornell University Press, 1971.

Samuel, Edwin. *British Traditions in the Administration of Israel.* London: Vallentine, Mitchell, 1956.

Schurz, Carl. *Speeches, Correspondence, and Political Papers of Carl Schurz.* Ed. F. Bancroft. New York: Putnam, 1913.

Seidman, Harold. *Politics, Position, and Power.* New York: Oxford University Press, 1970.

Siffin, William J. *The Thai Bureaucracy.* Honolulu: East-West Center Press, 1966.

Snider, James G., and Osgood, Charles E., eds. *Semantic Differential Technique.* Chicago: Aldine, 1969.

Strauss, Erich. *The Ruling Servants.* New York: Praeger, 1960.

Suleiman, Ezra. *Politics, Power and Bureaucracy in France.* Princeton: Princeton University Press, 1974.

Taub, Richard B. *Bureaucrats Under Stress.* Berkeley: University of California Press, 1969.

Thompson, V. *Modern Organization.* New York: Knopf, 1961.

Tilman, R.O. *Bureaucratic Transition in Malaya.* Durham: Duke University Press, 1964.

Truman, David. *The Governmental Process.* New York: Knopf, 1964.

Van Riper, Paul P. *History of the United States Civil Service.* Evanston: Row, Peterson, 1958.

Verba, Sidney, and Nie, Norman. *Participation in America.* New York: Harper & Row, 1972.

Weber, Max. *Essays in Sociology.* Tr. and ed. H.H. Gerth and C.W. Mills. New York: Oxford University Press, 1958.

Weber, Max. *The Theory of Social and Economic Organization.* Tr. A.M. Henderson and Talcott Parsons, ed. Talcott Parsons. New York: Oxford University Press, 1947.

White, L.D. *Further Contributions to the Prestige Value of Public Employment.* Chicago: University of Chicago Press, 1932.

White, L.D. *The Jeffersonians.* New York: Free Press, 1965.

White, L.D. *The Prestige Value of Public Employment in Chicago.* Chicago: University of Chicago Press, 1929.

Articles in Books and Journals

Aleshire, Robert. 'Power to the People: An Assessment of the Community Action and Model Cities Experience.' *Public Administration Review*, Special Issue, September 1972.

Argyris, Chris. 'The Individual and Organization: Some Problems of Mutual Adjustment.' *Administrative Science Quarterly*, 2 (June 1957), 1-24.

Banfield, Edward C. 'The Moral Basis of a Backward Society.' *Political Corruption*. Ed. Arnold J. Heidenheimer. New York: Holt, Rinehart & Winston, 1970, pp. 129-37.

Bennis, Warren. 'Beyond Bureaucracy.' *Transaction*, 2 (July-August 1965), 31-5.

Bennis, Warren, and Slater, P. 'Democracy Is Inevitable.' *Harvard Business Review*, 42 (March-April 1964), 51-9.

Boim, Leon. 'Ombudsmanship in Israel.' *Edizone Dell'Instituto Di Studi Legislativi.* Rome, 1968.

Bonjean, Charles M., and Grimes, Michael D. 'Bureaucracy and Alienation: A Dimensional Approach.' *Social Forces*, 48 (March 1970), 365-73.

Campos, Roberto de Oliveira. 'Public Administration in Latin America.' *Readings in Comparative Public Administration*. Ed. Nimrod Raphaeli. Boston: Allyn & Bacon, 1967, pp. 283-94.

Cornog, Geoffrey Y. 'The Personnel Turnover Concept: A Reappraisal.' *Public Administration Review*, 17 (November 1957), 247-56.

Davidson, Roger H. 'Congress and the Executive: The Race for Representation.' *Congress: The First Branch of Government*. Ed. A. DeGrazia. New York: Anchor, 1967, pp. 377-413.

Dresang, Dennis L. 'Ethnic Politics, Representative Bureaucracy and Development Administration: The Zambian Case.' *American Political Science Review*, 68 (December 1974), 1605-17.

Dror, Yehezkel. 'Public Policy-Making in Israel.' *Public Administration in Israel and Abroad*, 2 (1962).

Eisenstadt, S.N. 'Bureaucracy and Political Development.' *Bureaucracy and Political Development*. Ed. J. LaPalombara. Princeton: Princeton University Press, 1963, pp. 96-119.

Eisenstadt, S.N. 'Bureaucracy, Bureaucratization, and Debureaucratization.' *Readings in Comparative Public Administration*. Ed. Nimrod Raphaeli. Boston: Allyn & Bacon, 1967, pp. 354-73.

Eisenstadt, S.N. 'Problems of Emerging Bureaucracies in Developing Areas and New States.' *Readings in Comparative Public Administration*. Ed. Nimrod Raphaeli. Boston: Allyn & Bacon, 1967, pp. 220-38.

Etzioni, Amitai. 'Leaders' Control and Members' Compliance.' *Organizations and Human Behavior*. Ed. Gerald D. Bell. Englewood Cliffs: Prentice-Hall, 1967, pp. 81-5.

Forward, John. 'Toward an Empirical Framework for Ecological Studies in Comparative Public Administration.' *Readings in Comparative Public Administration*. Ed. Nimrod Raphaeli. Boston: Allyn & Bacon, 1967, pp. 450-72.

Gouldner, Alvin. 'Red Tape as a Social Problem.' *Reader in Bureaucracy*. Ed. R.K. Merton *et al*. Glencoe: Free Press, 1952, pp. 410-18.

Grabosky, P.N., and Rosenbloom, David H. 'Racial and Ethnic Integration in the Federal Service.' *Social Science Quarterly*, 56 (June 1975), 71-84.

Gulick, L. 'Science, Values and Public Administration.' *Papers on the Science of Administration*. Ed. L. Gulick and L. Urwick. New York: Columbia University, 1937.

Heidenheimer, Arnold J. 'The Context of Analysis.' *Political Corruption*. Ed. Arnold J. Heidenheimer. New York: Holt, Rinehart & Winston, 1970, pp. 3-28.

Hill, Larry B. 'Institutionalization, the Ombudsman, and Bureaucracy.' *American Political Science Review*, 68 (September 1974), 1075-85.

Janowitz, Morris, and Wright, Deil. 'The Prestige of Public Employment: 1929 and 1954.' *Public Administration Review*, 16 (Winter 1956), 15-21.

Katz, Elihu, and Eisenstadt, S.N. 'Bureaucracy and its Clientele—A Case Study.' *Readings on Modern Organizations*. Ed. Amitai Etzioni. Englewood Cliffs: Prentice-Hall, 1969, pp. 231-40.

Kimche, Jon. 'Tel Aviv: Messiah in a Business Suit.' *Commentary*, 6 (December 1948), 528-33.

Kumata, Hideya, and Schramm, Wilbur. 'A Pilot Study of Cross-Cultural Meaning.' *Public Opinion Quarterly*, 20 (1956), 229-38.

LaPalombara, Joseph. 'Bureaucracy and Political Development: Notes, Queries, and Dilemmas.' *Bureaucracy and Political Development*. Ed. Joseph LaPalombara. Princeton: Princeton University Press, 1963, pp. 34-61.

Lipset, Seymour Martin. 'Bureaucracy and Social Change.' *Reader in Bureaucracy*. Ed. R.K. Merton *et al*. Glencoe: Free Press, 1952, 221-32.

Mansfield, Roger. 'Bureaucracy and Centralization.' *Administrative Science Quarterly*, 18 (December 1973), 477-88.

Meier, K.J. 'Representative Bureaucracy: An Empirical Analysis.' *American Political Science Review*, 69 (June 1975), 526-42.

Merton, Robert. 'Bureaucratic Structure and Personality.' *Social Forces*, 18 (May 1940), 560-8.

Nachmias, David. 'Coalition Politics in Israel.' *Comparative Political Studies*, 7 (October 1974), 316-33.

Osgood, Charles E. 'Semantic Differential Technique in Comparative Study of Cultures.' *American Anthropologist*, 66 (1964), 171-200.

Pai Panandiker, V.A. 'Developmental Administration: An Approach.' *Readings in Comparative Public Administration.* Ed. Nimrod Raphaeli. Boston: Allyn & Bacon, 1967, pp. 199-210.

Peres, Yochanan. 'Ethnic Relations in Israel.' *American Journal of Sociology*, 76 (May 1971), 1021-47.

Reimann, Bernard C. 'On the Dimensions of Bureaucratuc Structure: An Empirical Reappraisal.' *Administrative Science Quarterly*, 18 (December 1973), 462-76.

Reissman, Leonard. 'A Study of Role Conceptions in Bureaucracy.' *Social Forces*, 27 (March 1949), 305-10.

Riggs, Fred W. 'Bureaucrats and Political Development: A Paradoxical View.' *Bureaucracy and Political Development.* Ed. Joseph LaPalombara. Princeton: Princeton University Press, 1963, pp. 120-67.

Rosenbloom, David H. 'A Note on the Social Class Composition of the Civil Service, 1789-1837.' *Polity*, 5 (Fall 1972), 136-8.

Rosenbloom, David H. 'The Civil Service Commission's Decision to Authorize the Use of Goals and Timetables in the Federal Equal Employment Opportunity Program.' *Western Political Quarterly*, 26 (June 1973), 236-51.

Rosenbloom, David H. 'Some Political Implications of the Drift Toward a Liberation of Federal Employees.' *Public Administration Review*, 31 (July-August 1971), 420-6.

Rosenbloom, David H., and Nachmias, David. 'Bureaucratic Representation in Israel.' *Public Personnel Management*, 3 (July-August 1974), 302-13.

Smith, Gordon. 'A Model of the Bureaucratic Culture.' *Political Studies*, 22 (March 1975), 31-43.

Somers, H.M. 'The President, the Congress, and the Federal Government Service.' *The Federal Government Service.* Ed. Wallace Sayre. Englewood Cliffs: Prentice-Hall, 1965, pp. 70-113.

Storing, Herbert J. 'Political Parties and the Bureaucracy.' *Political Parties, USA.* Ed. Robert A. Goldwin. Chicago: Rand McNally, 1964, pp. 137-58.

Subramaniam, V. 'Representative Bureaucracy: A Reassessment.' *American Political Science Review*, 61 (December 1967), 1010-19.

Thomson, James C., Jr. 'Getting Out and Speaking Out.' *Foreign Policy*, 13 (Winter 1973-4), 49-69.

Wilson, Woodrow. 'The Study of Administration.' *Political Science Quarterly*, 56 (December 1941), 481-506.

INDEX